# THE SPIRITUAL SEEKER'S GUIDE TO HAPPINESS

## Rashana

This book is dedicated to all who are willing to look into the shadows and find their way back to love.

Published in Canada By:
Inner Nature Publishing

ISBN 978-0-9920307-2-8 (eBook)
ISBN 978-0-9920307-4-2 (Paperback)

## Get One of My Books for Free

How a face reading workshop led to the inspiration to write a book I will never know, but that is how it unfolded. In the summer of 2010, a couple of days after that workshop, I was inspired to gather questions from family and friends and channel the answers to compile into a book. At the time I had been channeling for years but not fully trusting my abilities.

That all changed in the process of writing *Healing with Love, Messages for the New Earth.* Every time I received a question I would channel the answer and send it to the person who submitted the question. The feedback repeatedly was that the message touched them deeply and was very accurate for their life experience. So much love came through that I decided to call it the LoveSpeak Project.

Now, two years later, I call myself a channel and am deeply honored to have permission to connect with others on such a divine and beautiful level. There are messages in this book that will touch your soul. One question came from a young woman in her 20s who has an untreatable brain tumor. She wanted to know about living so close to death. The answer was one of the most beautiful and moving messages I have ever read and it can guide us all when loved ones are close to death.

Other questions were about natural disasters and how to find one's life purpose. It is a diverse collection of messages offered as loving guidance for us all to find our way in this world. I trust that it will touch you as well in some level of your being and I am happy to share it with you.

**Go to www.rashana.ca for your free copy of the book**

# Table of Contents

# PREFACE

There are a couple of terms that are used frequently in this book that I would like to explain, from my perspective. When The Council of Nine speak of the Light they are referring to the essence of All That Is, Creator, or God. Whatever resonates as truth for you. The Light represents the love that created all life. We carry a spark of that love within us. We have the spark of the Divine which The Council of Nine often refer to as our Light.

They also use the word darkness or the dark often in their transmissions. From a deeper level of understanding there is no dark versus light, good/bad or right/wrong. All life is love in expression. When we move out of duality and into unity consciousness, as I believe we are now doing, we understand that more fully. I believe the Council refer to the dark to give us an understanding of the choices in life. It is used for the purpose of understanding the concepts that they are offering to us.

Ascension is another word that is used frequently. It is my understanding that we, as a human race, are in the process of changing in many ways. The resonance of the earth is changing. Scientists have recorded that the frequency of the earth is rising quite rapidly in recent years. We are moving out of the dense third dimensional reality into the higher vibrations of the fourth dimension and eventually into the fifth dimension.

Ascension is the process of making this change. Each soul has a choice here. Those who are engaged in hatred, war and hardship may not make the choice to leave what is familiar to them – the third dimensional reality. However, life in the fourth dimension will be much lighter and more joyful.  I believe most of the people on this earth are choosing to ascend – to rise up into these more loving energies that are available to us now.  It is to support us on that journey that The Council of Nine are offering these messages.

Most of the transmissions from The Council of Nine, or what I have chosen to call Essays, are presented in this book in the order in which they were received.  One of the first, which I offer in this preface, was to explain more about who they are.  This is a personal response to me.  I have added it here to give you more understanding of where these Essays are coming from. Here is their response to my inquiry about who they are:

*Oh Dear One we are so delighted to be called before you for the purpose of expanding your understanding of who we are.  We are the Light.  We are a piece of heaven on earth.  We come from on High to oversee the successful transition of the human into the next dimensional reality.  We exist in Love and our mission is always to be of service to the Light.  Thus it is that we have come to you.  For we see your willingness to be of service.  Indeed it is your mission.  And, in this year of 2012, you have stepped fully into that mission, given the gift of time.  You have used it wisely in service to the earth and humanity.*

*And so we chose to speak through you to support humanity in this transition into the Light.  Many souls are still asleep, lost in the fear matrix, unable to see their power that awaits within.  Our purpose in speaking through you is to support humanity in its awakening so that as many as possible will be ready to step into ascension when the opportunity presents itself on your planet.  By offering our daily essays as you have chosen to call them, we are giving information that will assist those who give heed to what is written.*

*We exist in the 12th dimension, much closer to the Creator Light. We cannot incarnate upon your planet without serious recalibrating but we can speak to the children of the earth. We wish you great success as a planet and all who walk upon her in your transition into the Light in this magical time on planet earth.*

Finally, I would like to speak of the title of this book, for what is happiness? Is it having a life full of only joyful moments? Is it acceptance of our experience of life, regardless of what it is? Is it a decision to be happy? Is it being of service to others? We all have our own understanding of what true happiness is. I see this book as a guide to happiness, for many reasons.

In some of the essays The Council of Nine are leading us to be of service and share our love Light with the world. In others we are being called to release our wounded past and let go of outdated beliefs. And some are exploring the concept of self-love. This book is not a how-to manual to happiness, it is a journey to happiness. Pay attention to what is being offered in each essay and take the time to answer the questions and consider what is written. The truth appears to be simple, yet is profound in its understanding. I invite you to take the time to get to the place of understanding.

# INTRODUCTION

One day, as I was sitting in meditation, I sensed a presence wanting to speak to me. As a channel, I am open to receiving information from the Higher Beings of Light. However, this was a different presence than I was used to. They called themselves The Council of Nine and they were asking me to connect with them daily to receive messages.

Being unfamiliar with The Council of Nine, I told them that I would think about it and get back to them. I wanted to be sure they were coming from a place of love. The irony in that is now quite apparent. Day after day they talked about love, especially the importance of loving the self. It turns out that love is the very essence of these Essays.

What the Council of Nine wants for us, more than anything, is to find our joy. They are asking us to do the healing that needs to be done so that we can fully move into self love. What you will find in these pages are deep, loving and inspirational messages that help us find our way back to our true essence. Once we have healed our wounds and learned how to truly love ourselves, then we are living a life of happiness. They want us to know that we are the creators of our lives.

If we do not know what that means then we can create lives of challenge and misery, without knowing how to change it. If we do not know the impact that our thoughts have on creation, we will simply keep repeating the old patterns and continue to re-live yesterday instead of allowing new opportunities into our lives. It is by understanding our power as humans that we can shift into a life of peace and harmony. Until we know how we create, we cannot turn our lives around.

Humanity is in the process of ascending. It is a beautiful opportunity to move into the higher realms of existence where love prevails. However, to make the transition, we must be prepared. We must release the weights that are the wounds of the past. Only then will we move into fully loving ourselves and all of creation. From that place of love we are then ready to rise up. You will know how you are doing by the nature of your life. If your life feels challenging then you are out of harmony with the truth of your existence.

You will feel the loving presence of these beautiful Beings as they lead you out of fear and into love. Their guidance will lead you out of the challenges of life and into stillness. As they touch your heart with their words you will feel the peace that we all deserve. As The Council of Nine say so often, to love the self is not selfish, it is the greatest gift you can give.

# Essay One: FIRST SESSION WITH THE COUNCIL OF NINE

And so it is that we come before the earthly plane this day to offer guidance and love. We begin by commending all who are reading this book for your monumental growth as a human being on this earth. You are magnificent and we wish you to pat yourselves on the back for all that you have accomplished in morphing yourselves into a new human. We invite you to look at your life just a short year ago. How different are you now?

We are certain that you will see great growth, great change in who you are now compared to a mere year ago. That is huge – an accomplishment not to go unnoticed. And yet we see that many of you are still punishing yourselves with what you think you should have done or who you think you should be and we say that you are perfect in every way. Please take heed of our words. There are no mistakes in your life – no wrong turns or mistaken paths. It is all unfolding just as it was meant to be.

At the same time we tell you that you can change on a dime and become someone new. You can drop all the old patterns of the past and create a more rewarding life in this moment. Most of you, up until now, would not allow yourselves to do that. You would not step into the fullness of who you are becoming. You had trouble accepting that life could change just like that. It can and you can make it so.

As you see yourself desiring something different in your life all you have to do is believe it is possible and you can make it happen. The difficulty is that you have to let go of who you were in order to become the fullness of who you are. This can be challenging. You have been one person for so long it is hard to imagine being someone else even though you want change in your life.

In order to bring that change, you have to change. We hope this makes sense. We hope this gives you greater understanding of what is required in order for you to redirect your lives and create the heaven on earth that you have been waiting for. You are the ones who will create it. No one else can do it for you.

You are humanity and you are a creator race. You have all the abilities to create but you have had those attributes robbed from you. Now it is being given back. Now we ask you to play with this idea of re-creating your life and stepping out of your smallness and claiming your brilliance. Believe in yourselves. KNOW that if you can dream it you can be it. It is true. This is not some fluffy whimsical saying. It is the TRUTH.

We leave you now with the deepest blessings of love that you can hold in these times. We wish you to know that you are dearly loved and the universe awaits your enlightenment. And so it is.

## Essay Two - BEING OF SERVICE TO THE EARTH

And so it is Beloveds that we have the privilege of being with you this day to offer this transmission of Light. We come before you with loving hearts to encourage you to walk into your fullness of being in these wondrous times on your planet earth. These are magnificent times indeed and it is required, for the ascension of all, that those of you who are 'aware', who are tuned in so to speak, to be of service to all.

It is required that those who have the understanding and spirit to serve, take up that call to be of service. For you see, for those who have not found their way to the Light, the darkness prevails and they cannot find their way out. It is like being lost in a maze and going in circles. They do not have the knowing to stop, be still, and check in to the inner wisdom to find their way out.

Because of this, those who do take the time to check with the inner self and use their intuitive abilities to lead them ever closer to Creator, must be the ones who step up and lead the way. This leadership is not accomplished through preaching or bragging. It is accomplished by being. When you are fully embracing the Light and walking in your truth, others will 'see' you. Simply by being who you are in your fullness of living, others will notice you and wonder what is different about you.

Then you may share what that is. You may share how your way of being allows you to find that internal peace. For those of you who are living this way, we ask you now to find a way to show yourselves more. To be more illuminated in the world. Find that something that is your own way of being, truly resonant with who you are, and offer it out to the world. This is the way to share your Light Dear Ones. We hope this makes sense to you.

Now we know that many of you, after reading this, will immediately be asking, but how do I find out what my special way of being is? It is a question that baffles many. Again, we wish to use Rashana as an example for you. We do this because she once asked that very question. And she did not find the answer until she was willing to fully accept what had presented itself almost 20 years earlier. For her it is this channeling work. Her first channeled message that she received was 19 years ago. And yet, she is just now willing to call herself a channel.

She struggled with believing in herself and the clarity of what she received. She struggled with calling herself a channel in a small, conservative community. It was not until she fully embraced what had been presenting itself for years that she came to the place of fully knowing that this is her work. And the beauty is, she LOVES doing it.

Nothing could bring her more joy and this is the blessing that comes from walking into your Light. So for you, the reader, we say, explore that which you have always loved to do. It might be decorating or writing or acting. There are no limits to what it is. The answer is that when you step fully into it and accept the joy that it brings and your abilities with it, then you will become a shining Light and that Light will lead others to their own brilliance.

Oh it is really so simple but so many try to make it difficult. Do not give up in the searching, yet know that the searching is within. What is in your heart? Perhaps it is being an advocate for others that brings your passion alive. Do not use the mind to regulate what comes forth as your passion. Whatever gets you excited in life is your passion.  Some people are here to stir up the political system.  Others are here to quietly create art that will awaken people to their true self. There is no judgement around what the 'right' way is. Your heart will tell you that, not your mind.

And so Beloveds, find your way of being a beacon in this world and shine your Light for all to see.  No longer can you hide behind the fog.  The time is here for you to radiate and share your blessings with the world.  Find a community of friends who truly support you in your mission.  Find like-minded people who understand you. You are not meant to walk this journey alone, especially now in these times of enlightenment.

You are here to walk together as one, loving and supporting each other.  If there are people in your life who do not offer that, then find those who do.  It is vital to your awakening to be supported and nurtured just for who you are.  Even those who carry fear and evil thoughts will soften when they are supported for who they are.  They are not their evil deeds.  They are loving children of God who have lost their way in the hardship of this third dimensional reality.

Love them free of their pain.  Do not love their evil deeds but love the lonely hearts hiding behind those deeds.  This is the way of it Dear Ones.  This is the way back to the Light, back to your birth right of being Creator Light upon this earth.  We love you so and wish you to absorb these words into your knowing.  Find the place in your hearts that knows the truth and allow our words to rest there.  Use your own discernment always in what is being offered as truth.  Your hearts know the answer. Love is the way. And so it is.

# Essay Three - SHINE YOUR LIGHT

The year 2012 was one of monumental change on planet earth. It was a year of great influx of Light and Love through the heavenly realms. And now we ask that humanity step up the game. Those of you who are awakening to the truth of who you are – stepping into the truth of your Divine Mastery – we ask you to be of greater service to the Light at this time.

We ask you, by your very presence on the earth, to serve in her healing. It is our deepest desire that this ascension into the higher realms be achieved by many. It is our deepest desire that the earth and all who walk upon her shift into the (heavenly) realm of the fifth dimension.

In order for this to happen those who are willing to be of service are being asked to amp up the game so to speak. You are being asked to consciously anchor Creator Light onto the earth every day in your meditations. You may do this by calling upon this Light to pass through you and into the core of the earth. From there Gaia (Mother Earth) can disperse it as she sees fit.

This may seem insignificant to you humans but we say to you it will be a powerful tool in assisting humanity into these energies that are being offered at this time. We ask each of you who hear this message to add this simple task to your daily meditations. Ask to be an anchor for the Creator Light into the earth for her healing and the benefit of all of humanity. This we ask in God's name. And so it is.

# Essay Four - YOU ARE CREATOR LIGHT

Greetings Children of the earth. Greetings from the Council of Nine. We are honoured and delighted to have this opportunity to come before you and share our Light with you. We are looking upon the new humans, for those who read these messages have already become new. You have already changed your DNA to hold the Light of the fifth dimension. It is for you that we offer great congratulations, great high fives as we look upon all that you have accomplished.

At the same time we say to you Dear Ones, that it is necessary to lift up those around you as well so that you may all move into the Light. It is our deepest wish that all of humanity will ascend when the time comes for the earth to take her children with her to the other side. She will lift up those who are in preparedness to ascend with her.

Those who remain will be left to incarnate many times over the next thousands of years in order to stand at the moment in time where you currently find yourselves. For you see, these are magical times. You stand at the change of the season, so to speak. It is an opportunity that only happens every 23,000 years or thereabouts.

So, for those left behind, it is not the end. It is not doom for them, it is just a deep disappointment. It is not us who bear that disappointment. It is their souls once they realize the great opportunity that they let slip by. Many who remain behind will fall into deep despair as they see the world around them - the third dimensional world that has them already weary from all the struggle and fear and darkness.

For those who are ready to walk into the Light we commend you Dear Ones. We see that you have worked hard to earn that right and that you have taken on your own internal battles to walk out of the darkness. And so you are welcomed into the higher realms having earned your right to be there. There will be such celebration when this happens. You will feel our love pulling you up. We are pulling you into our arms as you shift out of the density of the third dimensional earth and into the fourth and fifth dimensions of existence.

It is an exciting time indeed. It is a time of great magnitude in all of creation. But there is yet time before this great shift happens and so we offer this message with the hope that you will tell as much as others are willing to hear about the great transformation happening on the earth at this time. Do what you can to assist others in walking out of fear. Do what you can to help them understand that what they are experiencing is a great opportunity for change. Do what you can to show them by your example how to be a new human on the new earth. By walking in grace and trust of the Divine plan you are showing the way.

Oh, our beautiful way-showers, we are so proud. We stand before you and we admire you deeply. Your Lights are shining bright on the planet we fondly call earth. She is magnificent and she has created you. She wants nothing more than to take you with her into the fifth dimension. But she cannot wait much longer. Her time window has been extended on your behalf. She continues to sacrifice for you, for she loves you dearly. Even so, the time will come when she can wait no more. That time is swiftly approaching.

Be aware Dear Ones. Do not leave it until tomorrow to heal your wounds. Do not leave it until tomorrow to see the beauty that is you. Do not wait to start loving yourselves. Love yourselves out of the darkness that you may see the beauty of who you are. Dear Ones, we love you so. We see you. We see you. We see the reflection of the Divine in your eyes and we weep with joy.

You are Creator Light. Radiate your brilliance into all of the heavens. We await the opportunity to connect with you as individuals. We await the time when you can feel our presence and we can gift you with an energetic hug. We can gift you with the kiss of heaven as we witness the grandest experiment ever in all of creation.

Oh, such joy we have in watching this earth school - such joy in standing before the human. Dear Ones. Our love for you is infinite. And so it is.

# Essay Five - NOVA SCOTIA

**Note – This Essay speaks specifically of the province of Nova Scotia, Canada. It has been included here because it also addresses "… all who wish to ascend".**

And so it is we begin this transmission. And it is the province, the land on which you reside, that we would like to address this day. And so let us begin to speak of the intentions of Nova Scotia in the grand scheme of things. You have read in The Keys of Enoch that NS is part of the wing of the dove and we would like to give you a deeper understanding of what that means. The wing of the dove is the part of the bird that gives it flight. It lifts it off the ground. For indeed without wings no bird would fly.

And so it is that this province is paramount in the ascension of humanity and the planet earth at this time. The wings are where the energies of love are lifting the dove of peace off the ground. How appropriate it is that one of those wings rests over NS. For you see your people are gentle, generous and kind. Yours are a people who do not think of war but of supporting and loving each other. You are in a part of the world, a so-called have-not province, which is used to hard times. But, what do humans do in hard times? They support each other. They comfort each other. They reach out to each other and they offer compassion to those around them.

These indeed are qualities fitting of lifting a bird off the ground. These are qualities that have had minimal appreciation in the business world. And yet, in the universal evolution, they are the greatest qualities of all. The universe would choose a simple man who knows only love and kindness over a stealth business man who knows how to con with the best of them. Two very different energies as you can feel. And so we tell you that Nova Scotia is full of loving energy and that is the grace of this province and its role in the ascension.

Having said that, we would like to be clear that there is still great responsibility in accomplishing this Divine facet of the evolution of the planet. There is an influx of conscious humans coming to this province for the intent purpose of assisting in this evolution into the Light. The more there are holding the Light, the easier the job is for each and every one. For those of you who have been here in the beginning, you know how challenging it was to be here. As our channel would say, it was like walking through mud up to your thighs. Rather hard to move forward.

And yet you have held steadfast, always believing, never giving up even when it seemed unbearable to stay. There are many of you here and we commend you for your mission to the earth. You did not know that you were on a mission to the earth but we did and we do.

It is to you that we speak at this time. It is to you that we say well done. You have accomplished a great feat of holding the Light for all who were choosing darkness. Because of your grace upon this planet, earth is ready to ascend. She is ready to transform and to take you with her. In fact, Mother Earth has already made her transition but few are aware and few are residing with her there.

So she rests between two worlds, so to speak - one foot in the heavens and one foot on the ground, waiting for her children to take the giant leap with her. She is so patient. But the time will come when she can wait no longer. That time is soon approaching. This is one reason for our messages at this time. For now we will speak in this transmission of this province of Nova Scotia and all who wish to ascend.

Now is the time to heal the wounds of the past. It is time to offer forgiveness to yourself, for there is no other place that requires it. For all the hardship, all the pain, forgive yourself. For all the holding on to the past forgive yourself. Find whatever way you can to heal those wounds of the past, for they are like anchors into the third dimension. If it is your choice to rise above them then you must find a way to heal and release.

Anchors away as you let go of the pain of the past and allow your spirit, your soul, to soar to new heights. If this is your intention Dear Ones, then now is the time. There is a narrow window of time here – one that has already been extended – for you to make these choices and take the action to see them complete. Find the strength and courage to face your wounds. Look inside to where you are holding onto pain, despair, fear. Then heal those wounds. There are so many healing methods now that instantly release those old traumas directly out of the biology where they are stored.

These are gifts that have been brought forth to support you in this time of transition. You no longer have years to work through your pain in talk therapy. Choose the new therapies that instantly release the trauma. They work. And with each release you become lighter and lighter. And as you become lighter you automatically lift up off of the third dimension and into the higher dimensions.

This is the purpose of our being with you in these times. We are here to assist with lift off. But we cannot do the work for you. We can only guide you. We can put up signs that point in the direction that is most beneficial for your evolution. The rest is up to you. Are you going to sit at the fork in the road and wait or are you going to follow the clearly marked signs to your new state of being?

The choice is yours Dear Ones. We are waiting at the end of the well- marked road. This is not a threat Beloveds. It is a choice. Our desire is to lead you to the choice that you came here for. In the density of this third dimension it is easy to forget your chosen path. It is easy to get lost in the despair that comes with the earthly incarnation. That is our reason for offering this guidance at this time. There is no punishment for not choosing to follow the clearly marked path.

It is just that we know the despair of the soul having realized that the opportunity was lost. It is like losing a relationship because of words spoken that were regretted the moment they were said. You cannot go back and change those words just as you will not be able to go back in time and try to climb through the window. Once it is closed, it is a long wait for spring to come when the windows will once again open.

And so we offer this with love. There are some who will not pay attention to soft and gentle messages. There are many who only respond at the last hour when time has almost run out. It is to you we speak this day. Do not lose your footing when you must hurry so to catch up. And so it is.

# Essay Six - SIGNALS OF JOY

And so it is that we would like to speak to you today of harm. Harm and alarm. For you see, there are many in these times who are ringing the alarm bells, calling out to the masses and using fear to feed off their energies. This is causing much alarm in the minds of those who believe only fear-based reality. They are stuck in a place where they do not seek out the messages of the Light and so they only draw into their experience the fearful messages of what is happening on the earth at this time.

For that reason, their experience is almost all fear based and it becomes almost impossible to move out of that field of energetic experience. It is for this reason that it is vital for all the Lightworkers – those who know differently or think differently about these times of earth change – to speak out. Let your voices be heard loud and clear. Please send out the signals of joy of these times. Let yourselves be the ones who deliver the message of peace and faith in all that is transpiring on the earth at this time.

There is a need for more balance between fear and faith. Fear is winning out at the time of this channeling. In order for those who are lost in darkness to see any Light, that Light must be bright and burn through the many layers of darkness that surrounds them. As beings of the Light, those who believe and trust with the flow of life, we ask you to do more to be open about what you know to be true. Do not let the ridicule of those in fear stop you from delivering your message.

There are enough who will believe that will balance out your feelings of being condemned. This is a vital role for those who have found their way. There are so many who are lost and walking in circles. They will not see out of their circle until there are many who are standing outside of that circle pointing to another way, another direction.

For those of you who are willing we commend you. We commend you for stepping out of the comfort zone of remaining behind the scenes, so to speak. It is time to step up on stage and be heard. For which voice would you choose to be the loudest on this earth? It is time for your voices to be the ones that ring the loudest, to be the ones that are heard around the world. The more of you who step out to be seen, the more who will bravely follow in your tracks. There are many of you now. It will not be as difficult as it would have been only a few short years ago.

So, find the courage to be in your full brilliance. It does not require great oratory skills. It does not require large audiences. Just be speaking the truth of your own knowing, your own trusting in the way of the new world unfolding. You will find that there will be eager ears by your side, ready to hear something positive that will give them hope in what to them appears to be a world falling apart.

The more dismal it looks the more people will be willing to find a way that offers some hope. Even if they do not listen fully at the time, you will put the bug in their ear as you say and they will continue to ponder the possibility of what you have said.

This is a great way to be of service at this time. This is a great way to support humanity in walking into the new age of enlightenment. This is what we ask of you this day. And we see many who are willing. We commend you Dear Ones. We offer you our Light as you illuminate the world. And so it is.

# Essay Seven - LIGHT ON THE SHADOWS

It is with great honour and delight that we come into the world this day and we say to you, the reader of this message, these are times of great magnitude in all of the universes everywhere. You humans are changing the playing field for all of creation. All of the heavens watch over you as you play this game, as you unfold the layers of time into the creation of the new earth. How are you playing Dear One? Pay attention to the ways in which your life is unfolding.

For what you see is a reflection of the thought processes you put together that create your life. We know this message has been put out there many times in many ways. We know that you have heard it before. And yet we say to you, we would not be repeating it if it did not need repeating. How many times must you hear this before you really take the time to look at what you are creating in your life and ask yourself if you like what you see?

For many the answer is more than obvious. It is glaring. So, if you do not like what you see, when will you change what you think so that you may change that which is your experience? This is all that is required. It sounds simple but it requires intention to accomplish.

So, what will be your deepest desire to accomplish in this lifetime? What is your purpose in being here? Is it to be love on this earth? Is it to be a great composer? Perhaps it is to be a business person who brings integrity into the workplace? Whatever your goal, let it be one that will bring Light into this world. Let it be one that will see each Soul as divine. May it be your goal to realize that each person you see on your path is a reflection of yourself - those you like and those you do not like. They are all a reflection of who you are.

And the reason you have brought them into your experience is so that you can see that reflection and learn and grow from it. If you like what you see, rejoice in that aspect of yourself that you hold dear. If you do not like the person before you, explore where you have those traits within yourself. Allow yourself to heal what those traits represent. Let yourself explore where those behavior patterns lie within yourself and look at them so that they may be released out of the darkness. The shadow side of yourself, the side that you hide from, cannot remain once you put the Light upon it. Where there is full radiant Light there are no shadows. Such it is with the shadow side of the human. Once you look at that side it is like turning on the Light and the shadows just disappear.

Behavior patterns and beliefs only remain in the shadows when you are not willing to look at them. Releasing those behavior patterns is not difficult. All it takes is a close look and it simply dissolves. Humans spend so much time running from the hidden aspects of themselves. It takes more energy to avoid it than to look at it and release it. What takes more energy, to run a marathon or to sit and reflect? The answer is simple. What we speak to is akin to this. So step out of the marathon and sit on the sidelines and look inside to the hidden pieces of your personality that await your awareness. Once you find them and say hello they will say goodbye.

This is our transmission for this day. We support you so that you may fully resonate into your brilliant Light. And so it is.

# Essay Eight - WHAT IS LOVE?

And so today we would like to speak of love. It seems to be the theme of the day (based on a group meditation this morning). And what a wonderful and wondrous theme it is. Wondrous. What does that mean to you? We use that word because we feel the word love is deeply misunderstood in the times in which you live. Actually, we could say that for most of the history of humanity on the earth, love was misunderstood.

Love has been many things. It has been used to bound people together when they could hardly tolerate each other. It has been used to abuse people and claim it is in the name of love. It has been used as protection so that you don't have to be alone in the world. It has been used in almost every manner but the truth. For what is love? You cannot see it. So is love like faith? You cannot see faith. Is it dependency? Is it giving of yourself to someone else? Is it adoration? Is it lust?

None of these are the truth about love. So let us talk about the truth of love. We can say that very few of you have truly felt love, the love that comes without any conditions. Where is this love? Well, Dear Ones, it is in a place where you seldom look. It is like going into the attic and looking for something but giving up because it is too dark and there are too many cobwebs. Love for many is hidden so deeply within the heart that there is no true understanding of what it is. And so where do you find it or how do you find it? You find it by having the courage to search.

You find it by having the determination to clean out the cobwebs and peer through the darkness until you see a glimpse of it. Like a frightened child, it slowly begins to show itself. But how do you know it is love? What do you look for if you have never known what love really is? This is the key to your discovery and this is the key which we wish to make clear to you this day. To find true love you cannot look to another. You cannot decide who you are by what others respond to. Real love is the love of yourself.

And so we invite you to ask, do you love yourself? Do you ever condemn yourself or compare yourself or scold yourself or judge yourself? Of course you do. Your society has taught you very well how to self-manage your brilliance by burying it under guilt and shame. No more. The time has come for you to learn to love yourselves but it will require much discipline.

It requires years of unlearning who you are. However old you are that is how many years you must unlearn about who you are. For you see, the messages that you were given from the time of birth have written your script for who you are. Your parents were wounded. We can safely say that to pretty much every human on earth. So, their vision of you came through a cracked lens. How could they reflect back to you the purity and grace of who you are when they were looking through cracked lenses? They could not.

Therefore you must unlearn everything that they created you as. And you must unlearn everything your friends created you as and everything your coworkers created you as and everything your partner created you as and everything your children created you as. Are you getting the picture? You have to search deep within yourself, way past the dark shadows and cobwebs to find the truth of who you are, which is pure love. You were born onto this earth as pure love. And the moment you were born that love became diminished.

We wish you to know that now is the time for all of that to change. The world requires empowered people NOW. There is no time to wait. And in order for you to become empowered as who you are, all the false ideas of love and the false perceptions of who you are must be erased so that you can shine your true brilliant Light out into the world and be all that you came to be. You will see this happening slowly. It is a huge mission for humanity to make this shift.

It will begin with the new generations who demand that they be respected and seen for who they truly are. They will be labeled as rebellious. Good for them. They have to be rebellious to hang onto their deep inner knowing of who they are. No longer will the children of the earth sit back and question who they are while society tries to de-create them. They are clear as a bell about who they are and they will not allow anyone to stop them from ringing their true being out into the world.

But you can help. You who are reading this can help all this along by first looking with great courage at what you believe about yourself. Catch all those critical thoughts. Explore where you feel guilt in your life. Be honest about what you are angry about. Look inside and explore all those things you believe about yourself or where you gave up your truth for the sake of someone else. Look back and find ways to release it. There are many healing modalities that pull the old belief systems out of the body. Find them and use them so that you can find your way back to your true Light. This is the beginning.

The next step is to understand your children. Do not think you have ANYTHING to teach your children, other than not to run in front of traffic! Anything that you teach them based on how you were raised will only diminish who they are. And the world does not need or want any more diminished people. So, see in them their own innate wisdom and honor it. Ask your children questions instead of telling them what is. Ask them what they think is right or wrong for them and then give yourself time to truly consider it.

This does not mean that you allow your children to run the household with no boundaries between being a parent and child. This is not what we are talking about. We are talking about HEARING your children – honestly with an open heart and then deciding what is best. If what you decide is best is different than what your child has shared with you, explain this to your child so they clearly know why their inner knowing was not followed in this instance.

It is important for them to understand this so they can learn but also know that their thoughts were seriously considered. You see, they come with much wisdom and less forgetting about who they truly are. When their truth and self-worth is diminished they become discouraged and must act out in other ways to be seen.

There is so much that is changing. And it all starts with love. We will speak of this subject more in the future. We wish for you to have a deep understanding of what we are relaying here through this message. And so it is.

# Essay Nine - CHANGE

And so it is that we come before you this day with our deep admiration and appreciation for who you are in these significant times on your Mother Earth. For you see these times are of high significance in the entire universe – in all of creation you could say.

For each part of a system affects another part of the system. You know this and this is proven not only in your scientific community but also in other systems such as a family. It is known and validated that if one person in a family changes, then it affects everyone and the family system itself must change. So it is with the earth and her impact on the systems that she belongs to which affect larger and larger systems.

This is why there is such focus on the earth at this time and it is why you have attracted the attention of galaxies all over the universe. So this brings us to the matter at hand today - change. Oh it brings up much fear for many humans. So many view change as being similar to death. For they are so attached to what it is that they are losing that it is like losing life itself. And yet we wish you to understand that change is a constant. It is always there. By accepting it and greeting it as you would anticipate a wonderful vacation, then you could easily move through it.

Change is necessary. In order for a system to thrive, it depends on change. You can see in stagnant water that when there is no change the system begins to die. It becomes clogged and is unable to thrive. Such it is with the entire system of the universe. And, of course, then it is also true for this system you call the earth and all creatures and plants upon it.

Even the rocks change. Something that looks as solid and bold as a rock also changes. So how could you expect to live your lives without change? Think of it. Without change your babes would never grow up. Your plants would never mature to provide food. Your air would hold the pollution that is pumped into it and you would die. So why so much trouble accepting change? It is vitality itself.

If you could see that change in your lives is truly vitality you may accept it more readily. Think of it. You lose your job. It is a great surprise so therefore it appears as unwanted change. But if you were to view it with the understanding that all change is vitality then you would see it differently. Instead of falling into worry and despair you would look upon the situation as one of wonder. You would know that a new opportunity awaits.

That is the only way when you accept that change leads to vitality. And so you would rest easy in the knowing that something wonderful was about to appear in your life - new growth, new opportunity. With that appreciation, you would see the new opportunities as they present themselves. When you are lost in worry and despair then you try to duplicate what was and you look for work just like you had before.

In this way you become lost because the change was intended to lead you to something new. The lack of faith that the change is leading to something better put blinders on and you do not see the new, fresh opportunities that await you. You do not see the opportunities that would lead to your newest desires being fulfilled. Instead of embracing change most humans rebel against it and to cling to the stagnant past. A piece of them dies in the process.

And so, in this discourse about change, we also wish you to know that change brings evolution. You know that the plants and animals on the earth evolve over time. Your scientists have seen this in their archeological discoveries. Even the human species has evolved over time. This is also a vital part of the history of the earth. And so this sharing is to give you the understanding that the earth is in the pivotal moment of one of the greatest changes ever to happen upon your planet and you have no option but to embrace it.

The more who embrace this change the easier it will be for everyone. Many who are reading this know that you are at the end of a 23,000 year cycle that has been repeated many times on the earth. It is a natural part of the system. It is like your moon cycles but of course a cycle of a much longer timeline. And, considering that this cycle comes so far apart it only makes sense that the changes that it brings would be much greater than the cycles you see with your moon.

However we would like you to consider the cycles of the moon and the effect it has upon humans, animals and the plant kingdom. All are impacted and that again has been proven through studies. So imagine the magnitude of a 23,000 year cycle. The change is paramount. Nothing else is possible. Such a time lapse between the turning of the cycle means that, when it shifts, the degree of change is magnified. And so it is that you are seeing these changes on the earth increasing and magnifying because of this time that you are in.

It is our desire for you to understand this so that you will be aware of the need to allow yourselves to flow with this change. Do not stand and scream about all the change and see it as destruction. Remember – change is creating vitality. If you do not flow with these changes your own vitality will be diminished. You can see these times with new eyes. It is your thoughts that envision what it is you see in this world.

Look at someone who is always happy. Some would say they are lucky and that is why they are so happy. We would say that they are happy and that is why they are so lucky. If you are resisting that which finds its way into your reality you are resisting creation itself. In fact you are resisting your own creation. So open your hearts to accepting that you are in a time of great change on the earth and know that it is a grand opportunity.

Those who understand what is available in these times are celebrating. They see change out of the ages of darkness. They see the chance to lift themselves out of the heaviness that has been the human existence for far too long. They see Light pouring its rays upon the earth. And what is Light? It is life itself.

How long would you survive without your sun? And so we invite all of you to follow those with open hearts and smiling faces and peace in their lives. When you see such a being ask them how they came to be so at peace with life. Do not miss the opportunity to find out how you too may find this grace in your life. It starts with accepting change and seeing the opportunities that it brings.

We ask you to give some meditation to this discourse that you may fully understand the meaning of what we say and the impact it will have on your life. These messages are delivered to support you in your growth and in your movement through this time. You can clearly see that what we speak of is truth. Ask in your heart if you are ready to hear this truth and embrace it in such a way that you will welcome change as growth.

May this be your quest this day, to find the answer within your own heart where all wisdom lies. We are here supporting you, showing the way out of the darkness. You have only to follow. And yet we say, follow not out of fear but out of the place of deep understanding of the truth of what is being spoken this day. That is why we ask you to search within your own heart for the truth of this message. We love you so. And so it is.

# Essay Ten - SHINE YOUR TRUE LIGHT

To those of you who have been clearing the sleep out of your eyes, we commend you. We commend you for taking the steps to find your wholeness - for taking the steps to be the brilliant Being of Light that you are. The more of you who shine your radiant Light into the world, the more you bring along with you. And what do we mean by shining your Light?

We mean, accepting the fullness of your potential as a human and stepping into that. We mean standing up and claiming your rights as a human and stepping into that. We mean knowing who you are with such surety that nothing will knock you off your center. These are the attributes of a human who is holding their birth Light within themselves. It is, in a sense, knowing who you are and appreciating that.

Some of you look at pieces of who you are and say, unconsciously, that piece of me does not fit into society so I will hide that into the darkness of my subconscious. And even though you shove it aside there, it keeps creeping up, looking for some light, like a new seedling seeking the sunlight. And then you step on it so it will not grow.

Instead we encourage you to love all those pieces of yourself. You have been misguided. It is not that those qualities of you are not worthy. It is that they did not fit into the societal norms that have mastered the suppression of your true self – your true Light. Those who set up those norms, the church and governments, have done such a good job of suppressing your true Light that you control yourselves. Your parents, with every good intention, taught you how to suppress those aspects of your being that did not fit within the norms.

Now we beg you to find those pieces of yourself that were suppressed and let them shine. Rashana is thinking of a friend who knows what she wants for herself but was always told that it was selfish to want for oneself, so she suppresses the very essence of who she is that would get her exactly where she wants to be.

So Beloveds, we ask you this day to look at the truth of who you are and love every part of yourself. Are you super sensitive and feel like the world is cruel and overwhelming at times? Love that part of yourself. Are you aggressive and know how to get what you want? As long as you can come from love in your actions, honor that piece of who you are and go get it. This is the time for you to claim who you are.

Explore all the little pieces of your history that have taught you to suppress who you are. Ask yourself what is suppressed that is ready to come alive. This is how you become whole again and step into the fullness of who you are. Rashana this morning saw a new group on FaceBook for sensitive people and she rejoiced. It took her back to a time when she was told that she had to toughen up to be prepared for the world. She knew that no one could toughen the sensitivity out of her.

So to read of a group that identified with that trait and made it OK to be sensitive and even just the labeling of it brought her great relief. This is what it is to love every aspect of who you are. Why should someone else determine whether it is worthy or not? This is how you find your way back home to your heart.

When you think of 'going home' do not think of leaving the planet but of finding your way back to your heart. When you are living from the heart and loving yourself and knowing yourself from the heart then you will feel like you are home. You feel like you have found heaven on earth. It is the lack of love on this planet that has you yearning for something different.

And so we wish you to be gentle with yourself and all those around you. When you see someone lost in the pain of being on this planet, embrace them with your love, even if it is just sending a loving thought their way. It will be felt. It will be a touch of grace in their day. And so we leave you this day with the encouragement to see yourself.

Truly find out who you are and then love every bit of you. Even the pieces of you that you do not like, with love will dissolve into softness. Anger cannot exist in a loving heart. Fear cannot exist in a heart that sees only love. Give it a try. Love all of you and see who you become. Make it your goal for people to say, "Wow. You have changed." Smile and say "I have stepped into the brilliance of who I am." Their response will be an invitation to share what you are doing and invite them to do the same. And so it is.

# Essay Eleven - HARMONY

So let us speak to you today of harmony, for indeed harmony is an aspect of love that is diminished in your society – in your world today. Harmony is the essence of grace. When one is living in harmony with all that is, they flow with the understanding that life comes to them. Those who live in harmony love themselves enough to know that they do not have to push to create, but simply to express that which they desire to have in their lives and then rest easy, knowing that the universe will provide.

In that knowing, when something presents itself, then they say yes to the opportunities that resonate as truth. This living in harmony is a way of living that is in essence, giving up the belief that one must do and do and push and fight for what they want. This does not lead to harmony. Harmony in living is... asking ... resting... receiving... asking... resting... receiving. The resting is the state of patiently knowing that your request is in the process of being fulfilled.

Asking and then asking again and then wondering when it will show up and then demanding that is show up now is not harmony. Living in harmony requires that vital zero point of rest where there is almost a forgotten state of what has been asked for. It is in that space of emptiness that the request may be fulfilled. It is in that place of resting that magnetizes the request to the one who has asked. This is a new way of being for many of you and so one that will take some practice.

Whenever you find yourself wondering when and why your request hasn't shown up yet, remember the state of resting. It knows the request it is on its way. The knowing is another aspect that allows the state of resting to be easier to reside in. When you are knowing, absolutely knowing, that what you have asked for is on its way, then you will find that it is easy to let go of the how it will show up. You simply wait.

The next step is to see your request when it does show up. It is easy to form an idea in your mind of what your request should look like. When it appears it may look quite different than what you have imagined it would look like. Because of this, many miss their greatest joy because they do not see it when it appears. This is why it is better to have an essence of the *qualities* of your request as opposed to the finer details.

For example, if you are asking for a life partner, what qualities would you want to see in that person? List your qualities as opposed to the specific features. We would see specific features as physical appearance, level of income, career, family size, location and such. On the other hand, qualities would be defined as loving, sincere, kind, generous, compassionate, adventurous, etc. We trust you can see the difference in the two.

When you focus on the qualities then you are more likely to see them when they show up. If you say that your partner must be handsome, rich, well dressed according to your standards, then you may not see him when his hair is blonde instead of dark brown and he wears sandals instead of a business suit. He may be the person with the qualities of character perfectly suited to your heart's desire but by focusing on the specifics you will have missed that.

On the other hand, if you are looking for one who is loving, compassionate and generous, you would be open to seeing those qualities in whoever comes into your field. Then you would begin to wonder if this person is indeed the one you have been looking for.

This example is just but one that people can relate to. The same principle applies to all aspects of your life when living in harmony. Perhaps you desire a new way of making your living in the world. You tell the universe you would like to earn your living in a way that uses your special talents which you have identified and in a way that is of service to others and allows you freedom and flexibility.

By defining your new position this way, it allows the universe to create something for you that may look like nothing you have ever imagined but you will recognize that it does give you the qualities that you have requested and you will know it is right for you. This allows your life to flow. It allows the harmony of ease and grace to flow in and through your life.

This is the harmony of which we speak. This is the harmony that brings joy into your way of being. It is so easy once you start using it and seeing your requests begin to manifest in your life. Start with small things that are almost insignificant so that you do not have a lot of emotional attachment to the outcome. Once you see those things showing up in your life it will be easier to accept that you can create in this way and start testing your ability to receive and flow with more important aspects of your life.

This is the new way of it Dear Ones. This is the new way of being human on this planet. It is preparation for the higher dimensions that you are moving into. In the fourth and fifth dimension of living, every thought is a creation. There is no time lapse. It is vital to begin to work with these energies so that you begin to make the connection between what your expectations are of your life and what you see as your life. They are intrinsically tied. No exception.

You have the grace at this time of a delay between some of your desires and the manifestation of that desire. This is grace itself. It is like a child learning to hold onto things. You give them small, soft, Light things to grasp in the beginning so that they do not hurt themselves if they drop the item. Such is the way of being in the third dimension. The time delay gives you time to see the correlation between that which you think about and its manifestation in the world.

Many of you have noticed that you are creating faster and faster. Let us give you an example. Let us suppose you are driving through your town or city and the speed limit changed to a slower speed but you did not slow down immediately. You see a police car on the side of the road and as soon as you pass on goes the Lights and siren and it pulls out behind you.

You realize you are about to get stopped for speeding. You accept that as your current reality (a key to switching realities). Then you state that you just didn't slow down fast enough but you did intend to slow down and *you would like the police car to simply drive by you*.

However, you also accept the apparent outcome without attachment (another key), so you start to pull over to the side of the road and, to your delight, the police car speeds past you and keeps going. Did you change your reality or was the car going to pass you anyway? You may never know. But, the more you play with this and see the seemingly probable outcome change, the more you will believe in your impact on the outcome.

Every aspect of your reality comes from what you believe your reality will be. Every piece of it. Your angry boss is only acting out what you believe your boss to be. Your troubled child is only acting out a reflection of the troubled child within you. Because of this belief about yourself you project it onto your child who has no choice but to act it out for you.

Change your belief about that child and the child will change. This is the way of it Dear Ones. We share this with you so that you can begin to take notice of these things in your life and learn to recreate your world through the awareness of your thoughts. For many of you this will be a challenge. You will have to identify all your fearful thoughts and search for their manifestation in your life.

Pay attention. Look inside and be brave. You have the courage to do it. After all, it takes more energy to continue creating a life that brings hardship than it does to search for the source of that hardship and create differently. Life has a natural affinity to health. That is health of the mind, physical body and human experience. That is the way that life wants to exist.

It takes more effort to hang onto fear and anger than to live in grace and harmony. Be easy on yourselves as you explore this. Be forgiving and loving like those who watch over you. There is no judgment in the heavens, only compassionate support. Be the same for yourself. It is hard work being a human in the third dimensional reality. That is why we are so delighted to see you moving toward the Light of the higher dimensions.

Though it requires a time of learning to be in these new frequencies, those who are already feeling the benefits will tell you how sweet the rewards truly are. We love you so and watch over you always. You are our brethren, for we are all from the same source. Understand that all of creation watches as you move through this grand time of lifting yourselves out of the density of the third dimension into the Light. We are ever so proud of your progress. And so it is.

# Essay Twelve - LOVE YOURSELF INTO WHOLENESS

In our initial contact with our channel, we stated that she would be writing a book about love. For is it not love that is the willingness to give your energies to the earth each and every day so that she can ascend with the greatest of ease and grace? Yes it is. And so this is what this book will be about. It is about us loving you and showing humans the way in which they can move into the Light and it is about you offering love back by being of service to the earth.

We know so many of you feel this great desire to be of service, this great desire to be part of the transition, the great change on the earth at this time. It is simple. It can be one simple act of offering Creator Light into the earth. You humans are the anchors of the Light. It cannot be forced upon you. You must ask for it. You must be willing to be the channel for the Light to pass through. And so, in your willingness to anchor this love Light into the earth, you are benefitting yourself, all of humanity, the earth and all her creatures.

One seemingly simple act has such great significance. This is the way of it. This is indeed how simple it truly is to be of service to the earth. And you will feel the rewards. You feel the pleasure of knowing that you are doing something to make a difference in this world. No one may ever be able to tangibly grasp what you are offering but do not doubt its impact. We say to you that those in our planes of existence will see the Light that you have created on this earth. We are your witness to your willingness and your intent to be of support to creation in this time of the great shift.

Oh what wondrous times are currently existing on this earth. What glory is ringing out in the heavens for those who see the Light. Celebrations are taking place every day for the changes that are influencing the earth closer to the great Light that she is. She is too precious to be lost. Some have tried. Some have proceeded without any consideration for the heart and soul of this planet on which you reside.

They have failed, for we say again, the earth is too beautiful to be destroyed. She is much more magical than you know. She is the culmination of eons of time in creation and the perfection with which she currently operates is the pinnacle of creation. And you, those of you reading these pages, those of you residing on this grand planet, have the honor of being here − of being witness to her beauty if you would but open your eyes to it.

So many have their blinders on, unable to see the Light. To those of you we say watch out. If you are not willing to lose the blinders you may not see the Light for a long, long time. This is not to scare you. This is to wake you up. Now is the time for ascension. If you miss this opportunity you will be living the third dimensional reality for a long time before this opportunity presents itself again.

Loud and long will be the cries of despair for those who realize too late that they missed the boat so to speak. This is not some cruel punishment for those who are left behind. This is simply the laws of creation. This opportunity comes approximately every 23,000 years at the Precession of the Equinoxes. Now is that time. That is why this is such a grand time on the earth.

If you are reading this and wondering, well, how do I make the shift? What is required of me? What am I to do? What does the shift mean? We say to you, the shift means that you will be residing in a higher plane of existence. The higher the plane of existence, the more love that exists. The more love that you are surrounded by, the more beautiful the life and the more ease and joy. It has been a long, dark road in the last few millennia on this earth.

Now is the time, through your willingness and desire to shift into the higher dimension, to take that giant step forward. It starts with the decision that you would like to give up the life that you are currently living for one that is less commercial and more 'natural'. Imagine a life where everyone supports each other and children are praised for their individual qualities and these qualities are nurtured as they mature. People see only love in each other. They have patience and understanding for each other. They reflect the best of who they are back to those who they interact with.

Imagine a world where everyone is provided for and everyone is appreciated for who they are. If this is a world that you would like to live in, then say yes to ascension. That commitment alone is the first step. Once you say yes, then you begin to do the work that is required to allow you to be in position for ascension. That work is healing the wounds of the past.

It takes a Light heart to move into the higher dimensions. And it takes a loving heart. And the first love should be for yourself. So many are deeply wounded on this earth. Begin by loving yourself into wholeness. Allow yourself to be vulnerable enough to admit that you are carrying deep wounds. Then be willing to allow those wounds to reveal themselves and be healed. You will find your way with this. There are so many books and healers available.

It is your commitment to healing that will lead you to the resources that are most suitable for who you are. This is all that is asked of you in order to find your way to the Light at this time. We say to you that time is running short. Do not decide to wait until you retire and have more time or wait until the children are grown, thinking that you are too distracted right now. The more you heal your own wounds, the more your children will benefit. As you grow and heal, all your relationships will be affected, whether with a partner, coworker or parent.

And so we ask you, how much of this can you read before you begin to get the message that the time is now? The time is now to step into the fullness of who you are. And in order to be in the fullness of you, healing must take place if it has not already begun.

You are clearing centuries of pain from the consciousness of the human being. Do not blame yourself for carrying these wounds. Rejoice in the willingness to release, for the sake of all mankind, the pain of the past so that you are Light enough to lift off into the fourth and fifth dimension of existence. We are here supporting you, holding you up, as you make your way out of the darkness into the Light. We love you so. And so it is.

# Essay Thirteen - WORTHINESS

Indeed, worthiness as an important subject of discussion. For you see, many of you humans walking this planet have been impacted by the ways of your society and its conditioning. It diminishes the worthiness in just about every human on earth. And so worthiness, for many, is something that must be learned. And in order to learn to connect with your worthiness you must first disconnect with all the patterns and beliefs that have been placed into your subconscious around unworthiness.

We wish you to know much you have accomplished and how revered you are on the other dimensions – on the higher planes of existence. You are a grand and radiant species of Light. Accept that as your birth right. Peel away the layers of the wounded soul and find your way back into your heart – back to the child who is waiting there. The child is waiting to be treated with tenderness and kindness.

The child is waiting to be embraced with love and accepted just for who s/he is. See that child within your heart and cradle it in your warm embrace. Tell her how beautiful she is and how delighted you are to be at her side. Soften her with your embrace so that she will feel safe to be out in the world. Comfort her with your words of acceptance for whatever she is feeling. Let her know that you understand and everything is different now.

Now you are ready to see her and help her feel safe. Now you are loving her for who she is – no need to change anything or be different or try to fit into any norm or try to be like everyone else. No, no - you love her just the way she is and nothing about her needs to change. Find this child within yourself and give it these gentle messages. The child will soften and feel safe to come out. As this happens the old beliefs will begin to fall away.

Whenever you feel the need to scold yourself, give it up for gentle acceptance for how the child is feeling. You cannot push your way through to love. You soften into love. Even if a child is 'misbehaving', if this child feels loved and cared for, it will want to do what is 'right'. It will want to do what pleases others because it has self-love that does not require any acting out. Acting out is only a cry for love. That goes for the adult self that is scolding itself and it goes for the young child that is learning how to be in this world. So do not punish that acting out but soften it with love.

How will you know you have found your way in this? You will begin to feel more love of those around you instead of frustration or a need to fix them. This is truly an acceptance of the self. What you see outside of you is a reflection of what lies within. When you see others with patience and acceptance, then you can be sure that you are treating yourself with patience and acceptance.

When you are frustrated at others or want to change them it is an indicator of what you are asking of yourself. Frustration is a great opportunity to see that your soul, the higher aspect of yourself, is asking for some changes of perception. This is your clear indicator light of where your soul wants to go.

It would be easy to not believe what we are saying. Many of you will make that choice. For those of you who are making a conscious choice to take advantage of the grand opportunity on the earth to ascend into the dimensions of greater love and greater joy, hop on board. Do the work of exploring your internal world and watch your external world change as if by magic. This

45

is the way of it. This understanding is what will lead you back to your worthiness.

It is the creative essence of the human and it is grand indeed. There is not much more time to grasp this understanding. Your thoughts are creating and manifesting faster and faster. Every thought of lack is showing up in your experience. Please know this so that you can turn it around. Believe in yourself, heal those wounds of the past so that your Light can shine once again, claiming the radiant brilliance that you are.

We are waiting, watching and supporting you every step of the way. Reach out to us and we will be there. We will show you who you truly are in your dreams so that you can bring that remembrance back with you. You are a magnificent Being of Light and now is the time to step into that truth. And so it is.

# Essay Fourteen - BEING IN THE LIGHT

And so this is the topic of the day. Kind of like the soup of the day only less sloppy. At least we hope that we can bring this information forward in a way that is manageable. And so we say to you dear humans, you are in a time of transformation back to the lighter way of being. And so, being in the Light not only makes you brighter, it also makes you lighter. As you transform into a less dense physical being you will also find that the heavy burdens of the past will also transform.

As you come to a greater understanding of what is important in life you will also release a lot of the pain and despair that came with the old paradigm. Everything is changing in your world. There is no choice but to change along with it. Many of you are understanding the need for change but not understanding the how. You realize that part of your life is simply not working but what do you do differently to allow life to flow more easily?

What do you do to release the density from the body? You release the emotions that are from the past. The emotions that are heavy literally hold the body in the third dimension. This time of transition is one into the fourth dimension. And yet, you cannot rise up, so to speak, when you are holding the heavy emotions of the past in the physical body. For those of you who do not realize, the emotions are stored in the body.

They appear as illness when the burden has become heavy enough for that to manifest. They also appear as resistance to certain ideas or ways of being. For example, you may think you want a loving partner in your life but you truthfully resist allowing someone in. It is not a cruel cosmic joke that you would ask for love and it not appear. It is a resistance based on emotions from the past stored in the cells as a memory.

Therefore, it is required that those emotions be released and you heal those feelings in order to allow a new experience into your current reality. This is what we refer to when we talk about releasing the burdens that will allow your physical being to become lighter which also means more full of Light.

For you see Beloveds, Light is the key. Light is love in a sense. The love of the Creator comes on a ray of Light. Just as darkness is dense, love is Light. When you make room in the heart for Light to enter, you will find your body changing. You will find your life changes as if by magic. As you release the burdens of the past and allow yourself to become a new person, everything you see in your world changes. This is the challenge of these times. You must forget who you were in order to be who you are. You are a new human on this earth. Your biology is different.

Look at the children of today. They are different as well. The children of the new millennia are born with a crystalline biology. What do crystals do? They retain and relay information. That is why these children are so knowing. That is why children who are barely two years old have a great vocabulary and are learning to count and the alphabet. They come in wiser and they do not forget what they know like humans did when their bodies were carbon based. This is the magnificence of these times. And so you may look to the children and their way of being to learn how to be lighter – lighter in the heart, less burdened and more radiant.

For those of you who are feeling that life is too challenging to endure we say to you that you must allow yourself to change. When you resist this new way of being, you will only draw hardship to yourself. The first step is healing the wounds of the past. We cannot say this too often. Without releasing the old wounds out of the body, you will not be able to fly.

It is like a hot air balloon with the basket full of heavy boulders. It cannot lift off the ground until those boulders are thrown out of the basket. The more rocks that are thrown out, the lighter it becomes. The balloon will not rise if only two or three rocks are removed. Most of the rocks need to be thrown out in order for the balloon to find the freedom of rising into the skies. And once it floats up it has a much broader view of the world. It allows an overview of what is below - a great perspective for moving forward.

And so Dear Ones, we use this analogy for you to see the weight that is your hidden emotions. Search them out and release them to the heavens for transformation. Once you do, you fly closer to the sun. And flying closer to the sun does not destroy you, it enriches you. The sun is the source of life. The sun is the source of Light on this planet. The closer you get to that source of Light the closer you are to your true essence. Now is the time to release yourself into that Light.

And once you lighten the burden of those outdated, outmoded emotions, you are able to fly into joy. There is great joy and peace and contentment on the other side of this work you are doing to change into a Light Being. There is great understanding of the truth of who you are. There is great trust in the way of it and what that means to the human existing on earth. Let us give you a taste of what humans will be a few generations from now.

You will be communicating through your thoughts. You will be creating with your thoughts. You will think apple and an apple will appear before you. You will be loving each other unconditionally because you will know that love is all there is. There will be no fighting among nations. Only peace will reside within your hearts and therefore upon your planet. You will understand your connection to All That Is. You will have deep appreciation for all that this beautiful planet is. You will feel your connection to nature and exist in harmony with it.

You will manage your weather patterns not only out of your needs but out of the needs of the planet. You will speak in communion with the animals and the plant kingdom. You will come together in communities of love, sharing what you have freely and receiving what others have to offer with great gladness. Life will be a continuous bliss of harmony; for even the seeming hardship that arises will be accepted with a deep wisdom that appreciates all experiences.

This is the life that awaits you Dear Ones. You are almost there. If this life sounds like the one you wish to be living then it is time to do the work to allow yourself to get there. Open your heart to loving yourself. This is the foundation of all love. Yours is not a task of saving the world. You must restore yourself and then your work in the greater world will begin. We can honestly say that the majority of those reading these pages will benefit from more releasing. Clean out the basket. The balloon is your heart. If it is heavy it cannot fly.

Release and clear so that you can be a part of the great new earth that awaits. She is here to support you and love you. She is waiting patiently, your earthly mother. She does not want to leave anyone behind as she rises into the Light of the Kingdom of God. Heed these words and do the work so that you may rise up with humanity into the grace of the higher dimensions of existence. All of creation awaits you there. And so it is.

# Essay Fifteen - THE DAY OF RECKONING

And so it is Dearly Beloveds that we are called to you this day with a message of deep significance in these times of transformation. For here you stand. You have passed the marker that was December 21, 2012. You have moved into a new year and you are still alive. Hooray! And yet, much is yet to be accomplished. The true transition into the Light was delayed. For not as many humans were ready to ascend as we had originally hoped for. And so this means, for those of you who are aware, that there is more work to be done to lift all of humanity into the energies of love and Light.

For those of you who are reading this message, we ask of you to be conscious and aware of keeping your thoughts with the Light. Keep your thoughts focused on joy. The more you are thinking positive thoughts, the more you are lifting all of humanity closer to what you would call heaven. The lighter the world is the easier it is to ascend or rise up. It makes logical sense to the human brain and so we like to use this analogy for you in these times.

So what do we mean by the day of reckoning? It is the day when the earth will have to make her transition into the fifth dimension. We say to you that she is already residing in the fourth dimension. Soon will come the day when she will again take another leap, another shift into the next dimension and those who are still residing in the third dimension will be left to finish many more incarnations on that level of being until the next Precession of the Equinoxes 23,000 years from now. That is why it is a day of reckoning. It is vitally important for any beings who are intending in moving into the higher dimensions to do the work that is required to allow you to rise up.

So when will this day of reckoning be? This is a question that is flexible with the creations of humanity. The more of you who are stepping into your brilliance and radiating your Light into the world, the sooner this time of transition will come. The earth will wait as long as she can, for she is your mother and she wishes that you will be able to join her. For this reason she is very patient. She waits and waits and offers her love to you so that you can find your way back to your true self.

Every single human being on the earth at this time came with the intention of ascending into the higher dimensions. And so it is our wish that those intentions will be fulfilled. However, the human experience still carries a lot of drama and density. It is easy to fall into the patterns that pull you away from your magnificence. When you connect with the worldly affairs such as war and hatred and you connect with your dramatic TV shows that focus on jealousy and greed then you are keeping yourself connected to the dark side of this incarnation.

You will not find the Light that way. Disconnect from all that heaviness. When you connect with these events or shows with your mind you are in reality creating such events in your life. Your imagination creates. When you watch these shows your imagination sees them as real so it must show up in some sense as reality in your life.

You must disconnect from these things if you want to rise up into the Light. The irony is that once you do you will soon find that you do not miss those things at all. You will find that your heart feels lighter and you will seek out other more joyful activities to fill your time. You may take up certain creative endeavors or find yourself connecting with more like minded souls that are also choosing the Light. Do not let the drama of the life of others make drama for your life. Step out. Seek that which comes from a place of love.

We know who is reading this message and we know those of you who say oh yes, I am a Light worker or I am an Indigo. But we say to you Dear Ones, you must do the work to make that claim. You cannot claim to be a Light worker and not do any Light work. You cannot claim to be a Light worker and gossip about every other person that you work with. You cannot claim to be a child of the Light and diminish your own Light.

Step into the radiance of who you are. Now is the time. This is the intent of this message this day. You are running out of time to play around and not be serious about your ascension. If it is your intention to ascend with the earth as she raises ever higher then you must be living with the full intention of disconnecting from the dysfunction in the world and see only love and grace. Seek out happy stories on the internet. Seek out happy people. Seek out loving thoughts of yourself and others. And most importantly, do the healing to release the past that keeps you from truly moving forward.

Your time has been extended. As we mentioned earlier, the earth is very patient. She cannot wait forever. If you have any questions about how you shift from the world you see before you that is full of war and crime and fear and into the Light, just read our messages *very carefully*. We are showing you the way. You must pay attention to every suggestion. They may seem simple on the surface but they will lead you to your place of grace.

However, it does require some doing. Step out of the drama and into your own life. Stop allowing yourself to be distracted out of your own life. Pull back in and discover who you really are. It is like your scientists exploring the moon and other planets when they do not even know of all the species that exist on this beautiful planet where you reside. If you could see the earth from our perspective you would never dream of being anywhere else. This is the way of it.

So where will you be on the day of reckoning? Will you have taken the steps to make it evident to Spirit that you are ready and willing to go with the earth? Fill your heart with love and you will find the way. Fill your heart with fear and you will be lost. Oh, we understand that it can be difficult to see the love in this world at times. We understand Dear Ones. And yet we say to you, it is all about where you put your focus. What you believe - you see.

If you believe the world is an evil place full of hatred and misdeeds that is what you will see. You must choose to see love. In every instance ask yourself where is the love here? And do not blame Creator for allowing hardship and natural disaster and a fallen economy. These are all creations of man. Those who are suffering through them are those who could not find the love. More than ever before on this earth you are creating your life.

There is great compassion for those who are suffering and that same compassion is the reason for offering this message to assist you in understanding that it is within your own minds that these events are created. So choose love and Light. Many have chosen to stop watching the news and stop watching movies full of killing and fearful drama. Many have chosen to give up friends who do not understand where they are headed.

Instead they have sought out a new circle of support that understands who they are and what they are choosing to create in their lives. Find your circle of

Light so it is easier to give up that which no longer serves your highest good. Your internet is a great place to start. It is like a great reflection of the earth. You can find love or hatred there.

For those who choose love, nothing fearful comes to them for literally, what you search for you find. Search for joyful events, happy stories, and communities of people ready to support you on your journey back into the fullness of who you are and who you came to be. Find your way back to the great shining Light that lies within your loving heart. All of creation awaits you. And so it is.

# Essay Sixteen - THE ASCENSION

And so it is beloved beings of the earth that we address you this day with the intention of supporting you in your journey back to the Light. For indeed, those who are residing here on planet earth have lost your connection to your source Light. You have lost your connection to your path to enlightenment. And yet, there lies before you a marvelous opportunity to find your way back.

The planetary alignments in these times around the year of 2012 have allowed great transformation in the human biology. This is to assist you in these times. This is to assist you in seeing the Light and claiming the Light and walking into the Light. This does require action on your part Beloveds. You must take up the guard and march forward with your own enlightenment. No one will do it for you. Everything is lined up to make it possible but you must take action to step into the reality of what you are choosing at this time.

All it takes really is your intention. Once you state your intention to move into ascension then, like dominoes, everything falls into place for this to happen. Like one domino knocking on the other, things fall into place, one opportunity leading to another leading to another to ensure your success. And yet we see many of you resisting this opportunity. We see you hanging onto your current reality as if there were nothing better available. That is the problem as we see it.

You have been in this third dimensional reality for so long and it is so comfortable that you do not even consider that something else could be better than this. And yet we say to you, what awaits you in the fourth dimension is beautiful beyond anything that you could ever imagine. It is a world full of love and beauty. There is no fighting, there is no war, aside from your internal battles. It is a world full of such grace and wonder that you will shake your heads for ever resisting it. But, from the human perspective, if you cannot see it and know what it is, you resist it.

So go into your imaginations and pretend that you have just arrived in a magical land. Everything is so bright. The colors are vibrant and there is so much beauty. The flowers almost sparkle and the sky emanates a wondrous hue of golden Light. Everyone looks peaceful and content. The houses are magnificent. There are so many different creations. It is as if everything you could ever wish for exists in this magical land. You wonder what it would be like to live here. People seem to be happy and they all know each other and share greetings and are happy to help one another out when needed.

They have gardens that are overflowing with vegetables and fruit. It is like heaven on earth. Go ahead and carry on with this vision. Make it as grand as you possibly can. Then ask yourself if it was possible to live this way would you say no thanks, I think I'll stay here where there is war and fighting and people gossip about you all the time and people struggle for money and work like slaves? We don't think so.

This is what it is like in the next dimensional reality. You can create all these beautiful things for yourself. This is what is possible. And this is why we are so intent in helping you understand what is possible. We would love to see you there. We are at your side supporting you in this transition.

And so Dear Ones, take the time to consider what is happening on this planet at this time. You are about to pass into another dimensional reality. It is kind of like the transition from believing that the world was flat, which is a two dimensional reality, into accepting that it is round – a higher dimensional perspective that is 3D. Now you have the opportunity to expand your horizons even farther and step into 4D. What awaits you there is magical indeed but you must make the choice to be there.

You must understand that the choice to ascend does not mean that everything will be left behind. You are not the only one on this earth who is willing to make this transition. There are many who are ready to step into the Light, tired of the weariness of this existence in the denser realities. And as you pass into the next dimension you will be so happy with what you discover there that you will not regret your decision.

We think this is a good time to relay to you that children will not be left behind. Their pure hearts will willingly ascend when the time comes. Do not allow that fear to hold you back from your choice. For those with adult children, ask yourselves, if you stay behind because you are not sure your children will go, will you be able to help them by being in the density of the third dimension? We say to you that there will be little you could do by staying behind.

If, however, you make the choice to rise up you will have affected your genealogy by doing so and created greater opportunity for those in your lineage to do the same when the opportunity comes again. Simply by making the choice and stepping through the veil into the fourth dimension you will be affecting those of your heritage in doing the same. This is the way of it Dear Ones. Every change affects the all, and especially those that carry your DNA, the genes of your heritage.

Rashana feels as if we are beating a dead horse so to speak. Repeating and repeating our desire for those who are reading this message to take the actions required to ascend. And as we have said, the biggest action is simply to say yes to ascension. In response to her concerns we say, she does not see the numbers who are hesitant to make the choice. She does not see the number of people who carry the awareness of what is happening but are hesitant to step into the unknown. She does not have the vision to realize the great disappointment of those souls once the door closes and they are running toward it.

This is what inspires us to be so committed to the weight of this message. It compares not to the despair of the souls on the other side of the door as the last opportunity to ascend slips away. That is the reason for our repetition and that is the reason for our serious transmissions. They will become lighter as we progress with these messages. In the beginning we feel the need to express what we are sharing so that you will feel the magnitude of this opportunity and the heaviness of a possible lost opportunity. And so it is.

# Essay Seventeen - THE COMMANDING OF THE LIGHT

There is much in the way of living in the fourth dimension that has not yet been revealed to humanity. But be revealed it must. For if you are to evolve into that dimension it is only fair to give you a heads up of what existence will be like on that dimension. It would be rather folly and thoughtless to let you fall into that realm without any understanding of what life like there will be.

And so it is that we are sending these transmissions. We are here to serve. We are here to guide you closer to the Light. We are here as your brothers and sisters of the Light, walking by your side, offering encouragement and hope when you feel lost. Our goal – our aim – is to be good enough guides that you do not feel lost. However, we also understand that until you experience something you cannot fully know what it is like. And so it is with this great transition that you are currently moving into.

We can teach you ways to be in the world you are entering into. We can tell you what to expect and how to think to manage your experience, but you will not fully know until you are there. It is our hope at that time that you will remember these transmissions and you will say to yourself, oh yes, I must be clear in my thoughts, for I am manifesting instantly. Oh yes, I must think loving thoughts and create a loving reality for myself. This is our intent here Dear Ones and so we ask you to pay close attention to our words.

We are going to tell you something that does not fall within the norms of your current society. And yet, in the fourth dimension, it is something to be aware of. Your way of being in the world is to fully integrate your love into yourself and not to consider others at all. This seems harsh from your current perspective but once you become a conscious creator, you will see the importance of this understanding.

When you make it to the fourth dimension, every thought is an instant creation. Knowing this, if you look at someone and wish something for them, you will influence their outcome and it may not be what the highest aspect of their soul is choosing. Instead you will understand that what you see before you is a reflection of your own reality. Therefore if you wish it to change, you will change your thoughts about yourself and not the other person who stands before you.

Do you understand Dear Ones? Do you understand that this is also true in this reality but not manifesting as quickly. So let us tell you another way. Let us imagine that your child is acting out, throwing toys all over the room in a fit of anger. In this instance you would not scold your child and demand that s/he pick up the toys. Instead you would imagine that your child was completely calmed down and picking up the toys without you having to say a word.

Because this is the reality that you are choosing for yourself, you would see that begin to happen. What you imagine would be your experience. If your child had anger that needed to be resolved, your child would figure out how to do that. You could certainly make it your experience to talk to your child and understand what your child is feeling to support her/his growth.

But the way of getting to that conversation would be different. We hope this offers a greater understanding of what we speak of. You are moving into an existence very different than what is currently the norm. The more you prepare here in this reality the more prepared you will be once you move to another reality.

And so what else can we offer you this day? We can offer you a message of understanding that changing who you have been for so long into a new way of dancing in this world can take some practice. We invite you to play with this. The next time someone is acting out in front of you, showing anger or upset, imagine them being totally calm. Let that play out in your mind and see if they calm down and change their behavior.

Let it be your little experiment and see how it plays out for you. You must expect a change in order for this to be successful. And, in reality, what you are changing is not the other person. You are changing *your* perception of what that other person is reflecting back to you. You are great creators and this way of being will become second nature to you once you begin to play with it.

Do not take it too seriously in the beginning. Just allow it to be light and joyful. That is what life was meant to be right from the beginning. Humanity was led waaaay off track. Now is the time to return to the lightness of being. Now is the time to pull yourselves back up to the Light that you call home. Every step up the ladder of ascension is another step closer.

And when you understand that *everything* is your creation you begin to understand that there is no right or wrong, good or bad. There is just creation. However, there is ignorance. You have lost your memory of how the game works. That was intentional. It is part of the game on planet earth and you agreed to play. However, now things are changing. It is a new game, played on a new field. It is now played on a higher field of resonance and so, in all fairness, you deserve to be retrained.

This new training is showing you how to work with the Light that you are and to help you understand that you are creating the dark and the Light. With that knowing, it is time to be aware of your decisions. Every decision, every thought, every action, is what is creating your life. There is no outside force of darkness that you can blame when things go differently than you think you would like them to be. Change your beliefs to match what you desire to experience and the darkness will disappear. It is a new game you are playing. If you do not learn the new rules, you're not going to win the game.

We send you great love in these transmissions. May your spirits be light as you progress through these ever-changing magical times on this, your planet earth. And so it is.

# Essay Eighteen - BEING IN THE LIGHT

Greetings Beloveds. Greetings from the Love and Light of the Creator energy as we come before you this day with gladness. For these opportunities to stand before humans and share our wisdom bring us great joy. We watch over you and we are greatly encouraged at the way in which humanity is moving into the Light.

So many are choosing to live from love and step out of the fear matrix that has existed on this Earth for so long. So many of you are ready to step up and be all that you have come to be with the intention of ascending with your beautiful and sacred Mother Earth. And so it is that when we are called to speak to you we are delighted to have the opportunity to express our encouragement and hope for success for all.

This day we have chosen the topic of Being in the Light. What does this mean for a human on this Earth? Being in the Light, to us, means that you are living your life with the intention of developing your spiritual self and with the awareness of the need for delving into the emotional blocks that keep you from moving forward. Many live their lives, once reaching adulthood, hiding from the emotional issues that keep them from moving forward in their spiritual development.

You are in the greatest learning school in the universe for spiritual development. To lose this opportunity by simply letting day after day pass by with the same routine and without any self-reflection is a sad waste of the chance for deeper learning. Know thyself is more than a mere trite saying. It is the foundation to being in the Light, living in the Light. Without taking the time to explore your pain you will not find your way out of suffering and darkness.

So what is suffering? Many of you would say I am not suffering. I have money to buy what I want, I have a good job and I can travel when I feel like it. Ah, but we ask you, what lies within your heart? Where are your daily thoughts? How often are you criticizing yourself or someone else? How often do you expect things to go wrong in your life? What are your relationships like? These are the questions to explore to help you identify the kind of suffering we are talking about. There is so much criticism on your Earth. Not many people are loving in every moment and seeing only good in others.

However, that kind of existence is possible and it is what you are headed for in the fourth dimension. Those who are not willing to do the clearing work to allow their thoughts to be loving, for themselves and others, will not be in resonance with the fourth dimension. And as we have already said, our intent in sharing these transmissions is for you to understand the way to ascend. We are sharing this information so that you may take the steps necessary to support your evolution. For when a species is evolving and a few of that species do not change, what do you think happens to them? Why do you think species evolve in the first place?

We will tell you that those who do not evolve will die away because the reason for evolution is to adapt to a changing environment. The fact that this planet on which you reside is evolving and changing is quite evident is it not? So it makes sense that the species that exist upon it must evolve as well. This is happening to the human right now even without many of you knowing that it is happening.

Your DNA is changing. And that is well and fine. We also say that you must change your way of thinking as well and your way of being. If you are one who would go to war and no one around you is fighting, what is the role of your readiness for battle?  Are you a support to that society that has chosen peace?  Will you break away from the norm and join up with other 'outsiders' who are ready to fight?  If so, where will that lead you? It will lead you into battle of course, when all around you is peace.

There is a similar scenario playing out in the minds of many right now on this Earth.  You are moving into an era of great peace and yet there are some who are continuing to battle within their own minds, where all battles begin.  This is an opportunity to step out of that way of being and choose to see peace in your surroundings.  It is a choice Dear Ones.  Whatever you *choose* to see you will see.  You can find the battles raging on this Earth if that is what you look for.  You will also see the love surrounding you if that is your focus.

We ask you to have compassion for those who are not ready to face their fears – who are not ready to look inside and find the wounded child there.  It takes great courage and strength to make this transition from despair into the Light.  To bring your dark and hidden secret existence to the Light of awareness is a great act of courage.  Be patient for those who are on this journey.

Try to understand what they are going through, revealing their pain, allowing themselves to appear weak in a society that looks down upon such character. In reality the vulnerable are much stronger that those who hide behind their pain with a brave façade.  In reality they are the warriors, doing battle with their own fears.  That is the only battle that is required.  When one fights the battles of the inner self there is no need for outward acts of war.

Resolving the war within allows the softness of love and acceptance to break through the darkness like a beacon of Light on a moonless night. This is courage. Support those who are in this place of revelation for themselves and have the strength to go there yourself. It is the only way. You must go it alone and you must take the journey.

There is so much to relay that we realize that many of these essays may leave you with more questions than answers. Keep reading. The more you hear and learn the more it will all come together and your understanding of what we offer here will expand. It is a journey that requires some time. Give yourself a full year just to begin this self-exploration.

That would be a very dedicated journey of being committed to healing all the wounded aspects of self. From there it just continues. It is a journey that is ever changing. And as you walk that path you feel lighter and lighter as the burdens of emotional pain are released layer by layer. It is a journey with deep personal rewards. It is the end of suffering. We hope that you will choose to walk that path. It leads to the Light – the greatest reward there is. We love you so. And so it is.

# Essay Nineteen - COMING OF AGE

Greetings Dearly Beloveds. Greetings from the Love and Light of Creation itself. Greetings from the heavens as we come before you in great joy and delight. For we see before us the queens and kings of the kingdom of humanity and we see before us the radiant ones who shine so brightly upon this Earth and it is to you that we speak this day.

Today we bring forth a message of love to those of you who are walking in your truth, walking the path of integrity and walking in the Light of your own radiance. Oh how you shine brightly upon this Earth. How you guide and lead others just by the presence of your Light is a glorious thing for us to behold. You cannot see yourselves as we do. We see the sparkling Light that you are upon the earth. Just as you look into the night sky and see stars, we look onto the Earth and we see your Lights shining like stars upon the Earth.

And she feels you. She feels each and every one of you as you walk her land. She feels your Light and she rejoices, for she knows that her children are with her. Your Light shows her that you are ready to ascend with her into the higher realms of existence. Your Light shows her that you are in resonance with her new vibration – the vibration of love. Can you feel it? Can you feel the giving back that your earthly mother sends to you each day? Stop. Take the time to notice. Connect with her and feel her love returning to you. She adores you so.

And so, children of the Light, come before us this day that we may offer you our blessings. We have to come to pour our loving grace upon you that you may feel our heart love touch your souls. We come before you to commend you for the coming of age. Oh yes, you have matured. You have passed the marker of being children upon this earth to being the great and powerful creators that you are. You have passed into maturity of spirit.

You have passed the test of the deepest level of darkness and you have passed with flying colors. You have aced the exam. For you are brilliant Light upon this earth. You are the will of God in human form, walking in service to the Light and walking to serve love. Your hearts are wide open to the bearing of this Light and you are radiating love out into the ethers – the sign of true Warriors of the Light.

Yet warriors you need be no longer. It is a time of the changing of the guard so to speak. No longer will you battle and toil to find your way back to love. The way shines brightly before you now. The darkness has all but fallen away. Oh we know that you can find it if you want to. What we speak of this day is the balance of Light and darkness upon this earth. The balance now stands with the Light and isn't that a reason to celebrate?

The earth resides in the overpowering energy of Love and Light. Hallelujah. The time has come for all who battled for so long to walk through this earthly school in search of the Light, in search for the way back to their loving hearts. The time has come when those who walked through the density shining their Light forward to celebrate and to reap the rewards of your great work. And what are those rewards? They are the grace of living life in harmony and with greater ease.

At the same time we say to you that you must know that you are creators and if you find that there is something lacking in your life, look at what your beliefs are around that lack and then choose differently. Believe the opposite to be true. Believe that you can have whatever you desire because you can. It is your beliefs that create the outcome. You are deserving. There is no doubt about that. It is not a matter of deserving, it is a matter of believing.

Being of service to the Light no longer means living as a recluse with a life of financial sacrifice. Oh no. Fill your coffers so that you have the freedom to live as you choose. Fill your coffers so that you can live the deserved life of abundance and bounty. Do not allow vows of many past lifetimes to carry forward into these new times and keep you humble. Step forward and claim who you are so that you are shining your Light brightly upon this earth.

And so it is that the coming of age is here for those who walk in the Light. Rejoice – sing – dance - play. It is time to celebrate. You have walked through the densest, darkest time upon the planet Earth back into the Light. How could anything be more worth celebrating than that? Love yourselves and love one another. Stand tall and proud. Be radiant for all to see your Light. Continue to sparkle Dear Ones, for all of the heavens rejoice in your great success – your passing into the Age of Enlightenment. It is ever so joyful. And we are your humble servants. And so it is.

# Essay Twenty - BEING IN THE LIGHT II

And so Dearly Beloveds, it is our deepest honor to stand before you once again this day. For we see all who will read these words and we honor you for your willingness to be here in these times of great change upon the Earth. For many of you it is not an easy journey. Your systems are falling apart with nothing apparent to replace them.

This is the way of it Dear Ones, for your systems will be created as you create them – one day at a time. It is the gathering of conscious thought on each and every nation that will recreate that which is crumbling. It takes time for the debris to settle before you can see through the dust and gain any clarity in what will replace that which has fallen. It will take time for new leaders to rise up – leaders who truly represent the people – who truly care for all and not just for themselves.

Those leaders are being nurtured now. They know who they are, although they are hesitant to step up just yet. And indeed it would be too soon. For the world is not ready yet for the change that will allow them to be seen. And so, for now, they remain hidden, waiting behind the curtain for the day when it is appropriate for them to step into center stage and pronounce their wishes to be of service through leadership. For indeed, in these coming times, leadership will truly be an avenue of service to the all.

No longer will this planet support those who care only for themselves with blatant disregard for the majority. Those days are gone and thankfully so. You are in a new age now. You are on the other side of the Precession of the Equinoxes and moving into thousands of years of peace and Light upon this planet.

71

Oh what a call for celebration. What a call for the rejoicing of the heavenly realms as we pay witness to that which is unfolding on this Earth that you call home.

And so what do we mean when we say Being in the Light? We wish to discuss this today so that you will have a greater understanding of what works and what does not work in this new way of being. The most obvious is that you are no longer in the dark. So what does that mean? We invite you to think of things no longer being hidden in the shadows. When the world is full of Light there are no shadows and therefore nothing can be hidden.

And so your politicians will find that all their dark secrets are being revealed. Major corporations will find that all their dirty tricks are being revealed. You will even find that, as people become more and more sensitive, that telepathically, people will know whether you are being truthful or not. They may not know exactly what you are thinking, but many are becoming more and more intuitive and able to read the overall energy of truth and lies.

And so you are in a time when it is necessary to clean up what is inside. Dust out the cobwebs and take a clear and honest look at how you conduct your life. Are you honest with yourself? For indeed all dishonesty is with the self. You may think that you are covering up things that are hidden only to others but the real lie is to yourself. When you put up appearances that are not the truth of who you are your mind becomes confused and you learn not to trust yourself.

It is not others you are deceiving so much as yourself. It is time to look honestly within at who you are and how you conduct your life. If you do not speak honestly about what you want and who you are you will find less and less tolerance among others for this way of being.

If you will not bring your truth forward willingly, others will call you on it and it will bring embarrassment. It is best to look within and start being honest with yourself. This is one way of Being in the Light.

Another way is to be more loving. And where does love start? Again, the answer lies within the self. You can only love another as much as you love yourself. If you have a beloved and you look at them and feel that they are not loving you the way they 'should' be, the only solution to this is to look within and see where you are not loving yourself. This requires forgiveness for all that has passed in your life.

Forgive YOURSELF for all that anyone has ever done to you - for in truth you chose that experience for yourself. Forgive yourself for choosing that experience. Forgive yourself for everything. Just start loving yourself as if you were a small child. Everything that you do that you would label as wrong or stupid or unkind, say, "That's OK sweetheart. You are doing the best you can and next time maybe you'll do it differently. It's OK to make mistakes, you are learning."

Speak to yourselves in this way as you would a child. You will feel it as soon as you do. It feels so soft and gentle compared to the usual harsh voice that many of you use when talking to yourselves. This is what self-love feels like and it is just the beginning of the process. The more you are forgiving and soft and gentle with yourself the more you will find you are ready to step into your truth and be more honest about who you are. You will find yourselves honoring more of who you are and finding the perfection in all your so-called imperfections. This is self-love.

You are each unique. Why would you want to be like *anyone* else? Why would you want to give up the Divine aspect of who you are to try to imitate someone else? That is such blasphemy from our perspective. It is as if you are saying, Creator you didn't know what you were doing when you made me so I, this humble human, must fix your mighty mistake! We think not. Be who you are Dear Ones and love every piece of who you are, even the not so pretty aspects. The more you love those darker aspects of who you are the more they will become love as well. It is only the absence of love that creates darkness.

This world is becoming more loving and that is why you must catch up with it. That is why we are offering so much guidance on growing and healing and allowing yourselves to change. The world upon which you reside is changing and so you have no choice but to follow suit or be left behind. That is the way of it. It is our deep desire for you to travel upward with Mother Earth. That is the energy behind these transmissions. Step into your brilliance Dear Ones. It is the time to be a whole, living Light upon this planet. And so it is.

# Essay Twenty-One - CLEARING WITH LOVE

And so beloveds we come before you once again with our message of Light. We come before you with loving hearts. We are here to help restore you to your original essence – your radiant and brilliant selves. For Dear Ones, the journey has been hard and arduous. We see and we know what you have been through. We know where you have been and how you have been impacted by this seemingly harsh and cruel world. And as a result we see your wounds. And so we again offer guidance on clearing those wounds.

This journey begins with recognizing your true feelings. So many of you, for so long, have mastered the activity of denying the emotions and hiding from them. This may work for a while, but for those who are choosing to ascend into the Light at this time, it is time to stop and look at what you are running away from. And so the first step is to FEEL those emotions when they come to the surface.

Ask yourself, what am I truly feeling here? Then repeat it ten times. By that we mean, for example, I am feeling so rejected right now. Say that same statement ten times and see how you feel at the end of that little activity. Do you feel yourself sighing part way through? That is the release. Just by repeating it in this manner you are allowing the true acceptance of what you are feeling and then it can be released. It is like a little child that wants your attention. It will keep pulling at your skirt until you look down and acknowledge and then it is happy and it will move on.

The same is true of those emotions that are hidden in the subconscious. They tug at your skirt until you really notice them and then they will move on. Of course there are many layers to this but this is one simple way to begin to acknowledge your true feelings. So we invite you to try this today. This same day that you are reading these words, give this a try and you will see its effects. You will not benefit from this activity by only reading about it.

And so this is one way to begin. You are to love that feeling and that emotion enough to say hello to it. You know yourself if you say hello to someone and they do not return the greeting that you feel rejected. The same is true of those emotions that come to the surface. Say hello to them with love and you can finally say good-bye. That is the irony.

Another activity in supporting this transition through old emotions is to pretend that they are already turned around. Let's say that you feel sad one day. You have a trigger that takes you back to a time when you were rejected by a loved one and you feel that sadness again. This time turn it around and see that EVERYONE you meet absolutely loves you and they are so excited to be with you and they admire all that you are, just as you are.

Imagine that everywhere you go you are running into people that know and adore you. See them stopping you on the street, so excited to see you and so happy to be able to spend even just a moment with you. See yourself walking away after saying good-bye and feeling so good inside, knowing that you are respected and cared for in this world. See the smile on your face and your happy thoughts about how lovable you are. Take this imagining as far as you like. The longer you stay with it the more your feelings of sadness will be replaced by happy thoughts.

The more you truly know that you are lovable, the more those sad thoughts will dissipate. We recommend this activity come after the previous one. First accept the sadness and send it love. Then see the happiness follow and feel the emotions connected with the happiness. These activities will help you be present with your feelings. However, the first step is to stop running from them with your busyness or your addictions that stuff them back inside.

It is time to face them Dear Ones. It is the only way to move forward in these times. It is like they cover your Light, so in order to shine you must release them. What is on the other side is so powerful and magnificent you will hardly recognize yourselves. From that as well come life choices that are much in alignment with the energies of the earth at this time. You have come to be whole, radiant Beings of Light. Why hide in the shadows when you can be the beacon for all to see? And why allow the shadows over your heart to diminish the quality of your life? You can shine - but you have to do it. No one else can reach into your heart and turn your Light on. You must do it Dear Ones.

Find the courage for change. Find the courage to look inside. When you judge others immediately look inside for where you have that judgment about yourself. Do not deceive yourself into thinking it is someone else's stuff. It is ALWAYS your stuff! Look for it. If you have trouble finding it, ask a friend to help. Say to your friend, I just had the thought that Susie is lazy and leaves all the work for everyone else, can you see parts of my life where I am lazy? Do you think that I sometimes leave the work for others to do? This is how it works Dear Ones.

So often you are not willing to see within yourselves what you judge in others. You believe that they are the ones that need to change. Perhaps change would be beneficial for them, but what you see is a reflection of you. If it were not you wouldn't be able to see it. You cannot see in your outer life what does not lie within.

It is like when Columbus came to America and the natives of the land thought the sails were clouds. They had no inner knowing of sails and so they couldn't see them as such. The same is true of your experiences. If you do not carry it within, you cannot see it. Therefore, if you can see hatred in someone else, you have hatred within yourself. The other person is expressing it for you because it is your expectation to see that in your experience.

Oh, there is much exploring for you in this essay. It is only useful if you use it and do an internal audit of your thinking. Like any audit, it brings forward any discrepancies and any untruths. This is always beneficial. Being honest with the self is primary in loving the self and moving forward into the Light. Allow it Dear Ones. Embrace it. Be it. For you are magnificent Beings and we wish to see you shining in all your radiance. We love you so. And so it is.

# Essay Twenty-two - LIVING IN THE LIGHT I

And so, Dearly Beloveds, we continue.  We continue with our transmission and we continue to pour our love over you, for we see you.  We see your radiant Light and your brilliant minds and we say, use them wisely.  Use them to create the world which you wish to see for yourselves.  As you say, be the Light you want to see in the world.  And it is now easier to do than ever before.

It is so easy for you to step into your Light now compared to times past when there was much less Light on the earth.  By that we mean much less energy of Light on the planet.  Only twenty years ago this planet held much more density than it currently does.  And so now it is easier for you to find your way.  We are delighted that, for those of you who choose to find your way out of the darkness, that it is easier to do so.  And so we say to you Beloveds, to lift your heads above the clouds and see the radiant Light that you are.

And how do you do this?  You do this by recognizing the latent abilities and talents that make you uniquely you.  When you see life leading you in a certain direction, say yes and step into your abilities.  When life is leading you, things simply fall into place.  People notice you for certain abilities and things just fall into place for you to be using those abilities.  That is when it is time to say yes and step out of your comfort zone and move fully into what is presenting itself.

After the first step it is oh so easy because you are doing what you love to do.  It is almost too good to be true and so many of you resist it, thinking that you must hang onto the old way – the old job – the old relationship – because surely this other way is just too easy to really work out!  And we say to you nothing could be further from the truth. It was ALWAYS meant to be easy. You just got lost in the density. And now you are so used to the hard way that you have trouble accepting the easy way.

Let that go Dear Ones. Know that Creator wants it to be easy and joyful and playful and fun. That is what life is meant to be. And so if you see your life rolling in this way, do not feel guilty! Please say yes and jump right in! What could be better than doing what you love and getting paid for it and finding that it sustains you and provides for all your needs and feels like no effort at all! Hallelujah.

That is the new way. That is the joy Dear Ones and we want nothing more than for you to be living in that joy with a life full of grace. Oh how Divine that is. It is your birth right Beloveds. You deserve it for no other reason than you are alive on this earth. Some do not have the self-worth to believe it and to you we say that everyone deserves it. Act as if you deserve it and then maybe you will begin to believe it.

And so this is the new way of living in the Light. It is by radiating your own Light out into the world. How can you help but be surrounded by Light when that is what you are? Beloveds, there is great truth in these words and yet many of you will dismiss them. You will continue going to jobs you hate, not believing that you can create something more fulfilling for yourselves. You will continue in unfulfilling relationships, believing that you would not find anyone else.

It is time to see beyond what is and create what it is you truly desire. Everything you desire can be yours if you believe it. That is the tricky part. Many of you think you believe it but soon learn that the faith is not there and you live the hardship of finding your way. This is OK Dear Ones. It is better than not trying at all. At least you can look back on your life and say I tried. Do not be one who looks back in old age with nothing but regret for not even trying. Have the courage to step out of what is and into that which you truly desired.

We wish you to know that if you can think it you can create it. In order to think it, it is already in your reality. You just haven't caught up with it yet! If you can think it, it exists. Now you just have to believe in it and know it is coming and watch for all the little signs that it is on its way. The signs will be small at first to see if you are paying attention. Every time you respond and step toward that which you wish to create, the signs grow. Every time you step out of what is toward what you wish to create, more and more energy goes into that creation.

This is how it is done. This is the new way of Living in the Light. It is so much fun. We really would like to see you try it. Start out with something small, something that doesn't have much significance to you. Perhaps you want a bouquet of flowers. Believe they are coming. See them sitting on your table in a lovely vase. And then wait. This is the playfulness of creating. Knowing, anticipating and receiving.

This is our transmission for today. We invite you to consider the one thing that you are going to create in your life in the next week. Ask for it, expect it to come and then sit back knowing that it will arrive. From time to time think of how happy you will be to receive it, mostly because you will see what you have created. This is the way of it. Believe it and love yourselves for all that you are. Magnificence is what you are and we are truly blessed to have this opportunity to address you this day. And so it is.

# Essay Twenty-three - LIVING IN THE LIGHT II

And so Dearly Beloveds, we come before you once again to share our love and grace with you. And we say to you Dear Ones, that it is our honor to stand before you and see the Divine human that now exists on this earth. For you are changing before your very eyes! Indeed, the human species is evolving in a way that, a few hundred years from now, those who look back to this period of time will see the great difference between who they are and what the human looks like at this time.

And this is wonderful indeed, for you are transforming into Light Beings. You are becoming more and more of what your potential is and we rejoice. And you will soon be rejoicing when you come to accept and see that the hardship is over and life is moving forward in grace and ease. This is coming but not for some time. For, again, your old systems must fall away in order for this to come about. We share this with you so that you can know where all of these changes are leading. It is not the world falling apart but moving into magnificence.

So what is it going to be like living in the Light? Pure joy. This is what you are moving into. This is what the potential is for every human being. Imagine a life with no worries, no fears, only love. Most of you cannot even imagine it at this time for it is foreign to this current existence for sure. It is however, the pure potential of what you have to look forward to. In the meantime we invite you to understand the transformation that is taking place.

As your DNA changes you must also be willing to allow your beliefs about yourself to change and everything that you believed to be true to be something different.

You hold many patterns of belief, many of them carried over from past lives. These are strong in your biology for they have existed on the earth for many generations, building with each incarnation.

Now you are in entirely different times when all of this will change. If you are not willing to change as a person, you will not allow this new way of existing to become a part of your experience. Living in the Light right now means letting go of the past which was dark. Recreate your lives Dear Ones. Morph into your brilliance. And so it is.

# Essay Twenty-four - THE COUNCIL OF NINE

Greetings this day Beloved children of the earth, or should we say adults of the earth – for indeed you are growing up. You are stepping into your power as individuals and it is beautiful for us to behold. We would like this day to share more with you about who we are and what we are here to accomplish with these transmissions and the words that you are reading.

We are of the Council of Nine although it is not accurate to say that we are only nine. There are nine who begin this council and many more have joined as they found their way back to the Light. They are part of our intentions and our programming for service to all of creation. We are an advanced civilization and we live mostly in Light bodies. We do not consume food or wear clothing. We are emanations of Light and we carry a blue hue in our bodies.

Our height is magnificent by your standards – ten to twelve feet in height. It is from this place that we look upon the earth and see the struggles that you have so valiantly been going through in order to find your way back to the Light. It is your deep and loving intentions as a species to find your way back to love that has called us to be here in service to your race. We are here to support you. We are here to help you become all that you are.

We do not want to scare you with this information. Many are aware that you are not alone in this solar system, not to mention all the other solar systems in the vast universe. We are millions of Light years away from you and yet we can be here with you in an instant. That is the way of it in much of the universe. This will help you to understand the nature of your planet and why you have been called children. And yet today we refer to you as adults – young adults in your universal evolution. We do not speak of the individual souls that are here mind you. We speak of the human race as a whole.

And so we, The Council of Nine, have come to help you to grow up in a sense. We are here to help you make your way out of childhood and into adulthood. You know from your own human experience that this can be a challenging time in one's evolution. The same is true for you in these times of learning how to become a human living in the fourth dimension as opposed to a human living in the third dimension.

It takes some understanding and a lot of changing of previous beliefs to allow yourselves to make this shift. You are learning to be a completely different being. What a wonderful opportunity. At the same time it can be confusing and challenging. And so we come to you with our daily transmissions offering our loving guidance for making your way back to the brilliance of who you truly are.

And we say to you Dear Ones, you are doing a marvelous job of finding your way. You are stumbling through, some of you, and that is understandable. Like a child finding his way in the world, you are learning as you go. How great is it to be a child again? How great is it to learn as you go? If you approach this time of transition in this way it will become more wonder-full for you to experience. Many adults wish they were children once again.

All it takes is an attitude shift. Release the burdens that you carry so diligently. Let go of the burdens that could be released. Give it up to Creator and let the great Light carry it for you. Many of you hold onto small insignificant matters as if they would change the world if you let them go. Just try releasing them and see what happens. The world will not end. Your world will feel lighter and brighter the more you let it go. Some of you also feel that you are the only one who will change the world.

You carry the big responsibility of being the one who heals the world and we say to you, do you really think that carrying life as a burden is of service? To whom? Only to yourself. It is only of service to the small part of the self that thinks it must save the world. The larger aspect of you knows that the only way you change the world into Light is to be joyful yourself.

Now if your way of being of service is Light and joyful then by all means carry on. But if you find that it has become a burden that is hard to bear you had best let it go and find a way of being in greater joy. Despair and heaviness is not going to lift this planet into the Light. It is those with light hearts that will elevate humanity, and how perfect is that? How great is it that by finding a way to let go of your burdens and live a light and happy life you are being of the greatest service? How could it be any better than that?

And so Dear Ones, we have, this day, offered a bit more of who we are and why we are here of service to you, Beloved humans. You are divine creation. Please look within and see that. You are the attention of all of creation at this time in your evolution for you are brave, courageous and determined to find your way back to love.

We watch in wonder and awe as you step out of the darkness into the Light. All of creation is rejoicing. You have accomplished what many thought was impossible. You have proven that creation is love by the choices you are making at this pivotal time on earth. It is glorious to behold and we, for that reason, are your humble servants. And so it is.

# Essay Twenty-five - LIVING IN THE LIGHT PART III

And so we come before you once again Beloveds to share our wisdom, our Light and our love with you and we say that the time has come for all upon the earth to be walking in their Light, to be shining brightly and claiming all the rewards of being a human on this planet earth.

This is much easier than you think. Many of you like to make things difficult. Some believe if it is too easy it is not worth accomplishing. Again, the opposite is true. That which is easy is that which is meant to be. If it is difficult and challenging then you are on the wrong track – you are lost. So claim the ease and grace that is being a human living in the Light.

So many of you are now asking, what the heck do you mean by Living in the Light? Good question indeed. We should not assume that you know what this means for it is a new way of being and many might describe it differently. And so when we say this what we mean is that you are fully embracing the fullness of who you are. You have healed all wounds, or are in the process of doing so, and you stand firm and strong in knowing what you desire from life and knowing that you have something to offer by being here.

That something may or may not be related to your career or that which brings income. Regardless, living in the Light is when you are fully in the awareness of your uniqueness and you believe in yourself. It is time to stop hiding behind a false veil of not knowing who you are. If you don't know find out. That is it. Time is running out for you to flounder about wondering and wishing and hoping. Get up, brush yourself off and declare who you are and go for what you want.

When you do the universe will have clear direction on what you want and will support you in getting it. When you are fumbling about in your mind wanting this one day but not the next, maybe that but not if I have to make changes to get it .... How can you be supported in that? Creator doesn't know what to give you when you do not have clarity yourself.

We would like to remind you that you deserve everything that you wish for. To think that you are asking for too much or are being greedy or denying others because you are asking for so much is rubbish that has been created to control you. YOU DESERVE EVERYTHING YOU DESIRE TO HAVE. That is it. No exceptions. And you will get it if you believe that you deserve and set out to claim it. That is the way of it.

Now you may find, once you receive it, that it is not exactly what you wanted. That is OK. Just tweak it and ask again. You are learning how to be creators (not that you have not always been). You are learning that you deserve all and by claiming that you will begin to step into your worthiness and by stepping into your worthiness you will begin to see your Light and by seeing your Light you will begin to fully live in the Light.

So, do not wait. Begin today. Write a list of everything you desire in your life. Don't forget anything. Look at your list and then say to yourself, I deserve to have EVERYTHING on that list and so shall it be. That is it. The beginning. Your intention has started it in motion. As you review your list and believe in it you will be reinforcing what you desire and then set into motion the knowing that it is all coming. It is all on its way because you deserve it all.

Play with this way of creating. Play with your imagination as you visualize all of those things coming to you. This is one step in living in the Light. It will get you started into stepping into your wholeness. For when you live believing that you shouldn't have too much or ask for too much you are keeping yourself diminished. How is everyone going to see your Light when you are keeping it hidden? So this is one step in moving into the fullness of you. One step that keeps you closer to the truth of what living on earth was meant to be.

We look forward to offering more of this to you. We look forward to seeing you shine in all your radiance for all the world to see. You are beautiful beyond your knowing. We see all the potential that is in each one of you and we say you would not recognize yourselves if you could see from our perspective. If you were to see what we see you would say naah. That's not me. But it is and we are doing all we can to help you see within yourselves all that you are. We love you so. And so it is.

# Essay Twenty-six - BEING IN THE LIGHT III

Greetings Beloveds. We come to you from on high with messages of love to resonate within the core of your Being. We come to assist in your ascension into the Light. As you rise to the heavens your bodies will become less dense and you will begin to grow. You will grow taller and wider because your beingness is not contained in such a dense vessel. This may surprise you at first, as you see others of such great size. It is one way in which you will know that you have made it into the higher dimensions.

It is one way that you will know that you are surrounded by loving beings. You can rejoice as you see this for, this is who you are. You can change and grow as your heart becomes lighter. Even some currently residing on the earth have seen themselves growing taller as they expand their awareness and lighten their emotional burdens. This is the way of it. There are other planets with beings as short as humans and shorter but there are many more where the residents of the planet are much taller.

And so to those who read these words we say to you that being in the Light is a whole new way of existing. It is a way of being that is instantaneous creation based on your thoughts. Why not prepare now for such an occurrence? It helps you to scrutinize your thoughts to ask yourself, if what I am currently thinking came true, how would that be for me? You often create negative scenarios in your daydreaming thoughts because you have done this for so long. It is because you have lived through experiences that would make you come to expect the worst.

Those times are changing Beloveds, but you must be the ones to actively change along with it. The energy is here to support your positive outcomes in every way, but you must change the way of thinking to expect positive outcomes. This is what we wish for you today – to consider your thoughts and turn them into the opposite if they are negative. If you find yourself thinking that you had best lock the door because someone might rob you, turn it around and say that you know your home is always protected and all your belongs are safe. You may still lock the door, but you have created a different possibility. It is this simple. And every thought needs to be scrutinized in this way.

So, you are thinking positive thoughts and all these positive things are showing up in your life. Suddenly you begin to make the connection. You begin to realize that you are indeed creating a beautiful, joyous life for yourself. There may not be any new situations or people in your life to create this, just your thoughts. In time these thoughts will most likely lead to new experiences and relationships as well. For what you think you magnetize to you.

When you emanate love, you attract love. The opposite is true of course. Existing in this way, you will begin to create more and more of what brings you joy. Eventually your life will feel very wonderful and you will allow all this goodness to come in. It begins slowly at first, mostly because many of you will not allow a great influx of joyful events. You are so used to struggle and burden that it feels wrong to be happy all the time. This is changing we are pleased to say.

Oh yes, there are places in the world where there is certainly not a lot of joy. This is the old dying out Dear Ones. This is the places on the earth where the last vestiges of the dense, dark energies are playing out. It is almost as if there is a hole in the earth where this darkness leaks out, as it empties itself of the last bits of density. Love everyone who is experiencing this war and hatred right now. Love the politicians who are also acting this out. Just send love to everything. Find the place in your heart where you feel love.

Perhaps you get there by thinking of your children or a pet. Then offer that love out to all the politicians who are leading their nations into war. Love the President of the United States. Love all who are in power so that they may act out your love and not the fear and hatred that is often bestowed upon them. Let them feel in their hearts what it is like to come from love. This is the greatest tool you have to change the world Dear Ones. You need nothing else. When this world is resonating in a place of love, like a pink blanket surrounding the earth, then the greatest choices on this earth will come from love.

That is the way of it and we see it Dear Ones. We see that beautiful pink haze coming off the planet earth - blue oceans and pink Light. How incredible. And you can pat yourselves on the back for accomplishing such a beautiful sight. And so as you Light up your own lives you can expand that Light out into the world. It is such a magical time to be a resident of your planet. Such a wonderful time of transformation into the Light. Find the joy Beloveds. Pay attention to your thoughts and enjoy the ride. We will communicate more at another time of Being in the Light. And so it is.

# Essay Twenty-seven - FALLING FROM GRACE

Greetings Beloveds of the Light. Greetings from the Love and Light of the Creator. We come to you from afar bearing messages of love. We are the witnesses of the Light, come to earth to offer messages to those who are ready to ascend. We offer messages to those who are ready to rise up into the heavens as Mother Earth herself has done and is doing. For you see, there have been many changes on your earth that many of you are not even aware of.

Many changes that the Legions of Light have undertaken to support you in making it to this time of transition into the Light. For you see Dear Humans, you are at a point in your evolution that is profound beyond your imaginings. We ask you to pay attention to our words and allow them to rest upon your heart. Search within for the truth of what we say. If it does not resonate with you then allow them to fall out of your sight. If, however, they speak to you, pay good attention to what we say. Your heart is the key to the knowing that is written here. Your world has gone through a major transformation that has allowed her to ascend into the fourth dimension, quickly on the way to the fifth.

This is the truth and it is the intention of all creation that humanity rise up with her. However, for this to happen there must be more commitment on your part. It is easier than ever before for you to ascend. However, it does require a little effort on your part. When you think of Jesus and all that he endured – forty years in the desert, in order to ascend into the Light, you will understand how easy it is for you at this time. And so we ask of you, those who would make the choice to ascend instead of dying and reincarnating, to make the conscious choice at this time to do the work that will prepare your physical body for that event.

The work that is required is simply to clear out all the debris and to honestly look at what is holding your pain body in place within the physical vessel. The more you clear the more you honor the physical vessel. If you find yourself making healthier choices for your food and drink, you will know that you are clearing out the emotional debris. If you find yourself living in more joy and contentment, then you will know that your efforts are paying off.

If, however, you find that you are living the way you always have, hiding from your pain and fears through addictions to food, relationships, sex, alcohol or drugs, then you must begin to change those patterns or you will miss your opportunity to ascend with your earthly mother. She has already moved to the fourth dimension. She is lally-gagging there, waiting and waiting for her cherished humans to step up and hop on board.

She is so very patient with you. She does not want to leave one person behind. But she cannot wait much longer. She must make the choice to step up to the next level when the time has come that it is her only choice. In order for you to be prepared for that moment it is vitally important for you to be in the space of clarity of mind and purity of heart that comes from the healing work that we are asking you to do.

We see many of you saying, but what kind of healing work do I do? How do I find those wounds? Some of you are wondering if you even have the wounds. We say that most of you have deep wounds. Some are well hidden. It is the willingness to see what they are that will allow them to surface. Do not continue to hide them behind deeply ingrained patterns of behavior.

Imagine yourself doing something that is radically different than your routine. Perhaps that would be a move to a different continent.

Imagine that and see what comes up as resistance. Imagine leaving your relationships and see what comes up as resistance. This is one way to see the patterns that may be keeping you from stepping into the fullness of who you are. These are the patterns to work with. This does not mean that you must make the move or give up the relationships. It is just a way of seeing what you could be doing to clear the deeply engrained patterns of behavior.

And so Beloveds, we invite you to take our words to heart. Allow them to resonate deep within your being and search for their truth within. If there is no truth there then these messages are not for you. For those of you who feel the importance of these words, find the ways to heal. Mend those broken hearts. Heal those unhealthy relationships. Move out of those distressing jobs. Make the changes by first seeking out the support that will help you open your hearts once again. When the heart is shut down, the connection to your fullness is diminished. Be vulnerable. Nothing is more courageous than that. Be vulnerable and release the ego that says you must be this and that. The only must is that you be true to yourself.

Who are you really? Not the face that gets presented to the world but the little child within. Who is that child? What does it want? What would it do if there was nothing standing in the way? What would it do if it knew that no one would make fun of it or ridicule it? What would that child do if it was fully supported and encouraged in whatever that was? These are questions to lead you back to the fullness of you. It is time to blossom. It is time to radiate your Light not only

to this world but to all of creation.  It is time Beloveds.
We love you so.  And so it is.

# Essay Twenty-eight - LOVE LOST

Greetings Beloveds. Greetings from the Love and Light of the Creator. Greetings from the Great Central Sun as we come before you with love and grace for the beautiful beings who read these words and who bless the earth with their presence. For Dear Ones, we say to you this day that those who read these words are the way-showers of the world. You are the ones who are leading the masses back to the Light. You are the ones who have the courage to step up and make a difference in this world. You are the ones who have the bravery to claim your truth in these times of great evolution on your planet.

And for all of that we commend you. We commend you for taking the steps to become all that you are. And yet we see many of you holding back. We see you intimidated by your own Light. We see you saying, who am I to claim this greatness? Dear Ones, we ask of you to turn that around and know that you are a child of God. You are Creation itself. You hold the brilliance of the Creator Light and that Light is asking for you to step up at this time and be all that you are. It is asking you to be your love Light in this world.

It starts with loving the self and that is where the love has become lost. For so many of you living in this world and growing up in the times that led you to this place, it was a challenging journey. So many of you grew up being told that you are not enough or that you should be like someone else. The messages of your childhood were criticizing who you are and expecting you to be like someone else. This message repeated over and over has led many of you away from a place of loving yourselves.

It has led you away from the beautiful Light that lies dormant within your heart. The love that you knew yourself to be when you were born has been lost to false expectations and sad rejections of your true self. In the order of fitting into society you have been lifted out of your true self, the self that fits you perfectly. In order to fit into the requirements of your parents you were pulled out of your true Light. Now, as adults, the way back to your heart is to release all of the messages that you are not enough and that you must be something other than who you are.

Dear Ones, we are here to tell you that you are perfect, and we mean PERFECT, just the way you are. You already are all that you came to be. You do not have to be leaner, keener, smarter or faster. You are just right. If you can, find your way back to the truth of who you are – all the aspects of yourself that you thought were right for you but the world made you questions them.

When you find that part of you that was so deeply buried say hello and embrace it like a child and welcome it back. Love it like a parent loving the wee child within. Tell it that it is perfect just the way it is. Let it know that you are ready to be that person now. Love yourselves Dear Ones. Every day know that you are just what Creator intended you to be. Creator did not want you to be molded into someone else.

Creator brought you into this world with all your quirks and traits that are uniquely you so that others could have the experience of that uniqueness. Believe in yourselves. Laugh at those aspects of you that are perhaps very serious or maybe silly or eccentric. The world needs all of us to be just who we came to be. Some in the world are playful and pure joy, some are serious and determined.

Each has his role to play in the Divine plan. The secret is to accept everyone with loving and open arms and appreciate all that makes them unique. This is the way back to love. It starts by loving the self and looking within and embracing your own uniqueness. Then and only then will you be able to look outside of yourself and love the originality of others.

When you criticize and judge others for their differences it is truly you criticizing that part of you that does not fit into what others have labeled as the norm. When you realize that you no longer criticize others then you can congratulate yourself for you have stopped judging that aspect of who you are that is different. When you love each person for who they are – even the ones who seem so deeply wounded – then you are truly loving yourself.

For when you have judgment of another it is a reflection of your self-judgment. This is your map to success. This is your evidence of your progress. If you judge another then look inside again and find that small child within and love it and nurture it and let it know that it is just perfect. Keep on loving all the aspects of self until you see no more judgment outside of yourself.

Love is lost in this world. To find your way back to love is to find your way back into your own heart. Each moment loving the self back to wholeness is a lifetime of pain erased. Be brave our Beloveds. Have the courage it takes to witness the wounded self. Take the steps to release that which has been placed upon you as 'correct' and step into the fullness of the uniqueness of you. You don't have to fit any mold. Please do not. Be unique. Be one of a kind, for that is who you truly are. Do not let any others tell you who you should be. Be who you are.

There are no mistakes in creating the life of a human. Accept that you are perfect just the way you are and step proudly into the world as your own Light. Those who are meant to bask in that Light will find you, but only if you are shining it out to be seen. Do not cover it with the concepts that others have placed upon you. Be your own brilliant Light and love yourself deeply. The heart yearns for love because the heart knows. Love is the way and the path to peace and joy. And so it is.

# Essay Twenty-nine - LOVING WHAT IS

What an interesting topic you may think, for us to bring forward this day. We hope you will find it interesting. It is a topic that will bring you to deeper wisdom and joy in your lives. For we ask you, how can you find joy in any part of life if you are not loving what is? You cannot. It is by loving what is in this very moment, moment after moment, that life becomes joyful and graceful. It is when the mind leads you away from the what-isness of life that you find yourselves falling into depression and despair.

It is by wishing that life was something different than what you are experiencing that you fall into depression. The state of depression is wishing that life was different than what it is. Of course, we have talked to you about how to change your life. We have suggested changing your thoughts and choosing what you would like to see in your life and thinking accordingly. This one step. A deeper level of living this way is to accept what is regardless of what that experience brings.

You can ask, how could I love having a cold or being sick? We would ask, how do you feel after you get better? Are you not more grateful for your health? Do you not appreciate more the ability to go about your daily activities with the energy and health to do so? So, when you are sick you could be thinking of how great it will feel to be well again. You could appreciate the fact that it slowed you down for a while because you must have needed the rest. You can take deeper levels of illness and still see the gift that comes from the experience. It is by looking for this gift in every moment that you find yourself loving what is.

Some of you will say that it is impossible to love what is, being in financial difficulty and worrying every day how you are going to feed your children. This is a challenging existence indeed and it takes great courage to see your way out of it. However, it will not change until you are willing to find the grace in it and then turn it around with your thoughts and expectations. Sometimes loving what is can be so challenging that all you can find to be grateful for is the fact that you are alive and have the opportunity to experience what it is to be human.

Many who wanted to incarnate at this time were denied. Just the mere existence on earth as a human is an opportunity to find something to be grateful for. You see, when you are living in struggle, you are of the frame of mind that creates more struggle. You must find a way out of that frame of mind to find a way out of that experience. More than ever this is true. It is only by finding SOMETHING to be grateful for and appreciate each day that you will start to lift yourself out of your current experience.

There are many inspirational stories of people who have turned their lives around. Oh, when you listen you wish for the formula. Please tell me, step by step, how did you do it? We say to you Beloveds the answer is within you. The first step is willingness. The first step is a sincere desire to make your life different. Step two is to take action. You cannot simply stay in the same way of existence and make change. You must do some things differently than you currently are.

Take action toward what you are choosing to see differently in your life. When doors open walk through them. This may sound like a simple statement but we say to you, many of you do not walk through those doors. You ask and yearn for something different and when the universe sends you the beginning pieces of that something different you do not walk through the open doors. You say, oh no, I can't do that. Oh, I'm not ready for that. Well then Dear Ones, you will stay just where you are.

You cannot ask for something different and for life to change and then not step into the opportunities that the universe sends to you in response to your request. It then becomes quite apparent that you are not ready or willing to receive that which you have asked for. The universe listens and it responds in kind. Are you willing? Look at your life and consider opportunities that have presented themselves to you and ask where you walked away from them.

There are many reasons that you come up with, oh, it is too generous of the other person to give this to me. Oh, it would take too much of my time to do that. Put your reasons aside and just look at what you have passed by. Now, be clear on what it is you are wanting in your life. Write your clear list and then ask the universe to bring to you opportunities for these things to come into your life. And now, when you see a new opportunity presenting itself to you, step into it. Do not allow ANY excuses to stop you from walking through that door.

In the meantime, while you are waiting for spirit to bring your request to you, love what is in your life. Everything that you can find to be grateful for and happy about will move you closer and closer to that which you desire. By loving what is, you set it free. If you are in a relationship that is bringing many challenges, love that relationship. Love every challenging aspect of it and you will soon find that your state of mind changes. You will either give up the relationship or you will see it change. By loving what is you are not resisting what is. As the saying goes, what you resist will persist. So, by loving what is you are setting it free.

If it is a good thing it is free to bring more and if it is a so called bad thing it is free to leave your life altogether. This is the wisdom of this way of being. We do not speak of loving something negative so that it will repeat in your life. That would not be wisdom. It is loving it free. Loving that which is either multiplies the beneficial because you are so grateful or releases the unbeneficial because you have stopped running from it. We encourage you to bring this into your practice of living and find out for yourselves how this works in your life.

These tools are being brought to you at this time to support you in your growth into the Light. As we have said many times, this is the time to rise up with the earth into a new way of being. By releasing through loving what is, you will be dropping those weights from your lives that you carry as burdens. Play with this Dear Ones and discover for yourselves what is possible with this work. It is work. It requires your attention to change from who you are into a greater possibility of you.

It takes consciousness to catch how you are thinking and being in the world and change it into something more aware. It is through this consciousness that you will change your lives. Now is the time Beloveds. Now is the time to step up and radiate the Light that you are. By loving what is you are leading yourselves into that Light and out of the darkness. Depression is hating what is. Use these tools to recreate your life and step out of the darkness Beloveds. We are sure that you will find success over time. Try it, you'll like it. And so it is.

# Essay Thirty - THE WAY OF IT

Greetings Beloveds. Greetings from the Love and Light of the Creator once again. We come to you in love and joy, for we are the lucky ones who get to share our words with the most magnificent Beings in creation. Oh yes, at this time in the evolution of All That Is, you humans are the prize creation. For you see, what you are accomplishing on the Earth at this time is what many of you would call miraculous. Indeed, you are changing your very DNA as you continue to walk around, many of you oblivious to what is happening within your bodies.

And you are becoming more and more connected to the Light without knowing truly what is happening. Such wonderful times you are in. And so it is that all of the heavens are witnessing what is happening on your planet right now. You are on the big screen Dear Ones so act accordingly. Let your every action be in the awareness that you are changing history. Let your every thought be as pure as you would have it be if you knew that Beings from all over the universe are witness to your thoughts, for it is true.

Oh, they may not be tuned in to each and every one of you, but you transmit an overall hum that is the message of human thinking. For eons that hum has been one of despair and darkness. But that is changing. More and more people are excited about the times we are in and more and more are awakening to the knowing that life is changing and they are living in the awareness of what they are creating.

Are you offering your great Light out into the world or are you filling it with pain and feelings of hardship? This is not a trivial question at this time. The answer to this question will tell you if you are supporting the earth in ascending into the higher realms or if your thoughts are hindering what is trying to happen. Nothing is insignificant in these times. Every thought is gathering in the collective and creating that hum that others are witnessing as they watch in anticipation of what is to be.

Talk about a cheer leading team. You have no idea how many are cheering you on, wishing and hoping that you will make your way into the Light. So, Dear Ones, please pause and give consideration to what we have just said. It is a Light matter but not to be taken lightly! These are times like no other and it requires all of your thoughts to be in the place of love and joy and grace and ease. We know, as we have said, that this can be challenging when all you see is hardship. We have also talked long enough about how you change those thoughts.

Those of you in despair, find someone to be with who is positive and upbeat and hang out with them as much as you can. Do not pull their energy from them, but learn how to be lighter and more playful in your life. Live in the moment where everything is always OK. That is the beauty of the current moment. No matter what lurks outside of the current moment, when you are immersed in the present, 99.999% of the time, everything is OK there.

And then as you connect more and more in the present it becomes more than OK. It becomes pure joy and delight. When you can keep yourself pulled in to what is and not worrying about what is not, then you can be happy. That is where happiness resides. Seek it out Dear Ones. Stay in the moment of what is joy and only let your mind wander to create more of the joy that you so deserve to have in your life.

Oh, these changing times can be hard to navigate - so many expectations and requirements. You have been enduring bodily changes and economic changes and system changes. Everything around you is changing and you are changing. This is the way of it Dear Ones. This is the way of this great evolution that you are in. Why do species evolve? Because that which surrounds them is evolving. The species must adapt or die off. That is it. And you are in such times and your species is adapting.

We will say to you that it is not the survival of the fittest but the survival of the willing. Those who are willing to flow with the changes and become someone new will be the ones that survive. Those who resist will be keeping themselves back with the energies that are dying off. We do not wish to scare you. Our deepest desire is to inspire you to become all that you are and change into the brilliant beings that you are capable of being.

Our deepest desire is to have every human walking the planet at this time step into the Light and claim their truth as a magnificent being of Creation. You do not do this by hiding in fear, afraid that your finances are falling apart and that the world is ending and that you will die. That which you focus on you create. You become brilliant by boldly claiming to the universe that you are a piece of the Creator and as such you are claiming your birth right to be whole.

You are claiming your birth right to be a powerful creator yourself and to create a life of joy and bliss. This is it Dear Ones. Be it. Claim it. Stand up and command it to be so in the glory of God. These are the times you are in. This is who you are! Be it. Say yes to love. Say yes to joy. Say yes to ease and grace. Say yes to life. Life is glorious and grand, you have simply forgotten that it is so. Claim it now Dear Ones. Claim it and command it to be so and it will. Awake every day saying yes to life. Put a sign on your mirror that says, I say yes to life!

Awaken the sleeping giant within. The giant is restless. Who are you when you are in the glory of your fullness? Who are you when you embrace all that is you? Who are you when you reflect all of your Light out into the world? Ask these questions day after day and the answer will begin to appear in your beingness. You will begin to morph into that fullness of you. Now is the time Beloveds. Do not wait a day longer. Heed these words and begin these simple steps of claiming who you are and stepping into the fullness of you. The world is waiting. The universe is watching. And so it is.

# Essay Thirty-one - COMMUNICATING WITH LOVE

Greetings Beloveds. Greetings from those who watch over the unfolding plan upon the earth at this time and rejoice in all that we see being accomplished with you and through you. For those of you who sit in willingness to be of service, we say that your intentions are well utilized by those on the other side. We take great advantage of your willingness to be of service by doing as much work as we can to support humanity in this time of great transformation on the earth.

And so, Dear Ones, as you sit in meditation and invite spirit to work through you we wish you to know that you are greatly assisting this transition into the Light at this time. For those of you reading this who do not currently offer this service but would like to, we ask you to call upon the Beings who work in the Light and state that only Beings with the greatest intention for mankind be permitted to work through you. This way you will ensure that you are keeping your physical body protected and supporting this time of transformation for all.

By doing so, you give permission for us on the other side of the veil to assist you. We cannot assist without an invitation through a human soul. This is the way of free will. By making the request to allow spirit to work through you, you are being of great service to the earth and all who walk upon her. We thank you for your dedication to all and your willingness to be of service in this way.

And so, let us get to our topic for today, communicating with love. The reason we have chosen this topic Dear Ones is that it is not the most common way of communicating on this planet and therefore many are in despair as they grow into adulthood. The way people communicate can often be quite harsh with little consideration of how it is received at the other end.

And we would also invite you to consider that every thought you have of someone else is truly a thought about yourself. If you have the desire to criticize someone, it is truly a criticism of self. Then you can consider why you would be so self-critical. Is it something you learned from your parent? Is it something you want to continue to put out into the world or would you like to change it? If you find that you would like to start being more gentle with yourself, then consider what you say to others. Only say what you would like someone to say to you. That is, be gentle, not only with yourself but with others as well.

Ask yourself how you could communicate what you are feeling in a way that would be gently received. And ask yourself how you would give the same message to yourself. Let us give you an example. Let us imagine that you have just had a conversation with someone that has left you feeling unworthy. You cannot put your finger on it, but something in what the other person said made you feel unworthy and not as valuable as the other person.

Your first thought may be to criticize the other person for making you feel this way. Now take that thought and ask yourself how *you make yourself feel* unworthy. This is the turnaround Dear Ones and it is a critical key in understanding this process of understanding where your true feelings are to be directed. Take time to explore your childhood and see where feelings of unworthiness may have come from events there. Consider how you compare yourself to your friends and coworkers. Do you indeed feel unworthy in the presence of others? From this exploration you will see that you truly have these feelings about yourself.

The person who just made you feel that way is just reflecting and showing you how you feel about yourself. Now, knowing this, what could you say to yourself, or to the other person, that would be communicating your feelings with love? To yourself it could be simply to say I feel unworthy when others appear to be more intelligent than I am. By recognizing the true feeling behind your unworthiness, you can then release it.

To another person it could be, 'when you spoke to me yesterday I felt that you were seeing me as less worthy than you'. There are no harsh words here – no accusations. The other person would only be able to respond in clarification of their intention. There is also no self-judgment in that statement. It is merely an expression of how you felt. Just speaking this way would help you to see where you are responsible for your feelings and that it is not the other person judging you but judgment of yourself. This is one way to communicate with love. The truly loving part is to acknowledge with deep honesty, how you feel about yourself.

Loving the self is accepting all aspects of who you are. Isn't that what you would want in a loving relationship with another? Wouldn't you want them to love all aspects of who you are? Would that not be real freedom, to be able to be exactly who you are in every moment and know you are loved always? So why not love yourself this way? Why not love the so called weak aspects of your personality?

By loving them you free them. By loving every aspect of who you are you allow yourself to soften. There is no need to have your guard up when you know that you are accepted for whatever you do and say. This is not to give little thought to saying hurtful things and accepting it as OK. The truth is that you would not feel

OK about that. When you are coming from loving the self there are no hurtful words in you.

Dear Ones, it is time to accept every aspect of who you are so that you can heal your deep held wounds and walk into the Light. The way in which you communicate with yourself and others is an aspect of claiming this Light within yourself. Deep and honest communication is a powerful tool to walk you out of the old and into the sincerity of who you are. It is time to stop pretending to be who you are not. You are only fooling yourself. Then the soul becomes confused and life is not able to support you fully.

Be honest with yourself and be honest with everyone around you. You can be honest in a gentle way. Others will actually have more respect for you when you communicate clearly and with intention. It is not something many humans are comfortable with. You have the power to communicate but it seems to be too much for you to bear. We love you so and we wish the very best for you in this time of evolution. Step into the fullness of who you are. Be honest with yourself about *everything*. Stop fooling yourself into thinking everything is OK when it is not. Stop pretending that you are someone you are not.

You will not be destroyed in the letting go of your false persona, you will be freed. You will find that the more you are honest about how you are feeling and communicate that, the freer you will feel and the lighter you will feel. When you feel resentful because you have been asked to work on your day off and you express that, you are being honest. Many will not express that because they are afraid of losing their job or they think they need the extra money. As a result, they talk to their feelings pretending that it is OK and they don't mind.

The body then becomes confused because the true feeling is resentment but it is not acknowledged. The honest response to the self would be to acknowledge the resentment and then even to say out loud to the body, I know you feel resentment about this. I have decided that we will do it just because I believe it will guarantee our job into the future. Talking to your feelings in this way will create a softness within the body because it acknowledges the feeling even though you are not following through on what the feeling requested.

It is like asking a child to do something. If you explain the reason for your request and the child understands it, then there is less resistance to doing as you have requested. We hope that you can feel the difference as you read this. Communicating clearly with your feelings in your body is communicating with love. The more you do this with yourself, the more you will be comfortable expressing yourself in this way to others.

The more you use this, the easier your life will become and the less emotional baggage you will be carrying around in the body. A lifetime of such baggage can be very heavy indeed. Lighten the load and you lighten your heart. A light heart is a happy heart and this is what we wish for you all at this time. Be happy and yet be responsible for your feelings and the face that you show to the world. Be in love with yourselves Dear Ones. It is where all love begins and ends. It is the way of it. We love you so. And so it is.

# Essay Thirty-two - BEING LOVE

And so it is Beloveds that we are called before you once again. Once again we commend you for being here, reading this book and taking in these words with the intention of moving forward in your life. Indeed this is vital at this time. We talk about love and we talk about love. Our channel hears about it from the trees, the other Beings of Light, so much about love. And we say why not? Love is beautiful is it not?

It is just that it has been lost on this planet to a great extent. So many have not truly felt love in their lives. Many are so lost in the illusion that they cannot find their way back to love. For those of you hold the love, we commend you and we say, shine that love brightly for the world is in need. The world needs you all to shine like beacons in the darkness. For those of you who carry your Light inside be sure to shine it out to everyone you see.

A simple smile can change someone's day. It is so easy Dear Ones. When you see someone in despair, dirty and ragged on the side of the road, do not condemn, send love. Bless their soul and gift them with your Light. When you see a parent angry at their child, do not condemn. Send them your love so that they will have love for their child. Everyone who acts from a place that does not look like love is only searching for love. You are all searching for love.

When you say you want only happiness, you are really calling out for love. For we assure you, living from a place of pure love is the deepest happiness that you will ever know. So, we call upon you this day to be love. Let it be your state of being on this planet. Let it be your focus for this day and the next day. As your head touches the pillow tonight, ask that when you awaken in the morning you will remember that the next day your intention is to be love.

Oh how the world would change if everyone reading these words would do but that one simple act. This alone would transform your world. This intention of sending love all day long would increase the vibration of the planet to a level where everyone would feel it. They would not know what they were feeling. They would just think that they had a really good day. You know those days when everything seems to go right. You can *create* those days Dear Ones and you can do it for the masses with your intention to do so. It is beautiful to behold from our perspective when we see the world light up.

We rejoice and sing out to all who are illuminating the earth. We send cheers to your personal cheerleading team. We commend you and we mark it in the heavens to be recorded for all of time. Oh it is delightful indeed and you are nearing the time when this is possible all the time, day after day. You are nearing the time when there is great possibility for the energies of the earth to resonate stronger in the Light than the darkness so to speak.

That time is upon you so rise up and claim your Light in the world. Stand tall and say I Am the Light. The Light reigns upon this Earth. Claim it Dear Ones, it is yours after all. Do not allow others to try and diminish your Light or say that you are thinking too highly of yourself. Send them your love so that they can find it within themselves. Send them your blessings and see them living fully in their own love and Light. What you envision you create. This is a vital tool in these times. Every thought is a creation.

If you see others in their highest Light then that is what will also be reflected to you. It will increase your own

Light in the process. It can all be a playful game. How many people can you love out of the darkness today? How much can you love yourself to rise out of your own darkness today? Every day is a new opportunity to be a beacon of love. Every day is a new opportunity and a new creation. In order to make your tomorrows something new, you have to change the patterns of thinking that habitually run through your mind today or else you will just continue to create what has been.

It is time to create what can be! This is the glory of it Dear Ones. *Anything* is possible when you let Spirit join your team. Tell Spirit what you want to create and then believe it. Day after day repeat the knowing of what you desire. I Am in a loving relationship, I Am so joyous, I Am so rich, I Am so fulfilled, I Am so happy in my career. Repeat, repeat, repeat. This is the way. The more you repeat the more you step into the possibility that it is true. It becomes a belief. The more resistance you feel when you make a statement such as I Am rich, the more you know that you are out of resonance with that belief.

If you find it hard to say then search back for the patterns of belief that were created throughout your life that do not support you being rich. See them so that they may be released and then repeat the new desire. Repeat I Am rich over and over until it feels like a possibility to you. The more you accept it the closer you are coming to that being a reality. The more you say it the more you will change your way of behaving to allow that possibility to come into your life.

Affirmations are not just silly statements that create on their own. They are the steps to changing your belief system. By repeating statements to yourself you are allowing the possibility of that to become your reality. There is much more work after that to make it manifest. That is the beginning step. Beyond that you must truly come to believe it to be true and along the way take actions that will allow your life to become rich.

When you reside in love, life is full of possibilities. It is only the lack of love that allows you to believe that you do not deserve to be rich or happy or in love. That is why we speak of love often and it is why we give you simple tools to use in your lives that will support you in coming to that place of living in love. Love for the self, love for family, love for community and love for the world. It grows and glows. And we love you so Dear Ones. We see your willingness. We are the teachers leading the way for the willing students.

Follow us so that you may find your way back to your true self. Use our teachings to change your life. Say yes to being all that you are. Shine brightly Dear Ones. You are creation itself and we love you so. And so it is.

# Essay Thirty-three - THE LOVE OF SELF

Oh Beloveds, it is such a delight for us to come before you this day and to sit in your Light. For we see those who are reading these pages. We see your Light and we rejoice in your presence here. For we know where this is leading. We see you awakening more and more as you absorb the energies of these words. For we say to you, these are not merely words but reflections of Light that you see upon these pages.

As you read you also become more and more of your true brilliance. You become more and more aware of the power of your soul on this human plane and you step more and more into the fullness of you being you. Oh, it is delightful for us to witness. We rejoice with each human who stands taller from the fullness seeping into their Being. You are kings and queens who are lost behind a veil of illusion. You do not see your true radiance on this earth but we see you. We know your glory and we know the great kingdom of Light from which you come. Stand tall and be proud Dear Ones. You are the Light. You are the Kingdom of heaven on earth. Rejoice in this and find your way back to loving yourself.

So much has happened on the earth over eons of time. The truth has been hidden from you. If you were to search out the ancient texts, such as The Emerald Tablets and the many books of your Bible that were hidden from you then you would come to understand more the fullness of who you are. You would realize that you were meant to be here in full awareness of how to manifest a beautiful life. You would realize that the intention was not to live in pain and suffering. That is man-made Dear Ones.

Creator never wished that for you. Your governments and religions have kept the awareness of your Light from you. They hid that which would show you the way so that they could manipulate you. It was hidden so that you would be controllable. No more. The time has come for you to find your way back to the fullness of what a human on earth was meant to be. All you need is the intention to find these truths and they will begin to reveal themselves to you. It might be a documentary you find or a YouTube video.

With the intention to learn more about what was hidden, it will be revealed to you. All it requires is for you to notice when it shows itself. Pay attention. When you ask it is given. Very often Spirit delivers in small steps. If you are paying attention then more will be revealed. If you ask but do not expect to find then you will not. It is that simple. It is not because the truth is not there, it is because you are not willing to see it. The truth is always there. Will you be brave enough to see it regardless of what it looks like?

Oh, so many of you ask for things but then do not like the process of getting there. You ask for healing but then do not want to look at the truth of what needs to be released. You ask for a better relationship and then do not take responsibility for your part in the challenges that the relationship is enduring. It is not a free ride Dear Ones. You must give some energy to that which you ask for. The irony is that hanging onto what does not work takes more energy than welcoming in the new. Holding onto the past for the sake of comfort actually requires more energy than allowing the newness of the present. It is just unfamiliar and you are habituated to think that the unfamiliar is frightening.

Change your perspective. Think of the unfamiliar as magical and fun. Oh boy, a new experience. Is that not the world of a child? Almost everything is unfamiliar and they approach it with great wonder and joy. What could be more fun than that child-like quality? So approach the changes in your life that way instead of being afraid of the unfamiliar. Allow change to grow within you. If you are not fully loving the self then change is required for that to happen. If your life does not reflect perfect love and joy and grace then you are not fully loving yourself.

Many will argue that point but we say to you, when you are *fully* loving the self it is not possible to see anything but beauty and grace in your life, regardless of what the outside circumstances look like. This is the truth of it. Self-love is reflected in your world, the world that you create. If you do not like what you see it is a reflection of something that you do not like within yourself.

The world is your mirror. The world is your creation. Oh yes, there is a mass consciousness and it is easy to get lost in the energies of that. But we say, that as well is part of your creation. If you do not like getting caught up in mass consciousness pull yourself away from the city to a place where there are less people. Oh, that is not easy you say. We are not asking you to do this, we are just showing you that your life is a reflection of your choices. If you say you could never do that then we say that choice will reflect into your world. You can do anything you want. It is just that you won't.

Most of you, not all, will not allow yourselves to recreate your world. You yearn for this and that but will not take the steps for this or that to come about. Can you imagine doing something totally radical like leaving your job, moving to some south sea island and living by doing odd jobs here and there? Most of you would say definitely not. And yet, you could be happier doing such a thing than you have ever been in your life. But, if you will not allow yourself to make the radical change

– or any change for that matter – then your life will remain the same.

The world is in a new cycle Dear Ones. Your Mother Earth is about to ascend into higher realms. She wants to take you with her. This is the reason for our transmissions to you. This is the reason for our encouragement for you to step into all that you are. This is why we ask you to stop hiding behind your smallness and claim the magnificence that you are. You were not created to be a creature of lackluster existence. Oh no, you are here to be Creator's reflection upon this beautiful planet called Earth. Be what you are. Find your fullness.

Every day we encourage and every day we offer you more tools for finding your way back to the fullness of your expression. By following our guidance and heeding our words you will find your life recreating before your eyes into more ease and grace. There will be growing pains as you make this transition, but every child wants to grow up. That is the reason for being. And it is your reason for being.

It is why humanity fell into darkness. It is so that you could find your way back to the Light. Believe it or not, that is easier now than it ever has been. The reason that is so hard to see is because the darkness is also more evident than it has ever been. We love so Dear Ones. We are here coaxing, like a life coach from heaven. We see only the best for you. Believe that for yourselves and allow the new Light to carry you to heaven; heaven on earth. And so it is.

# Essay Thirty-four - IN THE LOVE OF LIGHT

And so it is we come before you once again Beloveds. Once again we have the opportunity to pour our love out onto the page as you absorb the energies of our rays as you read these words. We come to you with the intention of lifting you up into the heavens with our love and with your own grace and ease. We are so proud of who you are and what you are accomplishing on this earth. Yours is a planet in great transition and one that is leading the way for other similar forms of creation.

Your beautiful Light in this universe is drawing attention. Crowds are gathered to see that which is to become the new planet earth. Many are waiting to see what humanity is going to create. It is all unfolding day by day. There is no predicting what will happen on this planet anymore because you are the creators now. Your mass consciousness is creating each new day. And we say to you that, more and more, you are creating joy and Light.

Oh, you can look around you and still see much darkness. And this seems to be the focus of your media. And yet, for those of you who are consciously choosing to see the Light, it is all around you. Your hearts are becoming lighter as you step into the energy of love and know that this is the way the world was meant to be. For indeed, that is true. Humans were meant to be living in the love of Light. In other words, one could say in the love of love. For the Light is Love.

The Light is the Creator Light which is the love that blesses all humans. And, if you look at all the awareness that your scientists are revealing about the connection of all species, you will see that the love is everywhere. If you are connected to a blade of grass and your thoughts have influence on plants and everything, then everything is love because you are love. You were created in the image of the Divine, which is love. And you are connected to everything. Therefore everything is love. This is the truth.

And so you may ask, how can love look like war and hatred and starvation? We can understand these questions Dear Ones. That certainly does not look like what most would consider love to be. And yet, you have been given so much love that you are allowed to suffer through that kind of existence. Only deep love could allow that. Only deep love could allow you to take yourselves to such deep levels of despair and not jump in and save you.

But it is the saving that would be pulling you out of your chosen experience. It is the saving that would be saying to you, you are not strong enough to find your own way out of this. In the saving would be the message that you do not have the skill and the knowing of how to find your way out and that is not true. If you are having an experience you have the solution to your experience. Only love could watch you live the same challenging experience over and over.

Yet, love knows that at some point, you will find your way. That is true love. That is the love of the Creator. That is the knowing that you have all that you need within you. After all, you are a creator as well. What you create is your choice. Lived long enough, everyone will eventually find their way out of such deep despair as you witness on this earth. The souls who are suffering to human eyes are experiencing what they have chosen in spiritual eyes.

This is not to dismiss compassion for others. We are not saying this at all. Love is compassion. It is to have compassion and to care for others in whatever way you are called to do. We are talking about the knowing that what you do is your path and what they do is their chosen path. It is a tricky matter for the human heart, to witness others in pain and living in harsh conditions and yet understand that it is not darkness.

Some can understand this. Love is everywhere, even in the pain and hardship. Rashana, just a few days ago, received such a deep healing that she finally understood the gift of this pain. That is when you can see the love in it Dear Ones. She fully understood that the pain caused her to disassociate from her body, for much of her life. She did not relate to humans fully because it was not safe. With this healing she understood that it was the yearning to be out of the body and connected to Spirit that allowed her to be such a clear channel.

Her connection to the spiritual aspect of her existence was an escape from the physical but there was a gift. Once you heal to the point of understanding the gift, you can see the love in everything. It is the same for all of you. Believe this, for it is true. When you have healed to the point that you can see the gift in your own suffering then you will see the love that the experience provided you. This is love in the Light and this is love in the darkness. There is no difference.

When all is love it is just a matter of finding your way through the darkness back to the Light. Like the sun shining above the clouds, the love is always there. It is never gone. It is just that it gets covered up so you can't always see it. Sometimes you just have to have faith that it is there. You awaken each day knowing the sun is still there whether you can see it or not. Have the same faith in the Light hiding in the darkness of existence.

The only method to find your way through this is in your own journey. Helping others is sometimes a great act of kindness. Sometimes it is a false sense of importance. Sometimes it is believing in the weakness of others and not seeing their strength. In this case, as always, the weakness is within the self. That is why the only way is through the self. You cannot help others improve their lives when yours is a mess. You cannot love others more than you love yourself. This is an illusion. Many think they are so loving and kind to others. In reality, many are looking for the love of self through others.

If they are kind and nice to others then hopefully those others will like them and approve of them and make them OK. It is a deep lack of love for self that reaches out so desperately to be loved and liked by others. Look inside Dear Ones. You are in a state of great weakness when your self-worth depends on others. Have you found it there? Do you feel fulfilled worrying what others think and if you are liked? It is as much a place of suffering to live this way as it is for those starving and living on the streets. Do not fool yourselves. The way out of the darkness is by looking at your own life and making the changes required of your life that will get you through. You cannot be a proxy for another. Each must do their own work.

As always, we have come with a deep and caring message. We have come to lift humanity into its rightful place which is to be living in love. Imagine a world where everyone lives in harmony. Imagine a world where everyone sees only the brilliance in you and honors you in every moment. Imagine a world where you are appreciated for your uniqueness in this world. Imagine a world where your quirkiness is loved and adored. Imagine a world where each child grows up knowing that they have a key piece to play in the world and they know they are important just because of who they are.

No changes needed. No repairs to fit in - just perfect. Oh what a wonderful world that is Dear Ones. That is where you are headed. You cannot see it in your manifestation but you can play and see it in your imagination. You can begin to create it by playing with it in your mind's eye and feeling what it will be like to live that way. Step into the future and create this beautiful life. See it in your now and you will bring it closer and closer for all. You are moving into such beautiful times. It will be safe for your hearts to be wide open once again. What a glorious existence that is. Expect it. Believe in it just as we believe in you.

Like the loving Creator that will not interfere, we have been standing by for eons of time watching and knowing that you would one day be right here. Right here on the cusp of becoming a whole new race of human. Oh, it is glorious to behold. All of the heavens are on watch, rejoicing and waiting. This time is here. How magnificent it is to see you in your power, ready to step into your rightful place with All That Is. We rejoice and we love you so. And so it is.

# Essay Thirty-five - THE COUNCIL OF NINE II

And so it is Beloveds that we would like to share with you once again a bit more about who we are and why we are here bringing forward these messages every day. For you see, we believe that, with more understanding of our role here on the earth, you will have more reason to understand our intentions in bringing these messages forward each day. So, let us begin by telling you that we come from a star system far, far away.

It is most unusual for us to be coming to the planet known as Earth. We would not have even noticed you if it were not for that which is unfolding on your planet at this time. For you see Dear Ones, you are the first. You are the first planet on which an experiment such as yours was conducted. To be given free will but no memory of the truth of who you are was a grand experiment. And, as many of you have read before, it seemed for a long time that the experiment would end in darkness. And then, at the last possible opportunity, humanity chose the Light.

The higher aspect of your soul said yes to all that the Light represents and bravely declared that you are ready to step out of the darkness. You declared that you are ready to put down the false weapons of hatred and choose love. And with this the support began. Light workers from all over the universe stepped in to support you in this great accomplishment. A horn rang out in the heavens calling for those who would be witness to this great transition and who would offer their loving to support to assist humanity in the move up the ladder of ascension into the higher dimensions of Light.

Oh, what a grand opportunity. It is a grand opportunity for those who are supporting you and also for you as a human race. You have declared your freedom and you have used it to look through all the darkness and claim your rightful place of living in the Light. Those who watch over you are so proud. We are so honored to stand before the souls who came into incarnation on this planet just to be here at this time with the determination to make the successful transition out of the darkness. We look at what you have endured and we see that it was not easy. We see that it was not easy to be a soul full of Light and compassion and deep love and reverence for life and walk into a planet of darkness.

Oh how they tried to diminish your Light. Right down to the last spark they tried to extinguish your Light but they failed. You held onto the knowing somewhere within your heart that Love prevails. Even though it was not evident in your physical world, you did not forget why you came and who you are. Oh, you may have forgotten for a time but it came back to you. The spark of Light in your heart ignited the pure love that you are.

This is why we commend you so deeply. This is why Beings from all of the universes have gathered to Earth at this time. This is why there is great celebrating in the heavens. You have walked through the density of enslavement into the dignity of royalty. You have found your way back to your brilliance Dear Ones. Understand that you are love manifest. Understand the glory of who you are. Be humble no longer. Stand in the Light of who you are with pride and dignity. See in one another the great humans that you are. It is time to be all of you.

And so it is our mission at this time to help you understand the fullness of this. It is our way of being at Ziluru to be a species of love and grace. Our bodies are Light – etheric, for we exist in the fullness of the Creator Light. We have not taken on the challenge of a fallen race the way humans did and we therefore have remained in the fullness of Creator Light.

It is your beautiful souls that have called us here. It is your beautiful souls that keep us here for we see you. We see you and we deeply admire the creation that you are. Oh if you only knew how magnificent you are. If you only knew the amazing accomplishment of humanity upon this planet. You have done the impossible. You have proven wrong those who saw the darkness on your planet 50 years ago and gave up hope. You will be heralded all the way back to the end of time for your accomplishments.

This is our transmission this day. It is our desire to help you see the magnificence of you. With this understanding we hope that you will find it easier to step out of the mundane into the radiance that you truly are. We hope you will find it easier to believe in yourselves as we invite you to step up to the fullness of all that you are. The time has come. It is the time to create the new Earth. It is time to decide what it will mean from here forward to be living in love. It is time to create heaven on Earth, for as above, so below. Let it ever be so. And so it is Beloveds, and so it is.

# Essay Thirty-six - LIVING IN LOVE

Greetings Beloveds. Greetings from the Love and Light of the Creator. Greetings from the Great Central Sun as we come before you this day with great joy and delight to be witness to the magnificence that is wo/man on this Earth. Dear Ones, we are celebrating today for we see that so many of you are willing to heal and move into the fullness of who you are that the colors of the planet are changing.

You are radiating more Light and brilliance into the world. Those of you who are intentionally growing and expanding are also growing and expanding the auras of all those around you. You do not grow alone Dear Ones. Every soul who chooses to move more fully into the Light of love also takes those around them to a higher level of being. That is the way of it. That is what energy does. As you know, your bodies are electric and magnetic.

It is this field that surrounds the physical body that also impacts those around you. The energies of the world do not remain in a tiny, closed box that could be a description for the physical body. They expand far beyond the physical body and so you impact those around you. If you live in an apartment building then your energies are being shared with those in adjacent apartments – above, below and beside you. This is also good to know for the cleansing of your own space.

If you feel that those around you do not hold the same integrity of living that you do, cleanse your space with incense, sage, good music … whatever speaks to you. You may simply use your intention for this cleansing. As well, if you have an argument with someone in your home, be kind to all and clear the energies out of your space and the space of those around you. It is always good to keep your space cleansed just as you do with the physical body. This makes it easier to keep your thoughts and intentions pure, with less interference of stagnant thoughts and mass consciousness.

Dear Ones, you are powerful creators. You have much greater abilities than you know. Merely intending these things to be so ensures their success. Your level of connection to the higher aspect of your soul will have impact on these intentions. Also the degree of love that you come from in your intentions will reflect back to you in what you create with those intentions. Be in a pure heart space when you make these intentional shifts in energy. You do not want to magnify that which no longer serves your life or supports your growth. Cleanse and clear your thoughts and then cleanse and clear your space.

Fill your home and the hearts of all those around with love. Have the intention of blessing yourself and all those around you. These intentions will have an impact on the whole of the earth. Everyone will feel the love in some way. It will brighten their day. It will make your home feel like the sanctuary that it should be for you. Be aware of your surroundings and what you connect with. For example, do you leave the TV on with the news playing while you prepare dinner? What are the messages that are coming into your field of energy as you prepare this meal? Is it about war, shootings, robberies, political upheaval, and economic downfall?

How do you think these messages, even when heard by the subconscious as you prepare your meal, impact you and the thoughts that are going into the food that will nourish your body? EVERYTHING has an impact on your life. And if your children are running around the room with these messages they will feel it even more. Children are sensitive souls who are very aware of the energetic field in which they live. Be kind to them and put on playful music as you prepare your meal or something that is more pleasing to your family.

All of these little aspects of daily life have an impact on your overall state of wellbeing. Love changes everything. Ask yourself daily how can you more fully love yourself? And think of simple things as we have just mentioned as your answer to that. You can play soft, gentle music as you drive to work. You can walk around outside for five minutes before you enter your home after work and your next level of busyness begins as you prepare meals, etc. All of these things impact your life.

We offer these messages to support you in living a more loving life. All love begins within. It is how you treat yourself that reflects how much you love yourself. Please do not confuse what we are saying with narcissism. That is not the love which we speak about. We are talking about kind, gentle, caring love of self so that your loving is balanced between caring for family and friends and caring for yourself.

Balance is key here as in all aspects of living. If you love others more than yourself, always doing for others but not for yourself, you are loving no one. You are deceiving yourself. If you are loving only yourself and always putting yourself first and expecting others to do the same, then you are not loving yourself from the heart. That is a dysfunctional love learned in childhood. Balance again is the key. If you can feel the love that we transmit in these words then you know what true love feels like. Those who connect deeply in meditation know what this love feels like. It moves them to tears. It is a love that touches the heart without any associations of want or need. It just drops into the heart and resonates truth.

The more you use the tools we give you in these transmissions, the more you will come to understand the love of self. These seemingly simple steps will make exponential changes in your life. That is to say, like the ripple on the pond, a little change will impact out into your life at an increasing rate. Then another little change will step it up once again and so it goes. Each little change for the better means a leap for the better once it impacts the various levels of your life.

Also know that as you change, so must those around you. This can be disturbing for others so have patience. As you change others must adjust to the new you. They must allow adjustment in themselves to integrate who you are and allow you into their existence. Do not allow this to stop you from improving your life. This is a gift to all around you. If you find that some people cannot tolerate the change, it is only because they are not willing to make the same changes for themselves. Because they do not see themselves reflected in you, they will look elsewhere.

This is their choice. You have given them an opportunity to grow into more self-awareness. It is their choice to say yes or walk away. Simply by changing who you are others around you will change. You do not need to preach about what you believe or ask others to change. Your responsibility is to yourself and others for themselves. You know that you do not take well to others telling you what to do. Each must make their own choices in life. By respecting that, you are not interfering in the life plan of another.

It has been our great delight to bring this message to you this day Dear Ones. We delight in every moment that we can express to you our understanding of the way of love. We delight in every moment when we can connect with the humans who read these pages and say yes to moving into the fullness of these times and the opportunities that lie before you. These are magnificent times of great transition. You are in the midst of the greatest shift ever known on planet earth. How fortunate to be here. And so it is.

# Essay Thirty-seven - HOW TO BE A HUMAN IN THE NEW TIMES

And so we gather once again Beloveds into the hearts of man, embracing the heart of heaven. And we say to you Dear Ones, that your Light is a reflection of the Divine. Therefore it means that you are a reflection of the Divine. And so what does it mean to be a reflection of the Divine? Do you see what you would consider to be Divine within you? Is it lying dormant in the heart, ready to awaken? Is it love? What is love really? Let us tell you the answer to these questions. Love is the softness of knowing that you are perfect and that the world provides all of your needs and that every aspect of who you are is what the world needs.

For many of you this softness is lying in waiting because the world has been a challenging place to be. Life has been cruel at times and so you have closed down your heart in order to be able to stay on the planet. And, to speak of the connection between your earthly mother and you, her heart chakra was also shut down for a long time. It is opening now, and so is the heart of humanity. For you see, you are deeply connected. It is because humanity is ready to step into the fullness of an open and loving heart that the earth is able to do the same. And it is the energies of these times that are the invitation.

The planetary alignments in the year 2012 and the years leading up to it had a HUGE impact in aligning humanity into becoming a new human. Look at the children being born today. Just barely two years old and many know their numbers and letters of the alphabet. Were they able to speak sooner perhaps you would discover more. They are of a different DNA and so are you. Your DNA has morphed and you are a new human.

Know this to be true. Do the research and find out for yourselves. How does knowing that change your perspective on what you can do and who you are? Knowing that you can change your biology do you doubt that you can change your life? After all, your life is truly the illusion that you create from your mind. So change your mind. Ah, that is the task. For so many of you that is the most difficult challenge. How can you see life as different as what it is? This is what we have spoken of many times.

This is the act of seeing what you believe, so change the beliefs. That is why we have just shared that your biology has changed and the children are changing. If the children are coming in with greater skills, a different intelligence, what do you think it means for your earth? Of course, it means that the earth is changing? Why would a species evolve without need? It is the need to adapt to a new environment that a species evolves - and humans are evolving. That tells you that the earth is evolving. In order to keep up with evolution, it is necessary to allow yourself to change as well.

What should this change be? To see only your greatest dreams and desires as your reality. It should be to believe that you have everything you would ever choose to have. It is to connect your feelings to that belief. Say yes to your desire. Witness yourself celebrating at the attainment of it. Imagine your happy dance as you celebrate the success in achieving it. This is how you change your reality. Keep doubt at bay. Quickly grab onto doubt and turn it around.

This is the beginning and yet we say to you, healing is a huge aspect of this as well. Until the old beliefs are cleared out they will lurk in the shadows and affect your outcome without you even seeing them. Rashana had a belief that was so deep within her subconscious that her healer had to spend an hour helping her get to it. She finally was able to see it and it was cleared. How many of you are willing to stay with it to clear out those old beliefs that can hold you back in your life?

Do not let the ego delude you into believing that all is cleared when it is not. If you have *any* fear, examine it and find the source and clear it out. It is those fears that keep you from success. You can trick yourself and think oh I have this cleared and I'm going to quit my job and start my own business. If your business is not a success within a matter of months, you had not fully cleared the old beliefs that would repeat old patterns in your life. It is a challenging piece of being human in these times to discern when you have done the clearing work and when you have not.

So, we suggest starting small and working up to the big stuff. Start with little things that you would like in your life, and allow spirit to lead you to it. Do not say, oh I want a new shirt and go and buy a new shirt and think you have done it. Ask for something and let spirit provide. Tell spirit what you desire and then wait and see where it appears. Then you can ask for things that stretch your belief system more and more and see when and where the manifestation stops. That will tell you where the hidden belief systems are and what still requires more clearing and healing.

Dear Ones, we know we have spoken of this many times, but we say to you that it is vital to learn how to manage this way of existence, for it is the way of it in these new energies in which you reside. Your life is a reflection of your beliefs. Our desire is that you are able to create a life of pure love and grace. This is our desire for you Beloveds and this is why we are here watching over you and guiding you in this way. This is why we deliver these messages with clear intention.

We see your success. We know you can do it. It may not be easy for all of you but you can do it.

Your success depends on your willingness to step out of your comfort zone that is really the old patterns of the past. We would ask why you would want to stay there when there is so much more that you can achieve which is a life full of everything you ever dreamed of. All it requires is to step out of what is comfortable and challenge yourselves a bit to step into that which feels like it is difficult. If you find it difficult to speak up for yourself to others, then that is what you must do to get through to your next stage of manifestation.

If you find it difficult to love yourself or to believe that you deserve anything good in your life, then you must conquer that belief in order to move forward. Whatever you find challenging in your life is a clear indication of what is holding you back. Please know Beloveds, that moving through these patterns can be terrifying. We know this. The illusion is strong because they were created as a form of protection. We trust that those reading these words are no longer living in the environment that produced the fear. As adults you can take on a higher perspective. As children you had to do whatever you could to make your way in a world that did not fully see you or understand you.

And so here you are, you have passed the marker that was December 21, 2012. You are still here. What next? What is next is that the world is morphing and what did not happen on December 21st will happen. The world is slated for ascension. What does that mean? It means that your earthly mother is moving from the third to the fourth dimension.

Do you think a mother would leave her children behind? Only if they were not willing to go with her. Are you willing? If so, are you clearing yourself? Are you in your space training program, so to speak?  Be prepared Dear Ones.  She is ready to fly and she would like to take you with her.  Release the old patterns and beliefs so that you are ready for lift off.  And so it is.  We love you so.

# Essay Thirty-eight - MESSAGES OF LOVE

And so it is Beloveds that we come before you once again. And once again we are delighted to witness the beautiful Beings of Light that inhabit this beautiful planet earth. What makes her so beautiful Dear Ones? It is your Light reflecting out that shines so brightly on this earth. Your earthly mother has deep appreciation for every loving thought that you send to her. Every time you appreciate something of the natural world, the whole earth shivers with delight.

This is the impact of your thoughts Dear Ones. This is the impact of one human thinking. And this is why we ask you to be very aware of your thoughts and what you are offering out into the world. It is not merely a passing thought but an electrical signal that travels the globe. Just like you do not see the electricity running through the wires that bring power to your home, you do not see the electrical signals that are your thoughts, but they are there. And, like the wires, they travel.

And so, if you want a world of peace then think peaceful thoughts. See peace all around you. Look for peace in every moment. Feel it. Feel it within yourself. Be at peace with yourself and feel it. Oh how soft and gentle it is when you think peaceful thoughts for yourself. You then put those soft, gentle thoughts out into the world and they caress all the thoughts of hatred into dissolution.

This is the way of it. It is so magnificent and delightful to play with this once you recognize the truth of it. And so we invite you to play with peacefulness. What is it to you? What would a world that was at peace look like? It must be clear within your understanding for you to create it. Once you are clear on what that is, you will begin to see it manifest within your life.

Let us say that peace to you is smiles from the people you meet on the street, and happy conversations within your family, and cordial communications with your coworkers. Once you understand that this is what peace looks like to you, then you can start noticing it. And when a coworker is friendly to you then you can acknowledge, I have peace in my life. The more you notice that you have peace in your life the more it will grow. As it grows in your awareness you will find that your thoughts of peace increase as you project out into the world. The electric current of thought that comes from you will be more and more full of peace.

This is how you impact not only your own lives but the entire planet. Never doubt your impact in this world. No drop of water in the ocean is insignificant, for each drop is what creates ocean as opposed to puddle. The same is true for your impact in the ionosphere that surrounds this planet. Peace starts within, as does all creation. It is by knowing what it looks like and then noticing it that you begin to create whatever it is that you desire to have in your life. This is the formula. Start small, noticing the simple things, like a smile. Then see it increase. The more you notice that which you are choosing as your reality, the more it becomes your reality.

If you are choosing a lover, notice all the other lovers and be happy for them. Oh, I see love is in my 'field'. Good. That is what I have chosen for myself, how delightful to see it is here. This way of noticing and recognizing that it is love coming closer to you will magnetize it closer and closer until the love you see is your own. Viewing other lovers with envy will push that same experience away from you. Your envy is really a statement of what you do NOT have in your life and so that will increase the not having of it. We hope this is clear to you. Notice that which you wish to see and it will come closer and closer.

And so that is enough about that level of manifestation. What we really wish to speak of today is the language of love. How does love appear in this world? Is it the love of a child? The love for a pet? The love of nature? Love of food? The love you feel for your partner? What is love? There are many levels or aspects of love so when we talk about messages of love, to what are we referring? Let us answer our own question Dear Ones.

We would like you to know that messages of love are thoughts of love of the self. Yes. This is where love begins. It does not truly exist in the mind although many of you will try to create it from this space. Look how sexy that woman looks. Look how strong he is. He earns a good income so therefore he will be a good provider. This is the language of the mind thinking it is recognizing love.

Does a man who earns a large salary always make a good provider? Definitely not. Does a sexy looking woman always fulfill every desire? No. So, when we talk of the language of love we would ask that you speak that language from the heart. Do you really want a sexy lover or a partner who honors and respects you and one who is fun to be with and shares similar values? This would be more of a heart-felt thought. Do you desire a man with a good income or one who is generous and supportive and gentle with your soul?

When you begin to ask these questions of yourself, in *all* aspects of your life, you will see great changes in your life. For, if you explore all aspects of your life in this way, you will begin to get honest with yourself about what you truly would like your work to be like, and

143

your family and your vacation time and on it goes. You could start with your method of employment.

First question to ask would be are you happy with your work. If not, what values are you looking for in a career? Not how much do you make and where do you work, but how are you treated and are your innovative ideas accepted? This questioning, when reviewed for everything in your life, can bring you great clarity of who you are. They open up the possibility to step toward what you desire as opposed to running from what you do not want. This is a huge shift of thinking and one that can recreate life in a very short period of time.

We invite you to do this activity. Get a notebook and make a title page for every area of life: partner, children, family, work, recreation, friends, etc. If you volunteer, add that. If you are a caregiver, add that. Even if it seems like you can't change some things, still add them to your list so that you are clear about them. That clarity alone will often lead to changes in your daily life. It will seem amazing to some. We say to you that it is the power of the mind. The mind is always searching for that which you desire. If you are not clear on what that is you cannot find it. And if you expect (through your thoughts) what you do not like about your life that is what the mind will be instructed to find for you.

Take time this day to begin this journey into this activity and we believe you will find that, more and more, you are offering yourself messages of love. Loving your life, loving yourself and loving the world you live in. Be clear on what you choose to see. See it. Appreciate it. This is the formula. Enjoy the transition into this clarity Dear Ones. We love being witness to all that is unfolding in your lives and are at your sides cheering you on. And so it is.

# Essay Thirty-nine - COMING OF AGE

Greetings Beloveds. Greetings from the Love and Light of the Creator. Greetings from the heavens as we come before you this day in joy and love. We come before the beautiful race that calls itself human and we say to you that there is so much love for you in the heavens. All of creation is celebrating who you are and what you are becoming. The world has changed. Never again will the earth fall into such darkness. Never again will humans be tested in the way that you have been in the last eons of time. Never again will you suffer the way you have, lost to the way of love.

That is over Dear Ones. You have crossed the marker and you are still here! You are still here in the flesh, although that flesh is changing. The point is that you did it. You held strong in the Light and won over the darkness despite all its efforts to keep you from your own true nature. You found your way back, like the story of the prodigal son. Now perhaps you know why the son was received so lovingly.

It is symbolic of what you are achieving on this time on your planet earth. And this is why we adore you so. This is why we come to you to deliver messages and encourage you with our words. There is more to accomplish Dear Ones. The journey has not ended, just passed an important marker. The next path of this journey is to grow into your fullness and be prepared for ascension when the time comes.

Beloveds, we wish you to know that you are Light – pure Light. That is what you are. And what is the Light? It is love. And so we can call you love and you can know that what we say is what you are. Knowing this, how can you ever doubt that you deserve to have goodness and gladness in your lives? How can you believe that there must be hardship? The old saying that you must work hard to achieve is simply not true. The less you work at being all that you are, the easier it is and the more you step into it.

What is work is to resist the fullness of who you are. What is hard is thinking your life must be disciplined and determined and controlled. Flow with life dear ones. If you work out today and it feels good, wonderful. If you do not feel like working out for the next five days, OK. When you are loving yourself you simply will not allow yourself to eat unhealthy foods and stop exercising. It simply will not be what you choose for yourself. When you are loving yourself fully you can go with the flow of what each day brings because your choices are always in the fullness of what a loving essence will choose for itself.

Then, when you do go for a run because you are inspired to do so, you are amazed how easy it is. When you are inspired you are floating. When you MAKE yourself run, every step is an effort as you push yourself forward. This is the difference. Flowing and pushing feel very different and it is not hard to see which you are doing. If it is a 'have to' instead of a 'want to' then you have your answer. It is that simple. Oh how easy life can become when you let yourself be in the moment of what wants to be. Step out of the 'must do' and the 'have to'.

Yes, we know that you must go to work when you hate your job. Or must you? Is there another way? We have discussed this with you. It is all in your mind, just like everything else. Change your mind and you change your life. Decide that you choose something different and something different will appear. Be clear on what that something different is so that it does not surprise you. Although we say, that regardless of what that something is, it is a new opportunity to learn, grow and expand.

Life brings fullness when you expect it and know that you deserve it. Life brings fullness to those who believe it is so for them. Sometimes you look at these people who seemingly have everything and you ask yourselves, why them? They are not kind or generous and here they have all this. The answer to that question is simple. They believe they deserve it so they have it.

The All That Is does not discriminate and so you receive what you expect regardless of your morality. The All That Is simply gives what you believe you deserve and can have. Knowing that, why not change things for yourself right now, in this moment? Take all that you have learned from us thus far and begin to put it into practice. Go over our essays and find the wisdom there. Use it for your own gain as a person and in your outward reflection – in your physical experience. This is why we are speaking to you each day. It is so that you can be prepared for ascension by believing in yourselves and moving into the fullness of living.

This world has been a challenging place for a very long time. You deserve – and indeed are given - medals for that which you accomplish by being here. This incarnation is the most challenging because in this incarnation you came here to change it all. And how do you change it all? - by changing yourself. You came here this time to do something different. You came here this time to reinvent the world right before your very eyes. This time you came to morph yourselves and the planet into a higher aspect of being.

You knew you could do it and we knew you could do it. That is why you are here. You are here because the heavens decided that you are the ones to be victorious in this grand mission on earth. You call this mission ascension for all. That is what we refer to in all our essays. It is the reason for our writing. For you see, the ascension has been delayed. Your earthly mother is waiting so patiently and generously. She is waiting for every last one of you to say yes to life. Saying yes to life moves you into the fullness of who you are and you are more ready for the shift.

When you are living in the drudgery of life and your burdens are weighing you down, this is not living in the yes of life. That is living in the fear of what might be. What might happen if I took a different job? What might happen if I chose a different relationship? What might happen if I am alone? These are drudgery questions. Life giving questions are more like this: how did I become so incredibly happy with my life? What did I do to bring such great success in my career? How did I ever attract such a perfect and loving partner into my life? How is it that I came to be so incredibly happy in my life? Oh yes, these are the questions to be asking yourself – over and over and over. Repeat, repeat, repeat and believe that they will change your life, for they will.

Be in the fullness of life Dear Ones. There are so many riches awaiting you. If you cannot see them you will not find them so believe that ANYTHING is possible and then you will see the unfolding of a whole new life. All that was lost will be found. That is to say, the fullness of you, the love that you are, will return to you. You must make the steps to achieve it. We cannot do it for you. That is the hardest bit Dear ones. Declare that this is the year that you step into the fullness of who you are, living to the greatest potential of who you are. That would make us rejoice, to hear those words coming from humans all over the world.

That declaration alone would change your planet into higher octaves of the Light. That statement alone could possibly be enough to lift all of humanity into ascension. That is really how easy it is. Believe it Dear Ones. We are here because we love you so. Feel us by your side. Call upon us to help you see your own radiance. Ask us for support whenever you are struggling and we will be instantly at your side supporting you and covering you with a blanket of love so that you can feel who you are – love in physical form on this most beautiful planet earth. Believe in yourselves Dear Ones. Believe. And so it is.

# Essay Forty - THE LOVE OF LIFE

And so it is Beloveds that we are called before you once again. We come in love and joy to stand before the beautiful humans who read these words, for we see you and we know who you are and we are delighted to be in your presence as you are with us. For you see dear humans, you are making the earth into a new experience. You are transforming the earth as you walk upon her and she delights in the sacredness of it.

She rejoices with every heart that offers her love and who appreciates her great beauty. She delights with every soul who feels joy and appreciates the smallest things in life. A child finds delight when playing with a bug. That is joy. You too can find such pleasure from the simple things in life. It just takes a slowing down and a connection to the natural world. There is not much to delight in when you are walking down a city street. All that you see is concrete or material misgivings.

But, when you step out of the city and get back to nature, you will find much to be joyful about. Your mere surroundings can open your heart and lift you to the heavens. This is the love of life. By finding your way into nature you will see that everything can bring delight - the feel of the sunshine on your face, the birds that fly overhead, the clouds gathering in the sky. There is so much that you can delight in. This is finding your way back to your nature, through nature.

Rashana is currently writing a book that is a collection of messages from a tree. Many would laugh at this and think it is folly, and yet we say to you, all of you have this ability and all of you would benefit from a deeper connection to the natural world. This is why, in some countries, even though they do not have all the commercial items that you have (and to you it may seem they live in poverty), the people are truly happy. They are more connected to the natural world and it brings them joy. There is also great contentment in living a simple life.

You would be surprised if you really knew how much your complicated lives lead to your misery. The busier you become the less quality of life you have. The more you own the more you worry about what you own. A simpler life allows you to get back to the basic nature of existence. We are not saying that you should all sell your homes and buy a log cabin in the woods. We speak of this simply so that you will explore this and get yourselves out of the city and see how you feel. It is amazing how two days out of the busyness and grind of daily life will soften your hearts.

For many of you, two days is not enough to forget the job and settle into your new environment, but if you go with awareness to be present in the moment, present with the natural surroundings that you have taken yourself to, you will feel the ease begin to creep in. Be present with the environment when you take yourselves into the natural world so that you can gain all the benefits of the experience. And what are the benefits? They are the stillness that comes from taking your mind outside of yourself. They are the appreciation of the complexity of nature and its ecosystems while appearing so simple. When you connect with this, you see another way of existence.

So many of you are now crying out for change. It is obvious to many of you that the current systems that you live in are no longer working for you, the people. This is appropriate. It is time for change. And yet, change begins within the self. It begins with appreciation of what is good in your life and expanding that. It begins with simplifying your life and exploring what is truly of value in this world. If you were stranded on an island for two years what would be more valuable, two good friends with you or five stores full of anything you wanted to buy?

When you isolate yourself from the world and explore your life in this way you will have a greater understanding of what is truly of value in life. Commercial investments are just distractions. They are a way of avoiding what is truly required for a full life, and that is to look inside. You distract yourselves away from yourselves. And now, with your telephones to your ears you are doing this more and more. You have all seen groups of friends all sitting side by side looking at a little box in their hand instead of looking into each other's eyes and seeing the beauty there. They are lost in the technology that pulls them away from reality.

And so our question would be, why do they want to step out of the reality that would be making human connections? Has it become too painful? Are you forgetting how to connect to one another? Answer these questions for yourselves. Parents, do you take the time to look into the eyes of your children and truly see them? Slow down. Let the fullness of life seep into your pores. As time speeds up it is even more important to consciously slow down. Leave Sunday free for family time. Cook a slowly prepared meal. Smell the food roasting in the oven as you prepare to sit together and enjoy each other's company. Find your way back to the treasures of life.

Here is a question we would like you to explore. Why do you think that you wanted to incarnate on earth? What was your purpose in being here? Do you think there was some purpose? Do you think it was to get lost in the complexity of living, simply striving to survive? Perhaps it was something more than that Dear Ones. Perhaps it was to discover the fullness of your soul and all the gifts that you have to offer the world. Perhaps it was to learn who you are by supporting your fellow humans and discovering the love of self through loving others.

There is so much to enjoy about the human experience. It is our intention that these questions and our guidance will lead you back to the fullness of existence and out of the mundane. Find the stillness that comes from quieting the mind or being in a natural environment. There is stillness in nature. That same nature is in your mind if you will sit long enough to explore it. Take the time to sit and simply breathe. Count your breath seven times and see if you do not feel just a little calmer.

It is not complicated Dear Ones so we ask you not to make it so. The desire to make it complicated is just the ego wanting to give importance to itself. The way back to your true self is found through simplicity. We would say that the more you simplify your life the more you will find joy creeping back into your existence. Find people who are truly happy and see how they live.

And so we leave you now with this thought for today. What is the one thing you could do this day to simplify your life? And then, if you remove some activity from your life, be aware of using that time for stillness. It is OK to sit and do nothing. Remember the day when people would sit on their doorstep and simply be? That be-ing was doing. It was the kind of doing that allows calm and stillness.

Find it Dear Ones. Allow it. Do not convince yourselves with your busyness that there is importance there. It is the stillness that is important because the stillness allows you to discover who you truly are. This is not what outward appearances would make it appear that you are, but what your heart says you are. Therein lies the truth – in the heart.  That is where the fullness of living is birthed.  Connect there Beloveds and find the beauty that is you.  We love you so.  And so it is.

# Essay Forty-one - HEALING IN LOVE

Greetings Beloveds. Greetings from the Love and Light of the Creator. Greetings from the Great Central Sun as we come before you as always with great joy and delight to be standing before the dear humans that you are. We see your Light beloveds and we rejoice. We see your strength and determination to make it in this world and we celebrate. We see your willingness to change and we celebrate even more! For you are the way-showers. You are the ones who carry the Light in your hearts and reflect it out to the world.

Oh, it is such delight to see you growing and changing and becoming all that you are. The more you heal the more you move into the fullness of this. It is a changing world. It is changing so quickly that many of you have trouble keeping up. And yet we say to you, it is going to get easier. The energies that led up to that magical day of December 21, 2012 were intense. They forced you to change whether you knew it or not. Now that you have passed that marker, things are settling down a bit you could say. Oh it may not seem this way on the outward expression of life, but in the planetary alignments and the celestial influences, things have shifted just a little.

The opportunity for ascension was the alignment of the planets. That marker has passed and yet you are still here. But, you are not here fully in the third dimension any more. The fourth dimension is creeping into your existence even though many are not aware of that either. And yet, they know their world is changing. They look around them and they see more tolerance for things that were forbidden in their childhood. They see greater acceptance of the more feminine aspects of life such as intuition, ESP and a more liberal belief system.

This is the awakening of the feminine and with it comes great healing from the vestiges of the patriarchy that has ruled this planet for hundreds of years. This is the healing that is allowing the fullness of life – the tenderness of life – to be rebirthed - and none too soon. The force of patriarchy almost overtook this planet. It almost destroyed the earth and all who walk upon her.

How glorious that you have passed this marker and you are still here. How glorious that the Divine Feminine is now amassing her energies upon the earth and softly influencing all that is unfolding at this time. It is indeed Divine grace that this be so. There has been much support for the earth that has allowed this to happen. We celebrate and rejoice this new beginning for you.

And so, you may be wondering how your world will change with these new more feminine energies growing into your awareness. It will change indeed Dear Ones. You will see more love in your world, more tolerance, more compassion, more understanding and less hardship, less dismissal of the lives of others. In the feminine energies the world is full of compassion and oozes the energies of loving grace – when it is in balance.

Your world once was led by matriarchal societies and, in the beginning it was very beautiful. As with all things, when one energy dominates for a long time it can become out of balance. This can cause despair whether it is feminine or masculine energies that have fallen out of the grace of a balanced existence. So, as you move into the feminine, you have thousands of years to look forward to where you are living in the balanced grace of the feminine.

And, with your ascension into the higher dimensions, you will not have the experience of falling so deeply out of grace as you have in this past cycle upon your planet. You will be living in a softer, more aware level of existence where you will feel the immediate impact of your thoughts and that is a very good governing tool Dear Ones. That alone is all that is required for you to learn how to manage your thoughts. When your hateful thoughts instantly manifest hateful situations in your life then you quickly learn to change your thinking.

We invite you to use this time to continually evolve by doing your healing work and stepping fully into loving yourself, those around you, and the world that you live in. Be the emanation of love at all times and you will enhance your preparation for the ascension that is inevitable for your planet. You do not have decades to prepare. You do not have time to dilly dally, for this healing work can take years of consistent intention.

Use the healing tools that are available to you and clear away the debris that stands in the way of your forward progress. Seek out a healer or a messenger that you trust. Ideally, you will have your own connection with your Higher Self and the spiritual support team that walks with you so that you can be receiving the messages yourself. Just be sure that you take the steps to fulfill the plan that you came with. We say to you, that you all came with the plan of ascending at this time, to be here for this great event and to grow and learn as much as is possible in this earthly school. You couldn't wait to get here. Then you landed and wondered what the heck you were thinking.

Oh yes we said it would be challenging but you are a warrior of the Light, there is no challenge too difficult for you. And that is true Dear Ones. That is why you are here. Do not ever doubt your success in this because it is your abilities that brought you here. You have particular skills to offer to all of humanity to support the successful transition to the Light at this time. You came here knowing this time would come. It is time to remember.    Be the Light Dear Ones.    The time of healing is upon you.  Be brave, be proud and grow into the brilliance that you are.  And so it is.

# Essay Forty-two - THE TIMING IS RIGHT

Greetings Beloveds. And so it is that we are called before you once again. And, as always, we are delighted to be here. Delighted to be offering our messages of Light to you and to share our wisdom and understanding of what is. We are delighted that you are here to listen, to read these words and allow the meaning and resonance to vibrate within your cells and lift you higher into the reality of who you truly are. For indeed you are creation.

You are the imagination of Creator allowing itself to be more than it is, in a sense. Your fragment of Creation is unique in itself, as are all Beings. In this manner, Creator or All That Is, gets to experience itself through expanded sparks of itself which is you. This is the beauty of life forms. This is the magnificence of all living things - not just humans but all species in creation. All species allow such diverse experiences you have no idea how much life there is in all the universes. It would boggle your mind, so we will focus on that which you are here on this planet earth.

You are God's delight. You are the essence of Creation and so we invite you to step into the fullness of that understanding. Does it make you ask (or consider) how magnificent you truly are? Does it make you wonder why you are living what appears to be such a mundane life? If it does, then also ask what can you do to change that? The first step would be to muster up all the courage you can find to be the person you would like to be.

Let us say you envision yourself travelling the world spreading your mission which is to be a messenger of love. What would that mean? What would it look like? What must you do to bring that into existence? It takes work. It can be joyful work because you knew it is leading you to where you want to be. It requires a constant shifting, releasing and adjusting. You cannot simply say, Spirit I am ready to spread love around the world and magically people will fall at your doorstep to hear your words.

No, you must take action to bring it into reality. We share this story with you so that you can understand how this all works. Action is required. If you are telling the universe that you are ready to ascend with planet earth, what is your action to get there? What is your declaration? Find it, speak it, focus and allow. You cannot *make* it unfold. That is spirit's job. Your job is to walk through the open doors. This is how your life journey can unfold when you have intention and allowing.

Now is the time Dear Ones. We have a short transmission today because we would like you to take the time to consider what it is that you are seeking in your life. Make a declaration. Give it a time frame. It requires commitment on your part yet we say to you, the rewards are great. Your life will change dramatically when you allow it to. Keep your faith that spirit is providing opportunity, not chaos. Your positive attitude will bring positive results.

This essay is entitled The Timing is Right. Why do you think we would choose that title? What does it mean to you? We leave this with you Dear Ones. What is it in your life that the timing is *ripe* for? We love you so. And so it is.

# Essay Forty-three - BEING IN THE DIMENSIONS OF LIGHT

Greetings Beloveds. Greetings from the Love and Light of the Creator. Greetings from the Great Central Sun as we come before you this day with messages of love. For you see Dear Ones, you are the Light upon this earth. Oh you thought maybe the Light was coming from the sun or reflecting off of the moon or even other stars in your solar system and yet we say to you that you are the Light in your experience. You are Light reflecting each other to each other. You are the Light that gives the sun its radiance and gives the moon its shine. You are the Light of the world and you don't even know it.

You have no idea how much Light you carry into the heavens and on your planet. It is such an interesting game of illusion that you are caught up in upon this great planet earth. It is such a brilliant game of deceit, but not in a harmful way. You knew when you made the decision to be here that which you were stepping into. It is not that you were deceived without your knowing. It is the forgetting that makes the game work and makes it so valuable to you as a soul choosing a tangible experience of growth and change.

And so it is that, as you walk this earthly path of being human, you have great opportunities for growth. And it is also that you can fall backwards in this game. For the dark is easy to find. The darkness can pull you in like the lust of a nymph playing with your mundane self. But, now is the time to turn your back to that lust. Now is the time to turn your back on the small self and step into the fullness of your full soul expression on this earth.

You are brilliant beings of Light. You are creatures of habit that must learn to close your eyes so that you are seeing from the inside and not what your human eyes show you. This is our invitation this day. Do not see the world from your physical eyes. Choose to see the world from your inner eye – the third eye – where the wisdom of your higher self resides.

For you see Dear Ones, this inner eye holds the wisdom of the beginnings of creation. When you look inside and find the wisdom of your heart, you are also connecting with all time. You are connecting with every aspect of your being that has ever been incarnate here on earth or anywhere else. It is all within the heart. Many of you will not find it because you are using your outside eyes instead of your inside eyes. Your outside eyes only show you the false reality that you created for this experience.

They are testing you. When you use your inside eyes you are connecting with the soul wisdom. Therein lies all knowledge. Therein lies all wisdom. Is it hard to find? Only if you think it is. As soon as you truly believe that it is easy to connect with that inner wisdom, then it is. Many are finding the way. We say to you that each and every one of you has this ability. It is actually so easy that you overlook it on your mission to find something that is difficult. You do it every day - every day, without exception, but you do not recognize it as such.

Did you know that all memory is retrieved from outside of yourself? Do you think that the brain actually has cells that have little drawers in them that hold information? What is information? What is knowledge? Is it tangible? No - just as love is not tangible. You love someone but you cannot put that love in a cup and give it to them. They FEEL it. So it is with intelligence.

You cannot put your knowledge in a cup and give it to someone. It is an interpretation of the brain.

So it is as well with this wisdom that is you in the universe and you on this earth and you connected to the higher aspect of your soul. It is not tangible but you can feel it. We know that you have had the experience of following your intuition which brought a favorable outcome. There was not a *thing* that guided you there, it was a feeling. Well, dear ones, we say to you that this feeling is the truth. This feeling is where the wisdom lies. It is within the heart and often accessed through the third eye – the intuitive eye.

Feeling does not come from the mind. Oh, the mind receives signals from the chemical systems in your body that indicate that it should respond in a certain way, but it is the heart intelligence that creates the feelings that are connected to the higher source of All That Is. So, when you have a feeling that you should not go with this person to the store, or whatever, that is the wisdom of knowing intuitively.

Many of you dismiss it as nothing and allow the mind to overtake the innate wisdom of the heart, but we say to you, this is not the role of the mind. The mind does not have the wisdom. It is a tool that searches for answers, but the heart knows the truth. When you listen through your heart, following its promptings, then your life begins to recreate itself. If you listen to your heart and respond according to those inspirations, then you are truly living a full life.

So many of you override the decisions of the heart, listing so many reasons that you should not or cannot respond according to its promptings. You allow the mind to override the promptings of the soul and therefore you live lives that are not as full as they could be. You live lives that are the same today as they were yesterday. If you were to follow the heart then every day would be a new day. You would be more child-like and follow the whims of the day.

It is so easy to dismiss this as childhood folly but we say the opposite is true. This child like quality is what would lead you to a life of riches. Oh, dear heart, you want to go to Italy. OK. Show me how we will get there. Be willing and watch what unfolds. Do not dismiss it with your many reasons why it could not happen. Sorry heart, we do not have enough money. Besides, we are married and our husband would not want to go. And there is my job. They wouldn't give me enough time off to make it worthwhile. Sorry, can't be done.

This is the *reasoning* that keeps you from the fullness of life. Throw that away and say yes. Where would yes lead you? Ask yourself that question when these opportunities and ideas present themselves. Simply ask, where would yes lead me? You can leave it up to Spirit to get you to that yes. If you have the willingness to get there then all you have to do is follow the open doors that would lead to that yes. Play with this Dear Ones. It is a new way of living for most of you.

Let go of the rules of life. They were created by loving souls who were restricted by dimensions of society that did not want you to live your fullest life. Let go of the old order of living and allow the fullness of your soul to express itself into this world. Oh what fun you would have if you were to allow this. It makes our hearts sing to imagine it for you. See it for yourselves Dear Ones.

Play with this with the small things in life and then allow it to grow and expand. It is yours Beloveds. It is your life. Live it as you see fit. Do not allow the norms of society to hold you in an imaginary box. Step out of what does not exist into the fullness of what you don't see. Life is grand. Find it and live it as such and you will pass with no regrets. And so it is Beloveds. And so it is.

# Essay Forty-four - THE GUIDANCE OF LOVE

And so it is Dearly Beloved that we come before you once again in the name of love. We come from the Love and Light of All That Is to resonate our loving vibrations through these words into the earthly realm. We come to lift your hearts with our words and to awaken a new understanding within you. Our channel Rashana questions the repetition of our messages and we ask her to be patient.

There is a reason that we are focused the way we are and there is a reason that we repeat the same message in different ways. It takes a lot of repetition for many of you to fully accept the fullness of who you are and the impact of your presence upon this earth. Many of you are so humble that it is difficult for you to accept the magnificence of your presence on this earth. And so it is that we repeat, over and over, these messages so that you may see from our perspective what radiant Lights you are.

Dear Ones, we love you so. We love you for your dedication to the Light or Spirit you could say. We love you for your persistence that has kept you in this world even though, for many of you, there is a deep yearning for home. We love you for your soft and gentle hearts that want only to serve. What beautiful gifts you are. Your presence is felt just by being here. It is our deepest wish for you to see your radiance, for you to accept what a wonderful being of Light you are and to step into the fullness of what that means.

It means that you are changing the world by being here. It means that you play a vital role in the ascension of the earth. It means that you have all the knowing and understanding that you need in order for this ascension to be a success. It means that you are the ones you have been waiting for! This is profound Dear Ones. Here, on this earth for eons of time, humans have been waiting for their savior and here you are it. You are your savior. There is no one else to wait for. There is no one Being who is going to descend from the heavens and rescue earth. You are it.

This is what we are trying to tell you. You know who you are deep within your being. It is time to step into that. Those who are alive on the planet this day, those who read these words in particular, are the ones who are lifting the earth into the fourth dimension. You are the ones who carry the Light that will allow this to happen. So, we wish you to understand that your presence is not insignificant. It is vital to the success of this time of ascension into the higher dimension and into a peaceful existence.

So beloveds, this is why we come to you. This is why we say, day after day, how important it is to love yourselves and to heal yourselves. Without doing so you will not see the meaning of who you are in this process of ascension and you will not be shining your Light fully into that which is. So, we encourage you with understanding and tools to support you in accomplishing this for yourselves.

It is for you that we ask this. It is for you to move up closer to the heavens where life is full of peace and Light. It is for you to be all that you came to be and to rise up into your own expansion as a soul. Oh, the human school can be a harsh one and it is easy to get lost. The darkness can overcome you very easily. And pain lives in darkness. Bring it to the Light so that it may be revealed and released. This is the way of it.

And so Beloveds, we come to you this day with a message of love once again. It is by loving yourself and those around you that you find your way. And yet, so many think they are loving when it is simply an empty act of habit. Look deep into your heart to see what love truly is. Do you feel it? It is not just an act with no feeling, it is a feeling which then inspires you to act. Love is a fullness that fills the whole being.

When you are residing in love you may actually find that you desire less food because the kind of love that we speak of is nourishing. It fills you up with its energy and fills all the spaces that would be seeking something outside of that love. And so, how do you find that love? You get still and call upon your higher self and your Guides and wait to feel it. Or, you sit and connect to Mother Earth and feel her love pouring back to you. Or you sit in front of a tree and send it love and wait to feel it back.

You get into the heart and you connect day after day after day until you can feel something coming back to you. You will know you have found it when you are moved to tears. For this love is very different than the process of acting without the feeling. When you feel this love you will know that you are connected through the heart. It is by being in this heart space that you change your world. When you declare or ask for things from this heart space it is creation itself.

That is what you are moving into in the fourth dimension and so why not practice now. Why not have this skill developed within you so that you will know how to navigate the fourth dimension? This would be a great gift to all, for as you develop this skill within yourself you will be able to share it with others and show others how to access that deep-felt heart space. Be the beacon Dear Ones, first for yourselves and then for others. It is for this reason that we come to you day after day with this message. It is for the assurance of the ascension of mankind.

Once you feel the love you will want to take all of your human family with you. This is our desire Beloveds. It is the willingness to change that will get you there. Step out of the darkness that is fear holding you back. Step into the Light that is willingness to be all that you are and heal. This is the way. The understanding is easy. The accomplishing requires some work, but like any job well done, you will be so proud of your achievement and you would not change the journey for anything. That is the way of love and that is why we come to you. And so it is.

# Essay Forty-five - THE COMING OF AGE

And so it is Beloveds that we have the privilege and honour of standing before you once again and we say that the time of evolution is upon you. The experiences that you are now having on this earth are like no other. What you are going through and adapting to is entirely new. Oh how exciting it is. Never before have we watched a humanoid species morph and change in the way that you are now. Never before have we witnessed the kinds of changes that are occurring on the earth right now.

You are living in a time of tremendous change and that means that not only are you changing as a species, but the earth is changing, her climate is changing, her rhythms and patterns are changing. It is a new beginning Beloveds. Let the celebration ring out in the heavens, for you have created something entirely new here. You have lived through the passing of the ages, the Precession of the Equinoxes and done so with grace. Oh yes, not everything on your earth looks like grace, but the Light that shines out from your planet into the heavens is grace. And that Light comes from you Dear Ones.

It does not come from your rulers or your patriarchal system – oh no – it comes from the so called ordinary people who walk the streets every day going to work and taking their children to school and greeting loved ones. It is you who is changing this earth into a thing of beauty. It is you who are taking up the anchor and sailing into the future of Light. It is you Beloveds who are brave enough to change right before our very eyes. How glorious and radiant you are. As the sun shines on your earth, offering you life each day, know as well that your Light radiates out into the ethers, offering

Love Light out into All That Is. It is Divine Grace in action.

And so, what we would like to speak to you about today is the essence of change that is happening on this earth. We feel it is vital for you to know what it is that you are truly accomplishing here with all your morphing and changing and willingness to recreate yourselves. You are creating the grand finale to an experiment unprecedented in the realms of heaven. You have grabbed the bull by the horns, so to speak, and pulled yourselves out of the depths of the third dimension and turned into crystalline Beings of Light that are about to ascend into the fourth dimension.

This lies not far in your future. That is why we are always speaking so much about healing. It is a vital step in your ascension, and it is about half way up the ladder. Then you must be prepared for the changes by practicing manifesting. So, first you do your healing work so that there is nothing holding you back from your possibilities. Second, you practice the game of manifestation. Remember the bouquet of roses that we spoke of days ago? Have any of you created them? This is the next level of the game.

Mastering this will prepare you for the fourth dimension in ways that you are not aware of. When you manifest instantly you soon become aware of your thoughts. If you have not taken the time to regulate your thoughts before then, you can stir up some scary situations. This is not what we would like to see happen, for it can be terrifying.

And so we invite you to begin now in the process of being aware of your thoughts by what is showing up in your life. Do you like what each day brings? Does life seem more and more magical? If so, congratulations. You have it. If not, take a look at your thoughts and your beliefs about life. If you don't like what you see we guarantee it is coming from your thoughts.

Everything you see in another you must take responsibility for. So, if you don't like what you see in your partner (for example) right now, you know what to do. Look for that quality inside yourself and accept responsibility for it. The longer you resist the understanding that it is within you, the longer your partner will have to act it out for you. As soon as you realize that you have the same quality within yourself and you release that characteristic by finding its source, then it will all change.

Look deep within to see if that quality perhaps came from a parent. OK. Where did you start believing in it and making it your own? Look inside, find it - truly see it, thank it and let it go. Then, what you see outside of you will change because what is inside of you has changed. This is your barometer for success.

And now, moving forward, having done all this reflecting and healing you are ready to move up the ladder. Now you are aware of what you are manifesting, yet you still see things in your reality that you don't like. You can't seem to find it anywhere within yourself. We understand Dear Ones. It can be challenging at times. And so we say to you, when you ask questions of the mind it immediately kicks into action and begins to search for the answers for you.

You can find the answer to *anything* for there are no limits to where the mind goes to search for the answer. It is only your belief that will limit the possibility of the responses that the mind will retrieve. So you are asking intelligent questions, like how do I find the solution to this? The less intelligent questions are the why me questions. Not productive! But the kinds of questions that send the mind out to explore that which you choose to have will lead you to success. What is this experience showing me about myself? Very good question indeed. The answer is there. Search for it for the sake of your happiness and your relationship.

Questions such as this will lead you to manifesting what is delightful and joyous in your life. How did I come to be so happy travelling all the time? Notice we put the quality of happiness in there. Often you can think that you love to travel and then end up travelling so much that it becomes a burden and you wonder why you asked for that. Be sure to put the qualities of life in your manifesting decisions.

And so here you are half way up the ladder. What awaits above you? This is a question to be answered after we have done more exploring of this section of the ladder. For yes, manifesting is in this middle area of the ladder and along with that comes responsibility. For you see Dear Ones, you must take responsibility for your own process and evolution in order to achieve what you are searching for. If you are still blaming your situation outside of yourself or if you are unwilling to make the changes that will lead to your success then you are stuck. You are stuck in the middle of the ladder.

There are others coming behind you who want to keep going but you are unable to climb any higher. You see, if you are on your healing journey and someone points out this one aspect of your life that is holding you back and you are unwilling to change, what do you think happens to your flight up the ladder? Dead stop.

Let us say that it has come into your awareness that your relationship holds certain qualities that do not resonate with the truth of who you are, but you are not willing to end the relationship because of fear of being alone and never finding anyone else. You have not only come to a standstill on the ladder, you may have to climb back down a few rungs. You seem to have missed a couple of steps along the way.

Every time you have an awareness of truth but you do not have faith in the truth of it to make the changes that have come to light, you are stalling your journey. We say this not to be cruel, but to be honest. There is not time to be kidding yourselves into thinking that your comfort zone is all that is required. If you ascend into the fourth dimension with this fear of being alone guess what? You will be alone .... and alone ..... and alone, until you figure out what your belief is.

It is soooo much easier to master this here where your thoughts do not immediately manifest the way they will in the fourth dimension. It is about living in the fullness of life. If you only knew the possibility that awaits beyond each courageous step of taking responsibility for your current reality, you would not hesitate for a single moment. Every time you step out of your fear and into faith that all is unfolding in your highest good, then you are stepping into happiness and an expanding life of joy.

You do not get there by staying in what is really fear that you like to call joy. If your joy can be taken from you then you are not there. That is to say, if your joy is because of your partner, it is not your joy. It is a dependency and that is not truly joy. If your joy comes from the delight of your children then it is not your joy. Oh we have put this one in here to get your attention. We are stretching you with this one. But it is true. Those who reside with the full knowing that *everything* in their experience is perfect and divine have joy.

They know that if they lost a child tomorrow, then it was in the highest good of that child and them as well. This is love without attachment. Your attachment to your children is not for love of them, it is a reflection of the emptiness within you. Your pride or shame of your children is not for them, it is your own pride and shame. If you feel shame about your children, it is truly shame living within you about you. And so it is with joy. If your children bring you joy, that is beautiful. If your joy depends on them, then it is not truly joy.

We tell you this Dear Ones to help you understand what your responsibility is in your own state of mind and where you are on the ladder of ascension. We invite you to consider our words. We will reflect on this a little deeper in future writings. For now we wish you to know that ALL reality lies within you. E V E R Y aspect of your life comes from within – your joy, your fear, your love, your happiness …. All is sourced from your beliefs and your state of being.

Long ago it was written, Healer Know Thyself. We say to you that you are all healers. You are your own healer. You can seek support in your healing journey, but you heal yourself. You welcome the healer into your life and that is you healing yourself. It is your willingness to change and take responsibility for your life that is you healing yourself.

We see you doing beautiful work in this regard Dear Ones and we commend you for that. Look to those who have found their way and ask them how they got there. Let go of pride. It has no role here in this ascension. Humility and vulnerability is the courageous path to healing. Step onto that path and begin the journey to heaven. We love you so. And so it is.

# Essay Forty-six - LIVING IN THE LIGHT IV

And so it is beautiful Beings of Light, that we come before you once again. Once again we get to dance with your hearts and share your Light with you. For just as we have written that everything is a reflection of you, so too is our Light dancing in front of your hearts a reflection of you. If it were not so, we would not be coming into your experience. Because you are reading these words then you can know that your beautiful Light is reflected here also.

It is your wisdom that we are sharing with you. It is your wisdom that perhaps is hidden deep within your psyche but it is there. For others it is more in your awareness and this is just confirmation of what you know to be true. Either way it is yours and we are delighted to be showing it to you. We know who will be reading these words and how you will receive them. There is nothing that is not known. We know also how you will respond to these words, who will use them to recreate their lives and who will sit with them for a while and come back to them at a future date.

It is all there – written in the ethers of time. And so it is our great delight to be here and share, knowing that these words are leading you higher and higher up the spiral of evolution. We are aware that these words are allowing many of you to find your way, where otherwise you would be lost, to the truth of these times. And so that leads us to our topic today, Living in the Light.

Yes, we have spoken of this before. It is a rather vague title is it not? That is why we can speak of it time and time again. What does it mean to be living in the Light? It is a question that you should be asking if you are not, for its meaning is vast or perhaps completely unknown.

And so we say to you that Living in the Light is living from the heart. It is your Light that we speak of. You are Light. All of creation is Light. And this Light that is you, lies within your heart.

There is a vast array of existence within the heart. This is why it has been hidden from you. There is so much power within the heart that those who would be your politicians and leaders have used their magic, their tools, to lead you away from it so that you would not rebel and stand tall and strong in the power that is you. No longer Dear Ones. The time has come for you to have full understanding of who you are and what you have to offer this world.

You are magnificent Beings of Light. You have the power within you to create anything at all. You are aspects of the Creator and therefore you are creators! It only makes sense. So, what can you create? You can create whatever you want. You do it all the time. You are always creating whether you know it or not. You create the love in your life, you create your job, you create the home where you live, you create your mode of transportation, you create your pets.

All of it comes from you. And so if you can create all that, why not believe that you can create that which hasn't shown up in your life yet. You can, you just have to know it is possible and then you will run with it. As soon as you learn to do math then you can do math. As soon as you learn to ride a bike then you can ride a bike – or swim – or dance. It is all in the knowing that you can do it and then you run with it. And so why not allow yourself to believe in the possibility that you are a creator and therefore you can create whatever you desire.

Do you desire a new job? Believe that you can create a new one and start listing what you would like that job to be like and then wait for it to show up.  Here is the key. You must believe that it is going to show up.  Your doubt is creation of a different sort.  Your doubt is the creation that says everything that is my life right now is what will be my life tomorrow.

Why not let go of that and believe in our words?  What we say makes sense if you will let go of what is not and allow your mind expand into the logic of it.  It is actually quite logical that you can create *whatever* you desire. We also wish you to know that our channel resists using the word want because it means 'to desire without having'.  So, instead of saying I want a new job, say I choose to have the experience of a new job.

Oh, this is so simple Dear Ones.  We hope you are feeling the energies of this.  Do not insist that your logical mind fully grasp what we are saying.  Allow it to sink into the understanding of your heart.  Did you know that your heart has brain cells?  Indeed it does.  Did you know that your heart responds to any situation seconds before the mind even knows what is happening? Indeed it does.  This is why it is vital to trust your intuition.

It is the heart sending its intelligent knowing to you. When you allow the mind to override it you often scold yourself later for not listening to the intuition.  It has a degree of knowing from the All That Is whereas the mind has to go out and search and then come back with answers.  The mind has much slower response and does not search with the basic understanding of the truth of the circumstance that the heart has.  This is more for you to consider.  There is much to learn about the heart.  You can search for this yourself and deepen your understanding here.

Beloveds, we come to you, as always, with deep love and respect for who you are and all that you are going through in your human incarnation. As always we come to support you in this journey and show you the easy route out of the third dimension and into the fourth dimensional reality that awaits you all. Heed our words. Play with our ideas so that you can see the difference in your lives and step into the fullness of what it means to be human.

You are not simple animals living on this earth. You have access to all of creation. You have access to everything in existence. Broaden your mind and understand this. It will become more and more evident to you in your world. The times of change are upon you and joyfully so. Who would want to stay where you have been in the darkness of despair and suffering? Lift your heads above the darkness and see the Light that is you. We are reflecting it to you here with our words and the energies that lie within the words. We do it with love. We do it with love of creation which is you. And so it is.

# Essay Forty-seven - LOVING THROUGH THE LIGHT OF LOVE

And so it is Beloveds we come before you once again in joy and delight to be called before the beautiful humans who read these words. We say to you Dear Ones, your commitment to being all that you came to be and to grow in the magnificent times is to be commended. We understand that these are troubling times for many and there is much darkness surfacing on the earth.

And yet, you hold fast to the Light, believing that all is well – as it is. You look through the darkness to the Light, like looking through a cloudy sky knowing that there is Light on the other side. It takes courage and a faith to All That Is to hold strong onto the Light in these changing times and we commend you for that Dear Ones. It, again, is your own Light that you see leading you forward. It is the Light within your hearts calling you forward. It is your faith and love that allows you to believe that all will be OK. It will work out, and indeed it already has.

You have already crossed the marker that would determine your future. You are already seeing more love in this world. You are already seeing more and more loving acts of kindness in your world. This is the Light shining forth. This is the love of all of humanity once again radiating out into the world. You see, for eons of time, it was not safe to love. The world was too cruel. Love and you would be sliced to pieces or burned to ashes. And so you had to shut that down. And now here you are in these new times.

It is a new earth on which you currently reside and on this earth it is safe to love. It is safe to be who you truly are in most countries of the world. And so, with this you can blossom and move into the brilliance of your true self. No longer must women depend on men to survive. This is no accident. This allows the feminine to grow in strength and to step out of submission. This is the way of the new earth.

You are moving into a cycle where the Divine Feminine will shine on earth for thousands of years. This is a very good turn of events, for the feminine is softer and more intuitive and more graceful and giving. The balance of men holding more of the Divine Feminine and women holding the same, will allow you to walk into more harmonious living. No longer will the aggression of patriarchy force you into retreat. That is the way of the third dimension but in the new dimensions where you are moving to, this will not be tolerated because it does not resonate with what is.

So Beloveds, once again we come with good news. You are Light in shining action. Perhaps your new comic figures will be shining Light, for this is who you are. Some are shining more than others right now, but all have the spark within them. Some of you have endured more hardship than others and have not had the ability to work through that darkness.

Be patient with those around you who are living this way. Offer them your love and blessings. See the child within that wants only to be loved. Do not resonate with their outer character. If you do not relate to it, then it does not exist. The more people in the world who only see the loving child in each person, the less darkness there will be in the world. You are doing yourself a favor and you are doing the other person a favor.

You are changing the world in the way in which you see others. Did you know you could do that? Did you know that you could change the world by choosing how you perceive others? When you see only love in someone else, that person must be more loving. That is the way of it. You may not see it outwardly, but, within that person, a little more of the spark is ignited. The more you do this and the more people who do this, the more you are changing the balance of love in the world.

You see Dear Ones, you are magnificent indeed. You are creators. Every thought that you awaken within you is a creation. Why not create more love in this world? And of course, every non-loving thought is a reflection of what you believe about yourself. So, if you find this activity hard to do, then look inside and find where you are not loving the little child within you.

Look inside to find the pain still residing within your own heart. There are many meditations that can support you in this regard. Use them until you find that you can see the love in everyone. Then you will know that you are fully loving yourself. Once you are fully loving the self, you have so much to offer to the world, you become love just by being you.

Much has changed on this planet in the last few decades, and it continues to change. These words are to support you in moving fully into the times ahead. Your bodies have changed. You are holding more Light in your bodies and therefore you have the tools you need to make these changes. Your bodies are more crystalline in nature now. And what do you know about crystals? What stores memory for your computers and phones? Of course it is crystals.

Did you also know that research now shows that water is crystalline in nature as well? This makes perfect sense when you consider that it has also been proven that water holds intention. And also when you realize that your bodies are mostly water. So, you are crystal beings and this means that you have antennae that are able to reach out into the ethers and access information. You are also able to store that information within your cells.

So, if you think negative thoughts about yourself all the time, you are storing those thoughts in the crystalline cells within our body and you are sending out a signal that attracts the same to you. Be aware of what you are. Use those crystalline cells to magnify beautiful, loving experiences into your life. Program yourself into love and Light. This is not science fiction we speak of, it is truth. The fact that you are crystalline means that you have incredible capabilities to manifest and create that which you deserve to have.

It was never intended for humans to suffer and struggle the way you do. Recognize what you are and step into the awareness that you can change your world and by doing so you change the entire world. This is what we speak of this day. This is Loving Through the Light of Love. It is a way of being that has not been fully recognized on this earth for a long time. You are awakening into the fullness of who you are. You are awakening into awareness of All That Is. You are being birthed into the next evolutionary stage of human existing on the earth.

These are remarkable times to be living in. Find the beauty in it. If you continue to see only hardship and despair, what is your signal that you are sending around the earth? Once you know who you are, and that you radiate your thoughts through your crystalline structure, do you feel responsibility to step into the Light and to find love in every experience? We hope so. We hope that these words will awaken the spark within that knows that it is Light and knows it is magnificent and knows that it is an aspect of the Divine.

This has been hidden from you for so long. Find the truth within your own heart. If ever you feel confused about the information being transmitted, look within your heart for the truth. Do not access the mind for this wisdom, that is not its role. The heart carries the truth. And we say to you, love is the truth.

Oh Beloveds, we see the splendor of humans changing and morphing before our very eyes and we celebrate. We dance in the ethers as you grow into what you truly are. All of creation is watching the earth at this time to join in the celebration. You have conquered evil and stepped fully into the Light. How wonderful. How grand that you have done this without interference that would push your free will.

You declared that it would be so and it is. We commend you again for this Dear Ones. We bow deeply before you for you have reclaimed the name of Love and Light in this world and all of the heavens are rejoicing. We love you so deeply and watch over you as you walk this journey back into the fullness of who you truly are – divinity into infinity. And so it is.

# Essay Forty-eight - THE HEALING OF TIME

And so Beloveds, we come before you once again. And once again we dance in the delight of being called before you and having this opportunity to speak of the beautiful Beings of the earth. And we say to you Beloveds, that you are in times of great change, as you know. It is all around you. There is no hiding from it. There is no pretending that change is not happening because it is quite evident.

And we say to you there will be more and more change on this earth. And that is because you are in a transition. As you move through the portal of the Precession of the Equinox you shift. There is no other way around it. That is what these times are about. That is why so many of you are here – you chose to be part of this shift. It is really a grand time to be a human on this earth and to be part of such a huge transition.

It gives you bragging rights, and fully deserved. It has been a long and arduous journey to get here. And now here you stand, ready to fully step up into the Light, ready to claim your magnificence. And we say to you Dear Ones, you cannot claim your magnificence if you are still playing small in this world and pretending that you do not matter. Nothing could be farther from the truth. Each and every one of you has a role to play in this world. Each and every one of you has a piece of the machinery that is ascension on this earth.

So we encourage you to step away from your smallness and even the belief that it is somehow commendable to keep yourself small so you do not outshine others. What folly. You do not show the way to the Light by hiding your own Light. Stand tall and find the courage to step into your great talents that you have brought to this world. What do others tell you that you are so good at? Find out. Ask your friends.

There is no doubt that it is related to your piece of this transition, your piece that you offer to the world so well. It is the fullness of you that perhaps has been held back. Are you afraid to move forward? Are you afraid to be seen in all your glory? Why? Ask yourselves these questions so that your awareness can release them out of the darkness of your psyche and bring them into the Light.

The changes that you are in, with more to come, are necessary to pave a new existence. Evolution does not happen without change and you are definitely at an evolutionary marker on this earth. We say to you that the changes will be gentle this time compared to times past. And yet, the changes still must occur at some level. The more of you step into embracing this change with the willingness to give up control and go with the flow of it all, the easier the changes will be.

If mother earth is clearing out the darkness, the more darkness there is the more clearing she must do. If more of you are embracing the Light, living with awareness and cleansing your own outmoded beliefs and unhealthy patterns, then there is less darkness for her to clear. With less to clear, the clearing is softer – gentler. That is why we are so encouraging you all to look inside and see where the cobwebs are.

Look inside and find the old trauma that still is held in your cells. Look inside and see where fear lurks, disguising itself as protection. The more you work on yourselves the less mother earth has to do it for you. This is not to bring fear to you Dear Ones. Each soul can trust that they will be exactly where they should be as changes happen. If you are supposed to be on a plane where someone becomes ill and you are a healer, there is no mistake there. If you are in a shopping mall and someone faints and you have smelling salts – no mistake (just an example clearly!).

So Beloveds, trust and know that your soul is placing you just where you should be in every moment. And be aware of your internal promptings, your intuition that tells you to be in a certain place. If you feel a strong urge to move – move! The universe is wanting to place you in the perfect location for you. If you have the strong urge to change jobs, do it. Everything that the heart is offering at this time is to support you in these times moving forward into the Light.

The time of the deepest darkness has passed. Now it is to walk fully into the Light. Do not bring any of that darkness along with you. Shrug it off as you walk forward. Allow yourselves to become someone new. Do not think for a moment that you must hang on to who you used to be. Let people say, you are so different I hardly know you. Good. What great willingness to change. Look at your life and ask yourself, why would you want to hold on to what was? If it was anything less than joyful, why would you not want to let go?

Be brave and step into the new earth. It is here. You are just about to walk higher on the ladder – into the clouds. You have never lived above the clouds before so everything is going to look new. Everything is going to be different. You will soon get used to the view. You will soon see your friends there and make new acquaintances. Soon you would not be able to imagine living below the clouds. You will wonder how you ever existed there. You will be able to look down once in a while, but you won't want to.

It will be hard to see at first. Once you adjust you will be able to look with more softness and compassion, but not in the beginning. That is OK. You are acclimatizing to your new situation, your new world. You won't be alone so enjoy it. Enjoy the change and feel like a child again, learning all over again what it means to be a human and what happens when you do this and that. Let it be playful and joyful. This is how children learn. They learn through play and wonder. They learn through sheer delight at everything that is new. They are amused and entertained. Find that within you again as you move forward in this new world.

Oh Beloveds, it is such a joy and delight to see what is coming. We see the Light shining brightly above the clouds. You may be squinting in the beginning, not used to such brilliance. Your eyes will soon adjust and you will be nurtured and restored by the Light. You will recognize that it brings more life – more chi. You will soon find that you need to eat less because you are nurtured and filled by the Light. You will find that your emotions shift and change because the level of fear that permeates the third dimensional earth does not exist here. You will feel softer emotionally and it is true.

It is the way of it where you are headed. That is why we are so delighted to be guiding you there. That is also why we are so adamant that you are prepared for what it means to be there. Follow our guidance Loved Ones so that you may reside in the Light. Only when you drop the burdens of the darkness will you be able to tolerate the Light so prepare yourselves and step fully into what is being offered.

This is creation at work. This is evolution. How does it feel to be changing what it means to be human? How does it feel to be one of those who were chosen to be here and make this magnificent transition into the Light? You should feel honored to be here because you are. The heavens are watching. Let the Light shine Dear Ones.  Open your hearts to illumine the world.  The Light shines brilliantly for you.  And so it is.

# Essay Forty-nine - LOVING IN THE LIGHT AND LIVING WITH JOY

We come to you with love and adoration as always. We say to you that you are growing and transforming in ways that would have been unimaginable only a few short months ago. And why is this Dear Ones? We say to you it is that you have passed a very important marker of time for your planet earth and from this you are changing and evolving even faster than before.

Because of having passed this marker, and residing more fully in the Light, you are moving ever forward to that time when all of humanity will be given a choice to move into the Light or stay in this 3D level of darkness. That time is approaching and that is the reason for our messages that we bring to you daily. Will you be prepared for the ascension? Indeed, we believe that most of you who read these messages will be ascending into the higher realms of existence.

And yet, that does not mean that there is no work for you to do in preparation for that. We wish you to know, again, that the more you do to prepare, the more you will lift all of humanity into the higher levels of existence. This is the reason for our messages and our encouragement. All of you know of people with whom you see great Light and yet they hide in their smallness, pretending to be less than they are. As they see you grow and change they are encouraged to do the same.

And there will be times when it is beneficial for you to let these people know that it is safe and appropriate to embrace their wholeness and to stop hiding by pretending they are less than they are. This would be a good thing to offer them when you see that they are allowing a slight opening for you to send this information into. You cannot overwhelm them with this information, for they will not receive it.  When there is an opportunity to share gently, then we would encourage this.

These times that you are currently residing in are times of great growth.  Those who are not willing to change are feeling the divide, lost in a sense, without knowing how to change or how to give up that which is familiar and therefore safe to them.  You will see some slipping away as you move forward and walk more fully in your Light.  This is the way of it Dear Ones.  Do not hold yourselves back for the sake of others.

Do not keep yourself small to make another feel more comfortable around you.  Stand in your brilliance without bragging or boasting about where you are.  Just to be shining your Light is what we speak of.  When you are in this state and you are carrying deep love and acceptance in your heart, then you shine your Light with compassion.  That is to say, you shine with love and not a boastful manner.

Even though you will see a greater divide among the Beings of the earth, there is no judgment on either side.  There is no better than.  There is just different choices.  Each has its role and each is fully appropriate for the individual.  It is just that we see that these words are for those who are fully embracing the Light and willing to grow and change.  You will see as you do so, that others will no longer be able to relate to you.  You may see that others seem to judge you.  Simply send them love.  It is because they do not understand who you are and who you have become that they judge what is unfamiliar to them.

Have this understanding so that you do not judge them in return.  Soften your heart for them to feel your love.  Not to lower yourself but to soften yourself so they can relate to you for a moment.  This is love Dear Ones.

And yet, we ask you to stand tall and proud in all that you are. You are kings and queens of the Light. You are royalty upon this earth and it is time to accept that about yourself and be proud of who you are, just as you are proud of others and who they are.

Oh Beloveds, these again are such changing times. There is so much to adjust to. There is so much that you used to be that no longer serves the highest good. Not only are you changing biologically but you are changing in your way of being on this earth and it can be a lot to keep up with. There are others among you who have mastered this in a sense, and so look to them to show you the way to work through these times.

Listen to what they say and choose what resonates with you as truth. Allow yourselves to have leaders, so to speak, those who share their wisdom, without giving all of your power to them. Stand strong in your own knowing and use those with the wisdom that we speak of to affirm what you know as truth.

In the beginning, when you are morphing and changing, the words of others can be very affirming of what you are feeling and act as a support that you are on the right path for you. May these words act as such a tool for you. May you feel the resonance of love that we bring forward to support you in this journey out of the darkness. Yours is a journey of love Dear Ones. This earthly sojourn, this time around, is one of transmutation into the Light and you are in the thick of it.

Many of you may be wondering where all of this is leading? Oh Beloveds. What a beautiful world you are creating with your beautiful minds and thoughts. All of this is indeed leading to heaven on earth. Once you move through the level of ascension into the fourth dimension and have settled into existence there, then you will know. You will know that what you have moved into is such a wonderful, loving, pristine level of existence that you will hardly believe it is real.

And, in truth, it is not real, it is another level of creating with your mind. You will find out how beautiful your minds truly can be and how you can create such incredible amounts of love and grace for yourselves. It will be like living in paradise. Everything that you ever desire will be yours and everything that you have ever dreamed of will shift into your reality.

Magnificent will be your lives as you evolve in the higher realms of existence. It will be a preparatory period for the next level of existence. It will be like being in school once again, learning how to draw only you will be learning how to create. You will quickly learn that your negative thoughts are instantly manifest and therefore will have to learn to think only the best. This may take some practice for some. It will be easy for those who began this practice in this current reality.

This is where you will learn to live in joy. It will come from thinking in joy. Why not declare this to be a year of joy? What a wise decision, for it is joy that you will be creating in the fourth dimension. The more you work on creating it here and now, the easier it will be when you ascend and create whatever you think. It is wise to start now and have it mastered. Then, when you ascend, there will be no need to try to change your thoughts when you are instantly manifesting. That can be a little tricky. Do it now and enjoy the fruits of your creations now.

What does a life of joy look like to you? Start imagining it now. Get clear on what it would look like. Put all the details in there. What would your relationships look like? What would your surroundings look like? What would you do with your time? Who will you spend it with? Where will you travel? Have a look at all the aspects of living that would bring joy and decide what they would look like. Then begin expecting to see these things in your life. Stay strong in the knowing that they are already there or you would not have thought of them.

Since they are already there, you will be seeing them in your experience very soon. How delightful! This is the way of it Dear Ones. Start now. Step into the knowing that you are a creator. Bring forward all that you love and cherish into your life. Why not? You deserve it. You deserve it because you are human - the greatest race ever created upon this earth. Step into the deservedness of it all and watch it flow into your experience. It is with this that we leave you this day. Know that it is our deep privilege and honor to come to you this day and share our messages of love. And so it is.

# Essay Fifty - LOVING IN THE LIGHT

And so it is Beloveds that we are called before you once again and once again we are commending you for all that you are accomplishing in these times of great joy. For you see Beloveds, you have found your way to the Light. You have found your way to the ascension and now it is time to shine your Lights brightly in this world. It is time for you to know that you are all that you have come to be in this world.

There is so much that lies behind the veil of your knowing and the more you realize all that you are, the more you will be able to peek through the veil and increase your understanding of that which you cannot see. Humanity is at a cross roads. You are at an apex where you can go in one direction or another. There is no more standing on the fence trying to decide which way it will be. You now have to make a choice. Either you are deciding to be an ascended being or you are not.

Now, you no longer have to go into 40 years of exile as Jesus did to prepare for this ascension, but you cannot expect to get there simply by doing nothing. You are being asked at this time to look at every thought, every belief. If there is fear ANYWHERE in your reality, it is best to have a look at where that fear comes from and clear it out Dear Ones. Any fear is going to keep you from achieving that which you want to achieve if you are choosing ascension.

Those who ascend from this earth have no fear. They have total faith in Spirit, All That Is and they are not afraid to die, for they know there is no such thing as death. If you were to die today, would you have regrets? Would you be sad to leave your children or partners? Would there be anything there that would bring sadness with the thought of death? If so, then what is that thing that would keep you back?

For you see, when you are living in full understanding of Spirit, you know that if you die it is perfect. You will connect with your loved ones at a different level. You will have no regrets because you are an independent Being on this earth with no attachments. Most of you have many attachments and this is going to make the ascension less likely for you. It is when you can let go of any attachments that you are prepared.

You will feel no sadness for children left behind for you will know that their souls are making their own choices (and we say to you that young children would not be left behind in a mass ascension.) So, look within Beloveds and ask yourself the question about dying and be honest about the answer. Pretending does not work in this regard. The answers must be honest. Then you can go from there to prepare.

We realize that coming to this place of being a fully sovereign soul unto yourself is not an easy task and yet we say to you that these times that you are in are allowing for that. It is possible for you to become sovereign in these times. This is what we mean about having the will to ascend. If you truly have the will for that, then you will have the will to do the healing work that will get you to that place of understanding that you are all that you need.

You are Creator Light. You come to the earth alone and you leave the same way. Oh, you are surrounded by Loving Beings of Light who guide you and support you and that will not change. It is just that we wish you to understand the process of becoming one within yourself, fully healed, fully loving the self, and fully ready to accept whatever happens because you have such a deep level of faith in All That Is that you know that everything is perfect and is given by Divine Dispensation. That is it.

If you have less faith than that then there will be fear. Explore what is within you. For many of you these words will be too much to comprehend. Just let them sit then Dear Ones. Leave them for now. Someday, when you are ready, you will come back to them. Someday when the soul has a deeper level of understanding of what healing is then you will come back to them and they will guide you at that time.

There is no judgment. There are no wrong decisions, we just wish you to make informed decisions. If you were ignorant of all the possibilities then it would be a decision out of ignorance. We prefer informed choices for you Beloveds. Then, whatever decision you make is honored and perfect for you.

There will be more teaching around this. We realize that what is written today is just an arousal of inquiry. That is the way of it. We trust that it will find its way to understanding for those who are ready to hear it. There is no one who reads it who was not lined up to read it. All is as it should be. And so it is.

# Essay Fifty-one - CALLING IN LOVE

Greetings Beloveds. Greetings from the Great Central Sun. Greetings from the Love and Light of the Creator. Greetings as we come before you with great joy and pleasure to be standing before the beautiful creators that you are. And we say to you Dear Ones, the time has come for you to be manifesting all the glory and happiness and joy and Light that you can possibly stand.

The time has come for all those who have struggled in the past, holding firm to love and yet struggling so much in the third dimensional world, to reap the rewards of your dedication to be of service. The time has come for your lives to fill to overflowing with love and peace and contentment. Such a beautiful emotion connected to the word contentment. There are very few who would not find solace in what that word means to them.

And so be prepared Beloveds for this to become a big part of your life. Be prepared to feel the joy and delight that is a life full of new opportunities and simple pleasures. Oh, this is the way of it. There is great delight indeed in appreciating and enjoying the simple pleasures in life. It may be a cup of coffee on a cold morning or the greeting of a smile from a coworker - simple and yet meaningful. This is the way of moving into contentment.

Also know that, as you heal and release all the burdens of the past, you are allowing more Light in to fill those spaces that once held darkness and despair. As you do, it only makes sense that you would feel lighter. Why do you think that term even exists in your English language? Oh, I feel lighter. Yes, you are carrying more Light so you feel lighter. Of course. This is the new way. The more you release the burdens, the lighter you become. And as you do so you also find that what you desire out of life becomes simpler.

There is more contentment in the daily activities. It is such a great way of being Dear Ones. It is so delightful for us to look down upon those who live in this way. We see their joy. We see their light hearts singing again and being playful. How wonderful that, as you release, you can find the way back to those childhood delights. For you see, a simpler life is a more joyful life.

For the average North American or European, life has become very complicated. You have so many possessions that they weigh you down. Each possession becomes a burden in a sense. It is more responsibility. The lighter you are with your possessions, the lighter you are in your mind. And the lighter you are with your worries, of course the lighter you are in your mind and body. The body becomes weighted with your worries – your burdens. You carry them upon your shoulders or your back. Your knees give out from the weight of it all. So release and fly Dear Ones.

This is the message for you today. Look around you. What do you see in your homes, your yards? Is it more than you need? Does it truly bring you joy? When you are lighter you are free to fly. We are not suggesting that you give up your homes and your means of transportation and let it all go. We are just asking you to consider what serves you and what burdens you. We would say that there is both for most of you. Those who have had to give up many of their possessions because of financial hardship actually find that they have more freedom in the long run. They also realize that it is easy to replace furniture and cars so why hang on so?

And we say to you, the true treasures in life have no burden whatsoever. What are your values Beloveds? What is the most important value to you in life? Is it to be respected? Is it kindness or honesty? These are the foundations of your character and they do not burden you at all. They define you. They are the basis of who you are. Explore what these are for you so that you can move forward with more clarity about what is truly important to you in life.

Once you have identified your core values, and you can easily find lists of values on the internet to assist you with this activity, you can look around you once again and ask yourself, what in your possessions matches your values? Are there things in your home, your office, your life that you could release because they are not necessary anymore? This one way of becoming lighter. It is like a cluttered home leads to a cluttered mind. It is hard to work or be still in a cluttered environment.

And so we invite you to explore this and have the courage to release possessions as you release the past from your body. It is time to be fully present in the now. This now has never existed before. What magic there is in today, because it has never been here before. Never, on the evolution of this earth, has there been this day. If you think about it, that could be joy in itself.

Each day truly is a new experience. If you stay within the parameters of this day and not in yesterday or tomorrow, then you can find the joy in it. You do not know what this day will bring. You do not know who you will see or what will happen. Knowing that there are no mistakes in the universe, every person you meet or walk by on the street, is part of your experience. What could you do with that Dear Ones? You could play with it. Have fun. That's what you're here for.

And so we would like to conclude today's transmission with this thought. You are pure love existing. That is it. It is pure love that brings e.v.e.r.y. experience into your life. It is pure love that brings the hardship and it is pure love that sees a loved one passing over to the other side and it is pure love that brings joy. All of it is pure love. Think about that. What does that tell you about life? Can you embrace all of it? Can you embrace the hardship and the pain, knowing that if it is pure love then it is there for a reason? And the reason is not just to give you a hard time and make life difficult.

If you were to view each experience as pure love would that change the way you look at things? We believe it would cause you to ask more questions about your experiences and to stop and look at each event in your life. Exploration is the key to discovery. If you never go exploring, well, life stays the same. Even a joyful life gets boring after a while when it stays the same.

And so we offer these messages in love, for your exploration. We challenge you to consider what is written this day. It would be easy to dismiss it all and just keep reading. The choice is yours. What is simple is also very complicated. What is profound is often simple. It is your dance. Is it a slow waltz? Is it a tango? Do you say, oh no, I don't dance? We love you Dear Ones. We are always willing to dance with you. There is no dance that we do not know. Call upon us when you need a partner. We are at your side. And so it is.

# Essay Fifty-two - BEING WHAT YOU ARE

And so Beloveds, we come before you once again. When you read these words it is not a story that you are reading that takes your mind into some fantasy. This is energy transmission. These words are awakening something within you. They are stirring up a knowing that you can't quite put your finger on but there is something there. This is true for all our transmissions, even the ones that seemed so repetitive to Rashana. They too were transmitting through the energy of the letters that made their way into words.

And so our message to you this day is one that is a little different than what we have brought forth in the past. We are rolling with a new theme now, for there are a great many things that we wish to accomplish with you in these essays that make up this book. We had a long introduction and now it is time to get to the nitty gritty. For some of you, we have been holding back, giving you time to get comfortable with who we are and what we have to offer.

That has happened now and so we are taking you to a new level now. Hold on and stay with us as we transmit the next level of our messaging. As we complete these essays, we say to you that each message will take you to a new level of understanding. These understandings will be developing a deeper awareness of who you are in these times and what this new level of being means for you. For you see Dear Ones, you are not the same people you were only a few short months ago. December 21, 2012 was a great shift. Some of you were fully aware of it and others thought it was just another day.

And yet, for those who are reading these words, you were prepared on some level to shift into the higher dimensions and the preparedness that would get you there. For those of you to whom we speak, you are now residing in a whole new level of awareness. And as such, you will find your understanding of what it means to be a new human is expanding as well. As we said, you may not be able to put it into words but you know something is different. You are creating in new ways. You are living in a deeper awareness of your ability as a creator.

This is what we speak of now. You are able to morph and change anything in your life very easily and swiftly if this is what you choose. You now have the level of understanding that you can simply step out of one dimension of this moment into another reality. It is as if each moment carried several different potentials. If you do not like the one you are in, simply decide to shift to something more favorable and it will happen. It is like, in the moment, deciding to have a different experience than what is apparently unfolding. It is a choice and it is that simple.

Once you are able to believe in the possibility of this, you will begin doing it. Let us give you an example. Let us say you are out to dinner with your spouse and an old friend of yours sees you at your table and you just know this person is going to invite himself to join you. But you just want a quiet dinner with your spouse and although you are happy to see this old friend, you do not want him to join you. In that moment you can decide that this friend is going to notice someone else in the room and quickly excuse himself from your table. Then you just pause and be present to see it happen.

It is your belief that it can happen, along with a certain detachment to the outcome, that allows this to happen. It is that simple. Play with this and you will see it happen. The underlying factor for this to work is the belief that it is possible. Each moment contains many potentials as we have said, it is just that you did not live at the level of resonance before to bring this into your lives. Now you do. Now you are living in a world that carries this resonance and so you can begin to use this to your advantage.

You can recreate every moment, and all life is a gathering of moments. Therefore you can radically change your lives using this tool. This is but one method of bringing what you choose to experience into your reality. There are some things that you will not be able to shift in this way because there is a bigger lesson for you in that certain outcome, but, for the most part, this is possible for you now.

And so we encourage you to try this and to decide, moment to moment, all day long, what it is you would truly like to have pop into your life. As you do this you will find that your relationships will change. Those who once thought you were crazy will finally come to believe that maybe you have something to offer. Those who thought all your experiences were just coincidences will finally have to consider that perhaps you are managing your experience somehow. The exciting part will be when they ask how it is done and begin trying it out for themselves.

This will not be something that you can force on people. Only those who are ready to begin experiencing life in this way will be able to relate to what you speak of. So, if you feel resistance, simply let it go. The person you are speaking to is not ready to live in this way. In time, more and more will come to recognize these abilities in your world. And as they do, you will already be onto the next activity that is awakening on the earth with these ascension energies.

It is a delightful game Dear Ones. Life will become more fascinating all the time. Rashana one day wondered what life would be like when you can create so easily. She thought it might become boring with less contrast. We say to you that there will be plenty of learning on how to be the new human in the fourth dimension that will keep you busy for quite some time. Simply creating with your thoughts is one aspect of what it will be to be living on a higher plane of existence.

There is much more that you will be discovering and exploring as you awaken to this aspect of who you are. It will be great fun and delightful. So, begin playing with this now with what we have spoken of here. Practice makes perfect. Use it and watch it develop more and more awareness within you. We are delighted to share this with you this day Beloveds. Enjoy. And so it is.

# Essay Fifty-three - LOVING IN THE LIGHT II

And so it is Beloveds that we are honored and delighted to be at your side once again. We are here with you, speaking these words to you so that you may flourish on this earth. It is time to truly expand and see how things are changing. Do you feel different than you did a year ago? We would think so, for indeed you are very different than you were just a year ago. You are in times of such rapid growth that many of you can hardly keep up.

As you prepare for this ascension, which is coming very soon, you are noticing changes in yourself that allow you to embrace more of your spiritual skills we could say. You are more aware of other dimensions. Many of you are seeing things out of the periphery of your vision that you have not seen before. These are things that have always existed in your world, it is just that you were not aware of them before. More and more you are connecting with the fourth dimension as the veil thins and so this is coming into your experience more.

There is nothing to fear. What you see was always there. It is like explaining to a child not to be afraid of the dark because it is the same as the daytime. Most of the energetic species upon your earth are harmless. This is not to say that all energetic beings on your earth have your best interest in mind. But, if you stay in the Light and believe only in love, they will not negatively impact your life. Remember what we said many times before. What you believe is your experience. So, if you see things in your periphery that you do not recognize, believe that you are always protected and that you are safe in the Light and that will be your experience.

This, again, is the way of it. As well we would like to add that the orbs and cigar shaped beings that many are seeing are beneficial beings here to support humanity. You are so dearly loved and there are so many beings working to support you in your journey back to the Light and into the fourth dimension. So many are cheering you on and watching to see where they can support you and provide their love to you. So, as you open up to new experiences, trust and know that it represents you becoming more aware of what was always there. In this way you will also begin to understand more of what these things that you are seeing represent.

And so Beloveds, we see that many of you are existing outside of love. You are searching outside of yourselves for love when it is within. For so long your society has taught you that the love of self is in comparison to those around you. Whoever is the prettiest wins. Or whoever has the nicest car wins. What is that Dear Ones? That is not love. That is pure pain. How could you ever keep up with that? It is division at its best. There is always someone with more than you and someone with less. Therefore, your worth is built up by being better than some and diminished by being less than others.

What a painful existence. It is for this reason that we wish you to understand that all the love of the universe resides within your heart and to look inside and reflect that love to all of you. Every bit of you is lovable and we ask you to begin to see that it is your uniqueness that is the most lovable part of who you are. You are like no other. Your face is like no other. Oh, to look in the mirror and appreciate that which is you, with no comparison to what society tells you a nose should look like or what shape your eyes should be. How could that be true when so few fit that model? Of course it is false.

The truth is that you are a perfect creation for your experience. Think of that when you look in the mirror. Your face was created exactly so that you could have the earthly experience that you chose. Your body size and shape was planned long before you were born so that you could have the experience in life that was just right for you. The more you love what is you, the more you will step into the learning that you desired from this incarnation. The sooner you step into the learning the more you will love yourself and your life will begin to change from that love.

Nothing is a mistake Dear Ones, or a happenstance experience. It was all planned *just for you*. How could there possibly be anything wrong about that? How could you desire something else when what you are is just what you asked for? Learn to love all of you and you will change before your very eyes. Oh, your nose will not suddenly become smaller or your hips shrink but you will see your nose as uniquely you and love it for all that it has brought to your experience. Your hips will not shrink two sizes but you will know that they are giving you life experiences that are perfect for you so how could they be anything less than perfect!

This is loving the self Dear Ones. This is also how you learn to love your children just for who they are. Love all the little quirks and demanding behaviors and know that they will be enriched in their lives because of those traits. It is what they came for. The more you step into loving the self and your children in this way, the more you change the world. We mean that literally. Do you want to change the world? It begins with you. It begins by fully loving yourself for all that you are. All the parts that you have disliked all your life because they were compared to some standard that you could not meet, love them.

Drop the false standards of society and make no comparisons. In this way you will change the world. For the more you accept *everything* about yourself, the more you will accept differences in others. Celebrate the differences and you have changed the world. No more discrimination. No more hatred. This is it Dear Ones. When you raise your children with this awareness that they are perfect just as they are, then the world will change.

We would like to add a note here in raising children. We are not talking about false praise. Do not praise them and tell them they are perfect even when they do something harmful. Children need boundaries and standards to live by. It is just that these standards should reflect your values, not those of a society that does not meet your core values. If honesty is an important value to you, teach your children honesty. If respect is important to you, teach your children to be respectful.

By doing so you are teaching your children to be honest with themselves and to respect themselves. It is just that you are not adding to that the need to look like Suzy next door or the ability to run like little Stevie. It is this comparison that steals away the confidence in who one is. It is the comparing that robs children of their sense of who they are and their confidence in what they have to offer the world. Teach your values only because they are your values, as parents, and not that of some outside standard. This is what we are referring to here. This is vital to learning to love yourself.

And so you see, there is much that needs to change in your way of being on this earth. The changes are coming whether you embrace them or resist them. Which group do you think will have the easiest time with it? Your resistance to change when it is inevitable will create much hardship and despair. Look around you.

Those who are struggling against the changes that want to happen in their lives are the ones who fall into depression and the hardship is reflected on their faces. The burden is weighted upon their shoulders. We can understand this resistance, for there has been much change upon your planet for many years now.

It can be hard to keep up with. Keep looking up Dear Ones. Know that every inch of change is a giant leap in your journey toward ascension. These are the times that you are living in. This is what you came for. You couldn't wait to be here. Oh, how you anticipated this very day. Those of you who are older, when you came in with your soul plan it was all you could do to know that you had to be here years and years before this magical time of evolution arrived. And now here you are. Embrace it Beloveds. Be in love with you. All that you are is exactly what you chose for yourself. Why would you not love that?

We love you so Dear Ones. We love you for your courage and your willingness to grow. We love you for your willingness to share your love and open your hearts to your brethren. We love you mostly for accepting who you are and accepting your vulnerability. There is great strength in that Beloveds. It takes great strength to be apparently weak. And yet, often to change, one must allow this place of opening the heart to possibility.

The barriers must come down so that the heart can shine forth. Whatever it was that caused you to lock down your heart, now is the time to explore and release all those emotions. Break down the walls so that you can step into the fullness of you. Love yourself free Beloved. Step out of the illusion by looking only to yourself for guidance of what is right for you. All the wisdom of all the universes lies within your heart. Go inside and seek it out.  Be your own shining Light.  And so it is.

# Essay Fifty-four - THE LOVE LIGHT LUMINAIRE

And so it is we come before you this day Beloveds with love and joy for this opportunity to stand before you – to speak to you in this way and we say to you Dear Ones, this is a day like no other on the earth. This day has never been here before. Oh, yes, there are many facets of this day that have existed before. Do you know why? Because you create the same things over and over and over. And yet, today is new.

It is a new opportunity to see the world differently. It is a new opportunity to have different expectations of your day and to learn new things. The pain and suffering comes when you do not learn anything new in your day. The old adage of learning something new every day was not as simple a statement as it sounds. The truth of that statement is that, if you truly learn something new about yourself each day, then you are changing and growing all the time. If that learning is not there, you are simply being caught in the cycle of living the same day over and over.

Is this resonating with you, this monotony of living the same day repeatedly? Then, what can you do to change that? What can you learn about yourself this day that will encourage you to be a different person tomorrow? Let us give you an example. Our channel Rashana had an experience today where she remembered that, when she looks through the eyes of love, she sees the best of everyone and she sees them in their healed, pure state of living Light. She has had this awareness before but forgot to come from that perspective in all her interactions.

She realized that when she first had this understanding, it was a fleeting thought. She did not grasp it and begin to work with it to the point that it became a part of who she is. Today, when that understanding came to her again, she realized that, if she goes too fast and does not integrate her learning, then it is just a fleeting thought. Today she decided that she would remember this so that she can be a healer in every moment, seeing the fullness of each person she meets. This is her intention.

We know that it will not happen just that way. It will take practice and remembering many more times, but this was a learning for her and therefore she will be a different person going forward. That is the fullness of the statement of learning something new every day. Then, when you begin to bring that learning into your life, tomorrow is a new day because you are stepping into it with a new perspective. That is the fullness of what we are speaking about here.

And so, here is some more learning for you. We understand that every day we are bringing you something new. So, what are you doing with it? Are you simply reading it and moving onto the next page or are you taking time to really understand what it means with the willingness to begin living that in your life? This is what we are offering you here Dear Ones. We are offering you a whole new way of existing in this life journey.

What seems simple is most often much more. We have embedded a transmission in this book that had very deep undertones that went much deeper than the words on the page portrayed. This is possible in all situations. What will you do with it? Will you allow yourself to go to the depths of understanding and grasp a whole new perspective on life? When you do everything changes. And we put forward that all change leads to something better because it leads you to a new understanding.

The more understanding you have the more you grow into all that you are as human. There is much hidden from the human understanding. If you are willing to see beyond what is apparent into the hidden realms of existence, you can completely morph your life. You can be a whole new person tomorrow if you like. And you can be living a whole new existence if you like. You do not believe it is possible because you put up so many resistances. I can't move because it would take my children out of the school system. Oh what a tragedy that would be!

It could be the best thing you ever did for your children. I cannot change jobs because I have this big pension waiting for me. Will there be any life left in you by the time you get to the pension? So many blocks that you put up to change and then wonder why life is so mundane. Step out Beloveds. Let life offer up something new. Dream big and wild. The time to live is now.

So ..... what's next? Good question. What is next for you as human on this earth? What is next for the earth for that matter? It is love Dear Ones. Love is next. Not that love ever left, but it was not so apparent. See it. Notice it. It is everywhere. Look only for loving acts this day. Turn off the news and instead notice couples holding hands and pets playing together and children playing.

Look for love today. It is everywhere. It is in the leaf hanging on the tree. It is in the snowflake falling to the earth. It is in the rain falling from the sky. It is everywhere. Nature is love. You can find it there always. If you are feeling alone or lost or confused, go in nature. It will soothe you. It will invite you to come back to yourself – to the harmony that is existence in love. That's what's next. Love. Find the love. And so it is.

# Essay Fifty-five - ACCESS TO THE LIGHT

Greetings one and all from the realms of the heavens. We come before you this day from the Great Central Sun and we say to you, this is a new day. There is no day like this one. Have you heard that before? Indeed. We do intentionally repeat ourselves so that you may give consideration to those words. We have spoken of their importance and we put them here for a reminder. Oh yes, you need many reminders, and this is fine.

It is just that we wish you to remember our words and the intention behind the words. What was the intention behind our sharing with you that this a new day? We hope that you can answer this. If not, you may cheat and look back. Indeed it is so that you will know that you are creating each day anew. Especially in these times upon planet earth with all the energetic changes, every day really is new because you are constantly integrating new shifts that continually happen for you.

These shifts and their integration can be challenging at times. If you find yourself needing a day to do nothing, give that to yourself. Often it is a null time that is needed to integrate something that you have transformed within yourself. This is the way of it in these incredible times of growth and change. You are morphing still. The new human is in the creation process. As you move ever closer to the Light and the higher dimensions, integration is required to fully grasp that which you have just elevated yourself to.

You are like computer programs that are being upgraded every week. You need to shut down to integrate and complete the new upgrade. And so it is that we are delighted to tell you that you are Light. You are shining brightly and growing and glowing more with each passing day. Your access to the Light is expanding as your energy bodies and your ability to hold more Light expands.

You see, the old human that was you only a few years ago, was not able to hold the Light quotient that you can currently withstand. Your system would have felt fried a few years ago by the Light that you are now able to withstand. It is because your earthly mother has moved closer to the Light that you are now able to hold more Light. You are in resonance with her and therefore able to withhold more Light in your being.

What does this mean to your existence on this earth? It means that life is changing. It means that you are creating in new ways. It means that you can create magic in your life if you choose. Decide this day to be brilliant and you will be. Decide this day that life is easy and flows with grace and it will be. Decide this day that you are surrounded by loving friends and family and you will be. This is what this transition means. It means that you can create and become more than you have ever been.

You will find, in these times, that you are able to withstand more change and more downloads than ever before. These downloads mean that you can heal instantly if you are willing and you have awareness of what that looks like and feels like. The more healing you do for yourself, the more you become a healer, just by being you. You see, everything is a reflection of who you are. If you are whole and healed, then you are that on the planet.

If you are in pain and suffering, then you are that on the planet. And so you see, doing for yourself is not selfish, it is the greatest, most generous gift that you could offer the earth. Let go of the old teachings that there is any such thing as selfishness. It is all there is in reality.

Everything you do is for you, even when it looks like it is for someone else. If you put others ahead of yourself, it is because it makes you feel good to do so.

It is because you maybe then think they will like you more or call you a good person, which is what you need to be happy with yourself. So, there is always a self-motivation for everything. So let healing be your motivation and then you are healing the world. When you are healed then everything you do is healing for the world. And the deeper the healing you have done for yourself, the deeper the healing in your work with others. This is the way of it.

There are many levels of healing just as there are many different people. There are those who heal the world and there are those who work closer to home. The important thing is that healing is your focus. Do not let more time slip away into lethargy. Be brave and step up to all that you have come to do. Be brave and see the truth within. Allow others to help you on your journey. You do not have to do it alone. Allow your friends to support you in your growth as you do with them.

Allow softness into your life. Allow others to support you. Expect that the journey will be easy, with lots of support, and it will be there. Whatever you intend you will find. That is why it is vitally important to be aware of all your thoughts. You should know in every moment what you are thinking about. This is awareness. It allows you to be living fully in the present moment.

Thoughts never end, but you are living consciously when you know what your thoughts are. When the mind spins out of control, then it is harder to keep track of the thoughts, although it should not be because the same thoughts just spin through, over and over. In order for inspired thoughts to come, control is required.

Stop the spinning wheel and instead flow down the river. Oh, there is a new thought. Fully aware watching it drift.

Let us get back to the topic of today. We wish you to know that time is shifting and changing and so are you. You are in a time of elevated growth and therefore great opportunity. This is why we so encourage you to pull up the ropes and move fully into the healing that will find you full of love and grace, living with ease. This is so possible now. Many of will find that, in these new times, life is beginning to flow so smoothly and things are unfolding with grace. Beautiful. You deserve it.

If this is not your experience, then following the guidance here will get you there. It is you that we share these words with to guide you into the new way living on this new earth. Do not give up or think it is too hard. Just try differently than what you have been doing. If what you have been doing leaves you feeling that life is a struggle and you can't do it much longer, do it differently Dear Ones. Like anything, it is easy once you know how. We are offering you the knowhow.

As always, it is your discretion that is your greatest guide. If these words feel like truth to you then embrace them and try our suggestions. Play with what we offer here in these transmissions, or essays. Allow your mind to go with what we say and have fun exploring it all. Take one piece at a time. Allow yourself to play with it and practice it until it becomes a part of your way of being. Then try another aspect to work with. Your life will slowly begin to change and transform.

You will begin to understand on a much deeper level, all that is available to you in these times. If you do not feel the depth of that, then play with the processes that will get you there. We offer this wisdom for your evolution. The time of change is here. Why resist it when that will only make the inevitable integration more difficult? Embrace all that it is and life will flow. We love you dearly Beloveds. Be well and flourish. And so it is.

# Essay Fifty-six - GROWING OLD

And great greetings to you Beloveds. We come to you in love and joy and delight. For we see before us beautiful humans who are having an experience of forgetting. So deeply did you fall into the forgetting of who you truly are that only now, after eons of time of the universe sending you love, beacons of Light, to help you find your way back, are you starting to awaken to the truth. And so it is on this earthly school that the fall is deep and dark.

But no more. Time is changing Dear Ones. You are changing before our very eyes. You are awakening to the truth of who you are. More and more those of you who are steadfast upon the path are seeing your lives grow and expand into joy and bliss. And with this comes change in the physical body as well. Your physical bodies were created to last for hundreds of years. Your biology is so incredible that it can heal itself of anything.

It is your thoughts that create illness and old age just as it is your thoughts that create your experience. The body is part of the experience is it not? There are stories of miraculous healing. The thing is that the miracle is that the mind shifted and allowed the healing to happen. That is the miracle. It is not that some spirit fell out of the sky and chose that one person to heal because they are lucky. It is because the mind allows healing to happen. The mind gains a new awareness that all illness and poor health comes from an emotional foundation.

Give up the emotional burdens and hidden beliefs, and the illness can simply disappear. It has been documented. The same goes for aging in the body. What causes the body to age? It is not that the cells are programmed to begin to die the moment you are born. It is the belief that it is so. It is the language you use with yourselves. Our scribe has met many people who call themselves old and they are much younger than her. And so they begin to look old. And because they believe they are aging, they begin to act old. They stop moving so much or sitting on the floor. That is only for young people. And so their belief then tightens up the body and it can't move because it does not get any practice doing that.

There are people on your planet who get younger as they age. Why is this so? Because they finally feel free. The responsibilities of raising a family and creating a living for oneself are over and they embrace the time they have and enjoy life and thus they feel younger and younger. Some take up jogging when they are 60. Why not? It may take a year to be able to run a mile but what does that matter? It is not as if they are running out of time. They are embracing the day – in the moment – feeling good and acting young.

Aging is a gift Dear Ones. It truly is a time of wisdom and grace. And yet, again, we go back to doing the healing work. You will notice some people as they age carry such wisdom and grace and others just get cranky and stop living their lives. The difference, again, is the healing work. When it is done it leads to joy and grace. When the pain is stuffed deep inside, then it begins to show up in the body as discomfort of some kind. And it shows up in the personality as well. Some, as they age, are very unhappy and miserable to be with. It is because they have not loved themselves free. Instead they have run from all that was challenging and so it continues to chase them.

It is like standing before a wolf, if you run you are a sure target for it will chase you until you can run no longer. So it is with your painful memories. The more you run from them the stronger they become as they chase you. Stand and face them and they simply fall away. That is the miracle Beloveds. Stand and face your past so that it may leave you and make room for a new and exciting future. This is our deepest desire for you. We would like nothing more than to see all of humanity standing in their pure Light, ready to rise up with the earth in her journey of ascension.

So, what will your choice be as you age? Would you like to age in a way that sees life getting better and better? If so, healing work is required. The sooner you do it, the more joyful life becomes. Why not make this year the one that is dedicated to healing? Your intention will create the miracles that will see you living a new life. It must be sincere and you must be willing to fall into vulnerability so that you can be strong enough to heal.

It is time to stop pretending. It is time to stop fooling yourselves into the illusion that everything is fine when it is not. The other side of the healing is so beautiful Dear Ones. If you could only see into the future and know what wonderful lives you create when you are willing to let go of the past. The universe wants to provide for you. It is ready to give you everything that you have ever desired. It is you who must make room for it. Clear out the closets so that more can come into your life. If your life is stuffed with the past, there is no room for something new.

If you are afraid of change, what is it you are afraid of? Is it being alone, poor, weak? What is it Dear Ones? Be honest with yourselves. Find what the fear is and then ask, where did that fear first show up? How old were you? Just let the answer flow into your mind and do not question it. The mind will try to reason away the truth. Once you know the age ask what happened to you at that age that created the fear. Was it a behavior that you learned from a parent? Does that behavior serve you in your adult life? Again we ask you to question and dig deep.

There are many gifts that come from the healing work, and one is aging with grace and ease. How lucky are those who enjoy aging. There are many who would not trade it for youth. They would not give a second thought to going backwards. That is because they know the peace that comes with maturity. You become more and more your own person. You each came here alone, unique and beautiful just the way you are. Why would you want to be like someone else? But that is what youth wants. Maturity has grown beyond that. Maturity begins to see the beauty in aging. You are coming into a time when society will shift in its thinking around this.

The beauty is within. This is the truth. The more you open your hearts, the more you will see this. That is the grace of aging. So Beloveds, this healing work that we ask of you so consistently is not just for the young, it is for everyone. And it is not just to make this moment better, it is so that you can age into grace and beauty and be comfortable with who you are. Then you have so much to offer. Then you are healing the world just by being here.

Love yourselves Dear Ones. We have so much love for you. We see your struggles and your pain and we understand the challenges of being human. And yet, we say that once you change your mind, everything changes. So why not? Play with it. Change your mind. Decide to be young for 500 years and see where it gets you. We are delighted to share these messages with you and to witness all that is unfolding on the earth. These are grand times Dear Ones. Enjoy the journey. We love you so. And so it is.

# Essay Fifty-seven - COMING TO THE LIGHT

Greetings Beloveds from the Love and Light of the Creator. Greetings from the Great Central Sun as we come before you in great joy and delight. For you see, we stand before the beautiful and magnificent humans who are embodied upon this planet. We stand before those brave and courageous humans who have found their way through the darkness back to the Light. We stand before those who were brave enough to fall into the density that was earth at the time of your birth.

And now look at you. You are glowing. You have called Love to your planet. You have stepped out of the burdens of the past and are creating a new earth as we speak. Oh, Dear Ones, it is such an honor to stand before you. It is such an honor to be with you, guiding you, supporting you, encouraging you. For we wish you to know that we are doing all that.

We are watching over you and we are here to respond to your requests for guidance and support as you learn how to climb that ladder. We are your cheering team as you find your way back to your magnificence. For indeed, you are doing it. You are recreating the earth, each in his or her own way. Each of you has a role to play. Each of you has a piece that makes a perfect pie. So we encourage you to believe in yourselves Dear Ones.

Know that you are love and nothing but. Knowing that, how could you have fear of following your truth? If you are pure love, it must be leading you back. The heart is the wise sage. The mind is the young student. Let your heart be your leader in your life and all is well. Let the mind lead and you may be led astray, for it does not hold the wisdom. It may be more reckless and less responsible in what it will bring into your life.

We desire you to have the best life you ever imagined possible. And believe us, if you can imagine it, then it is possible. Why not have it? Do you resist because it would require change? What is so fearful about that change? Write a list. What do I fear about this change that my heart would lead me to? Then take an honest look at the list.

Is it logical that you would allow those things to lead you away from your heart's desire? Let us ask you a question. If you were to hear your soul and all its desires, where do you think you would hear it - in the heart or the mind? If indeed the soul speaks through the heart, what does it mean to your journey to ignore the promptings of the heart? What do you think it means to your soul development? Are you going backwards or forward? This is for you to contemplate Dear Ones. And, if you are going backward, what does that mean for your soul plan? Ask and listen quietly for the answer.

So let us speak to those of you who are doing your healing work and self-exploration and internal cleansing. Dear Ones, the rewards that are coming in return for your great attention to preparation for ascension will be rewarded. Your work is leading you to great joy for you will be living from a healed heart – one that knows its truth and is willing to change and flow with these glorious times that are creating a new earth.

For those of you who are aware that you are creating a new earth every day, we commend you and we say, make it beautiful. As you sit in the magic of the self-love that comes from your healing work, imagine the most beautiful earth that you have ever seen. And then, when you look at others around you, see them whole and healed and beautiful just as they are. As you learn to fully love yourself then you are love in all your thoughts. As you are love in all your thoughts, you are changing the world. You are seeing through the eyes of love and so that is what you see.

And as you do that, you are changing those around you because they must respond to you according to what you see. This is the way of it. This is why we ask you to see love first in yourself, so that you can see that love reflected back to you from everyone you meet. If you see only love in others, they will be whole and healed and they will show you your love. Oh how beautiful it is when this begins to work. How wonderful it is when you begin to see how much you have changed because everything that happens to you flows and is joyous and expands you.

This is what you are moving more fully into in these times. There are some who are already there and there are some who are just beginning to see this. It matters not where you are on the journey. What matters is that you are on the path taking one step after another. It is not a race, although there is a time span for this to be completed. But do not look at it like a race. Just be committed to staying on the path and learning as you go. Be committed to honesty with yourself about what you see reflected back to you. If you like what it is, celebrate. If not, take an honest look at what requires change in order for you to like what you see. The moment you change everyone and everything around you changes.

And so Beloveds, we stand before you in awe. We are in awe and wonder at all that you are. And we commend you for your willingness to be here reading these words and for your willingness to listen to what we have to say and allow the resonance of these words to touch your heart. If it feels like truth, step into it Dear Ones. If it does not, allow it to rest. When something is your truth then it will resonate with you and you will know the fullness of that truth.

If not, trust what feels right for you. If you let it go and then you find you are thinking of it again, come back to it, for it is calling to you. Whatever your decision around these transmissions, they are filled with Light and the reading of these words also fills your soul with Love Light and that is the way of the new human. Every breath you take becomes a prayer - every sigh a healing and every word a blessing. This is the direction of humanity at this time and it is a beautiful, gracious gift to all the universe.

That is why we are here Dear Ones. That is why so many Beings of the Light are here assisting you. Be proud of who you are. You deserve great rewards simply for being here in the density of the Earth and for finding your way through. There is rejoicing in the heavens. Allow the bells to ring on the earth, for you are the new humans creating the new earth. And so it is.

# Essay Fifty-eight - CRAVING LOVE IN ALL THE RIGHT PLACES

And so it is Beloveds that we come before you once again. And we come in deep joy and gratitude for all that you are. We come with love on our wings so that we may bestow you with the grace of who you are. For Dear Ones, you are grace itself. You are the embodiment of love in its finest form. If only you knew how truly divine you are, you would have no doubts about anything that you are. Ah, but the veil has hidden your radiance and your Light and so here you are rediscovering who you are. And you are doing a brilliant job in that rediscovery.

For you see, there was a time when humans were living in resonant love with no fear of lack of love anywhere in their experience. There was a time when you were so sure of who you are and all the love that you carry that you could imagine nothing else. And then, things began to fall apart. You fell into despair that the darkness brought with it. It was a long and arduous journey away from the Light but there is rejoicing now. There is rejoicing because you have found your way back.

Here you are, living on this earth, embracing all that you are. Here you are coming back, ever closer to the truth of who you are in your fullness. You are awakening the full potential of being human, and we say to you that the potential of a fully awakened human is beyond your wildest imaging. The potential of a fully awakened human is to be likened to a James Bond type human in your physical abilities and angelic in your abilities to love and be love.

Do not ever doubt anything that you could become for we say to you that, there is nothing that you could imagine that you cannot become. There are things that are beyond your imagining that you could become as well. That will awaken in time, as you learn more and more of what you are capable of. For now, know that you are true magnificence and are capable of feats that are, in your minds, reserved for the few gurus and super heroes. We tell you this so that you will fully awaken to who you are.

We tell you this so that you will not limit yourselves with your beliefs that it is not possible. It is all possible, and it is possible now if you believe it. That is where the shift lies. The shift has already happened in the energies that would allow such brilliance. The shift now has to settle into your belief systems. Your thoughts have to shift to believing that you are all that and more. Your thoughts have to shift into believing that you can change into whoever you would like to be.

Want to be an opera singer living on some remote island? It is possible. Just see it and believe it. Even if you are now living in the most desolate of conditions, if you can believe it, the universe can deliver. You do not need to know how the universe will deliver it, just walk through the doors that will get you there. If a door opens that does not look like it is taking you in the direction of your dreams, walk through anyway. The universe knows what it is doing. The universe knows all the little pieces that need to be lined up in order for your dream to be fulfilled.

So, do not let your logical mind convince you that this door must have been a mistake. Walk through and see where it leads you. Then take the next door that presents itself, and the next one and the next. This is the way to your dream. So, do not allow your logical mind to convince you that you cannot have everything that you desire because you can. You can have it all if you believe it. Many of you will tell yourselves that is greedy to have all that you desire.

We would ask, how is that greedy? Would not having all you desire lead you to living a fulfilled life? When you are living a fulfilled life you are offering much more joy and happiness into the world than when you are down trodden and miserable. Which energy do you think is most beneficial for the earth? Understand that every thought you have is an energy pattern, and energy is not constrained to a physical body. It travels the entire planet. So, what other false beliefs do you have around having all that you desire? Explore them and use our logic to release them. They serve no one at this time. Step into possibility and fulfillment. Then you are radiant love Light on the earth.

How wonderful it is to see those gathered in joy and love. This is the new earth. All gathered in love and joy. All knowing that they deserve to have all that they would ever dream of. All knowing that the more they receive the more they have to give. You can only give from the fullness that you are. You cannot give more love to the world than you have within. So fill up. It does not require walking on other people to get what you desire. There is plenty for everyone.

The 'field' where all dreams draw for manifestation is unlimited potential. It would be like saying there is not enough stars in the universe. It would be hard to imagine there are not enough stars because there are so many. The same is true of the potential that becomes your dreams. There is no lack in the universe. The only lack is within your minds. Awaken to this truth and start planning your dream life. No limitations.

Our scribe Rashana is currently questioning our messages. She is asking why The Council of Nine would be delivering such simple messages. We are amused. She knows herself that simplicity is the truth, and yet it is the apparent repetition that is confusing her. And so we say, so many of you are awakening to the truth of these times. You are awakening to the ever changing energies of the earth and yet you are hesitant to step into the full expression of who you are in this journey.

It is for this reason that we send these messages, day after day, about how to step into your Light and embrace the joy that you are. It is for this reason that we repeat over and over, in hopes that you will fully understand that there are no limitations to who you can be. And you came here to be incredible Dear Ones. You did not come here to remain small as Marianne Williamson said so beautifully. You came here to be magnificent. This is the truth. This is your true birth right, for it is what you truly are.

Do not play small so those around will feel comfortable in that. Take them out of their comfort zone by being radiant. Your mere presence will then challenge them to be the same. Create that life full of fun and joy and prosperity so that you can challenge them to do the same. You do not challenge them with your words. Let your words be compassionate.

You challenge them with your mere presence, for they can see you. They see you in your complete joy and they ask themselves how you got there and how they could do the same. That is how you teach. It is the only way to teach. Answer only when they ask. When they ask, or attend a workshop that you are hosting for example, then you can teach, for they have chosen to listen. The rest of the time it is you being you in your radiance that challenges them to do the same.

You can change the world Dear Ones. Each one of you can and is changing the world. What is your impact? Are you leading the world to the Light that it is? Do it for yourself, for then you are creating for all of humanity. The more of you who step into your brilliance the more brilliant the world becomes. As you step into your fullness, you are showing the way and making it easier for those behind you for you are creating a resonance of fullness that others can connect to as they follow your lead. Be the new human Dear Ones. It is such a beautiful existence. We love you so and it is our desire that you are encouraged by our words. And so it is.

# Essay Fifty-nine - LOVING IN THE LIGHT III

Greetings Beloveds. Greetings from the Great Central Sun as we come before you this day in joy and love for this opportunity to be sitting before the dear humans who are reading these words and who are populating the earth at this time. Beloveds, this is indeed a time of great change and if you do not see it in your lives then you are not looking. Open your eyes and see. There has never been a time such as this for you to have this opportunity to ascend into the higher dimensions en masse. This is a first Dear Ones, and we commend you. For indeed, regardless of how many of you ascend, you are doing it in a way that it has never been done before.

Never before have you said yes as a complete consciousness of human on this planet. This is a time for rejoicing and to recognize the opportunity at hand. And we say, it is because of your great work that you are in this place. It is because of your willingness, as Lightworkers, to step into this opportunity and embrace it. And so, knowing this, would you let this opportunity pass you by? Will you continue to repeat your patterns of the past and not take this opportunity for change? This we ask this of you once again.

And so let us begin with the transmission for today. This day Beloveds we wish to tell you that you are magnificent beyond your comprehension. You are awakening to the All That Is and in that process you will be astounded to learn who you truly are on the higher planes of existence and what you have come to do upon this earth. You are changing the universe, for as every planetary system shifts, so too does the entire universe. Just as you are microcosm in the macrocosm of earth, so too is your solar system part of the All That Is.

Therefore, as you change, everything changes. And you think your lives are boring. From our higher perspective what is happening on the earth right now is a great show indeed. On each of your earth days we get to check in see what has changed. We see how your vibration has changed and who has grown to love themselves and who is believing in the illusion. It is a grand piece of theatre you are playing out and it all is leading to a new creation that will astound you.

And so it is our intention to offer guidance with these messages and our guidance for today is to be *in love* in every moment. We know that life offers up many challenges. We know that you get down on rainy days and sad with losses that you witness. And yet, it is possible to view all of this through the perspective of love which brings great understanding. You can have bad days. That is OK. Revel in your feelings for a day and see the beauty in your sadness.

That is the gold mine. When you can see the beauty in every experience you are creating a joyful life. Happiness does not come from a life that offers nothing but 'good' experiences. Life does not unfold that way. Happiness comes from viewing even the darker experiences from a place of love. It is the understanding that you are meant to have whatever experience it is you are going through. It is the knowing that, on the other side of the experience, there will be feelings of joy.

It is the awareness that each day is a new day and has a different energy and brings new experiences. When you can anticipate what your new day will bring, you step out of the sadness and move back into wonder. This is the flow. Waves on the ocean are not always peaking. They peak and they fall down. The flow of life lifts them up again and once again they settle back down. It is how you view the experiences of life that brings happiness or hardship.

Yet we say to you, the more you believe that you deserve a life of ease and joy and the more you expect it, the more such days you will have. It is a balance of going with the flow and expecting happiness and joy. Take what you get with grace and expect life to get better and better. My life gets better and better with each passing day. Say it and believe it. Then wake up tomorrow wondering what the day is going to offer that is new and fresh. Envision what the day is going to bring you. Watch a happy movie. Do what makes your heart Light. Color and draw to bring back the playful child. Create a happy life Dear Ones.

This is written mostly for our channel Rashana this day. She is faithful to bringing forth a message every day, even when her heart is not feeling its usual state of peace and joy. Even when the skies are grey and dragging her spirits down, she sits. Tomorrow is a new day and it will feel more joyful and the message will be deeper. And so it is.

# Essay Sixty - LOVING YOURSELVES TO SLEEP

And so it is Beloveds that we come to you once more. And once more we offer our love and grace to those who stand before us this day. Dear Ones, we are incredibly proud of who you are and how you are navigating these times. For indeed, there is much fear amassing around the earth, and yet you stand in the Light. You stand in faith that the All That Is has a Divine plan. And you know that the plan does not carry the demise of humanity, for indeed it does not. The plan is much the opposite of that. The plan carries the Light of Love in order to save humanity and carry you into the higher planes of existence.

That is what these magical times are about. That is what 2013 forward is about. It is the time for you to find your wings and realize that you are angels upon this earth. Not only angels, but great masters walk among you. You have all come back to support your earthly mother as she winds her way up the ladder of ascension. You stood in line to be here and support all of humanity into the wonderful time that you are in. And you are succeeding Beloveds. You have done it.

You have stood the test of time and the test of darkness and you have lifted yourselves above it all in search of the Light. The rewards are great Dear Ones. You have no idea what celebrations are happening in the heavens. We are recording your names, preparing your colors. We are waiting for the celebration when you find your way back to us and we can commend you fully for all your work. Oh, it is a grand time. All of the universes are celebrating. This is a time of great joy and so it is our great joy to come before you each day and offer our messages to you.

And so we are led to the topic of this day. What a strange title we have offered here and our scribe Rashana did not question it all. So what is loving yourselves to sleep? It is, basically, what you have just walked out of. For you see, in order for the experiment that is planet earth to be successful, you had to forget your brilliance. You had to forget all that you have been in other solar systems and other lifetimes. You had to forget who you were in Lemuria and Atlantis and start over again with an empty slate. Much like a person with amnesia forgets, so too you agreed to this so that you could test yourselves.

It was an experiment to see if you forgot all that you are, if you would find your way back. And you have Dear Ones. Not fully. Very few of you fully understand all that you have been and what led you to this experience that you are having on the earth right now, but you are starting to remember. You are awakening slowly to pieces of your brilliance. And so it was with love that you allowed the forgetting and it is with love that you find your way back to the remembering.

You have proven that you can fall deep into the darkness and find your way back to the Light. You have proven that Dear Ones, over and over on this earth. Time and time again you incarnated here to prove this to yourselves and all of the universes everywhere. And now here you are. You have succeeded. More and more people are awakening to the truth that life is much more than fast cars and new furniture. More and more are finding their way back to a simpler life where what matters is how many people they can offer their love to and how they can help their neighbor.

Instead of competing, more and more are choosing cooperation. Instead of fighting to make it to the top, more and more are waiting for everyone to come along.

The world is finding its way back to Love. This is such a grand and wonderful shift on earth. There is much rejoicing on our side of the veil, for if it were not for this shift then much would have been lost. If you had not found your way back to Love then humanity would have witnessed mass destruction and huge loss of life. It could have not been anything but, for the earth will not be destroyed.

And now, not only will she not be destroyed, but she is being rescued by the very species that almost brought on her demise. This is pure poetry Dear Ones. You are redeeming yourselves and this is why we celebrate so. This is what brings us such great joy. This day is a celebration. We celebrate you and we ask you to celebrate yourselves. Pat yourselves on the back for all that you have accomplished. Know that you have rescued yourselves through your love. How beautiful that is. There is more work to do Dear Ones, but now you know the way.

Support all those who take to the streets to demand change. Be among them or support them, for they are demanding a new earth. The powers that be are not going to give up all their wealth easily. They are not going to succumb without one last effort to claim what they thought was theirs alone. They are learning differently. What is for all shall now reign upon this earth. Business is changing to be more cooperative. People are changing to be more inclusive. The earth is waking up. No longer are you fast asleep.

Now you are awakening with the same love that put you to sleep. Now you are in the times when that love is bringing awareness to all and supporting all of humanity and all of the species of the earth. It is time to claim the rights of all and to protect the earth and all who walk upon her. We are rejoicing this day and commend you Beloveds. Do not think of love as a trite expression of folly. Nothing could be further from the truth. Love is creation and you carry love in your hearts.

Find it and shine it brightly. Shine it within and when you are filled to the brim – then it will pour out of you and onto all who cross your path. This is the new way of being human on this earth. Love is the way. Love is the Light. Shine it brightly. And so it is.

# Essay Sixty-one - BEING IN THE LIGHT OF LOVE

Greetings once again Dear Souls of the earth. Greetings from the Love and Light of the Creator. Greetings from the grace of the heavens as we come before you with love and joy to bestow upon you. For indeed, Dear Ones, we come in the glory of the Light of All That Is and we come with gladdened hearts, for you are on the road to success. You are winning the game of life and we rejoice. For you see Beloveds, the game of life has been very challenging and yet you have walked through the hardship and now you stand, ready to receive the rewards for your efforts.

And we say, for those of you who indeed have made the effort to become whole, to walk the road of a warrior, claiming the Light of their being and reclaiming their sovereignty, you are seeing the rewards begin to appear. For those who have done the work to heal the wounds and be in the fullness of who they are, you will find that many doors are opening. These are doors to the future in the Light. These are the doors that are leading to great joy and happiness.

For that reason we would say, when things unfold gracefully and seem to fall into your lap, do not pass them by. This is leading to the life that you have been dreaming about. You do not always recognize it when it appears because it often looks a little different than what you expected, or it requires a major shift and change in your life. And yet, when you look at the qualities of life that it will bring, we believe that is what will tell you that it is the path for you. So remember, it is the quality of life that you look for when the doors open.

Many people pray for wealth when what they really want is freedom to travel. Others pray for handsome lovers when what they truly desire is to be cared for and protected. So, do not let the cover of the package discourage you from the qualities that are inside the gift. This is how to discern that which is appearing to lead your life to one of fulfillment and joy. This is what many of you are now finding your way to. This comes to those who believe that life is grand and trust and know that life is delivering everything they have ever wished for.

Those who do not carry such faith will continue to create the life that they are currently living. You cannot ask for a new life with old thoughts and expect to see that which you are asking for. You must change your thinking and your behavior in order to change your life. There is no other way. So be willing Dear Ones, to make these changes. This is how your lives will unfold to be living in the Light of Love. It starts with love of self and expecting everything that you desire. Simply ask and know that it is coming. The universe wants only to provide.

We see that you are starting to get this message. We see that you are stepping into a willingness to change what no longer serves you in your life. We see that you are mustering up the courage to bravely claim a new life for yourself and believe that it is possible. We would recommend that you use questions again. How did I become so rich? How did I attract such a loving, kind, generous partner in my life? How did my life become so joyful? Such questions as these will get the mind working to find the answers. In searching out the answers, it will magnetize to you the experiences that will see your questions answered.

That leads to fulfillment of your wishes and desires. So, simply ask the questions, over and over until you KNOW that your desires are on their way to you. This is the way of the new human being. This is the way of creation. And you are magnificent creators Beloveds. You have not been aware of creating all aspects of your lives and therefore you have lost the understanding of how this works. This is why there are so many teaching these rules of the game right now. We are supporting you in the re-education of what it is to be human on this earth. We are leading you back to the knowing that is inherently yours.

Did we tell you that all thoughts are stored in 'the field'? (Note: they are referring to what quantum physics would describe as the field. It is an understanding that what takes form as matter lies dormant in the quantum field until thought influences it to manifest. It has been proven long ago that thought affects plants and more recently that water changes with our thoughts. This is because the particles in the field are influenced by thought. If you are interested, research into the Higgs Boson and quantum physics will lead to more understanding of this). Did you believe us Dear Ones? It is as if your mind is a computer. It takes commands and goes to the main drive to find the answers.

Everything that ever happened in creation is in that computer. Therefore, you can retrieve not only what happened yesterday, but anything! Anything that you ever want to know!! That is truly astounding and as soon as you allow yourselves to believe it you will begin to work with it and your lives will expand exponentially. It is the believing that will make it easy for you. Once you truly believe that it is true, go fetch. It is just that simple. As soon as you realize that it is just as easy as remembering what you had for lunch yesterday, then you will begin to use this tool and your lives will change. There is so much that is like this for you.

There is so much that the human is capable of doing that has been kept from your awareness. It has been so long since you remembered, that your beliefs tell you they are impossible. That is OK. This is the time of discovery. That is why it is so exciting to be on the earth in this time. There are so many new discoveries and so much is changing. You are growing into what you are. You are realizing that your DNA stores much information that is untapped and that it is malleable. Your scientists, because there are more and more who are open minded, will soon discover things that the human is capable of.

It will blow your minds and you will begin to believe and you will then embrace it and expand more and more. Just as computers evolved so quickly that year after year the previous version became obsolete, thus your human evolution will expand as well. Once you start realizing what is possible it will continue to expand and expand. In a matter of years you will look back to the human who existed at the time of the shift (referring to December 21, 2012, the end of the Mayan calendar) and you will consider them to be archaic. And you will be putting yourself in that category, for you will be among those who change and shift very rapidly.

You are the way-showers Dear Ones, and this is part of what your role will be. Your role is, being of open mind with expanded awareness, to embrace all that you are learning about your abilities as a human and working with them and showing those around you what is possible. They may not pay attention at first, but in time they will not be able to pretend any more that you are anything but incredible. They will see your lives and they will have to question how you got there.

And so Beloveds, we leave you this day. We leave you in the love and Light of heaven. We leave you in the arms of Creator Love to resonate as pure grace within your hearts. We leave you with the knowing that you are whole and complete just as you are. When you recognize the truth of you, nothing need change. That is what is coming, for you are stepping into the All That Is with awareness that humans are evolving. As you do, you are embracing more of your Light and you are embracing Love and not dismissing it as mere folly. This is a good thing Dear Ones. This is grace unfolding on planet earth and all the universe is rejoicing. And so it is.

# Essay Sixty-two - LIVING IN LOVE II

Greetings Beloveds, greetings from the Love and Light of the Creator.  Greetings from the Great Central Sun as we come before you, as always, with love and grace upon our hearts and great love for the Divine Beings that call themselves human.  And we say to you Beloveds that, this day we wish to speak to you of living in love.  For there are so many opportunities to find love in your day.  Even the most evolved souls do not always see when they are operating away from love.

Rashana, just this morning, is preparing to go to a social function where there will be people who she feels are different than she is.  And so her thoughts have gone to those differences.  When we said to her before this transmission to not judge them but just love them, she immediately understood that she was judging herself for being different.  Her thoughts were leading her to wonder if she would have a good time because they are not as spiritual as she is (in her mind) and their occupations are very different than hers.

In reality, it was self-judgment for being different.  Our invitation to love them totally shifted her thinking and so we invite you to do the same.  Every situation in your lives offers this invitation to love everyone, even when you do not feel that you can relate to them at all.  Once you have the intent of loving them, then your whole experience changes.  You feel loved!  Isn't that interesting?  Do you see what is happening here?  You reflect your thoughts back to you.  When you offer love out you see it reflected back.  When you offer judgment out, you see it reflected back.  It can be no other way.

Now, there are a few circumstances where this is not quite so simple.  Let us say you are a nurse in a prison, an attractive young woman, with a heart of love, it may seem different. As you walk among the prisoners, offering your love, you may not see it reflected back. Some are so wounded and broken that they cannot accept the reflection of love that you send to them and therefore they cannot send it back. Some, those that many of you judge as evil or criminal, are so wounded that the love that you all hold in your hearts, is deeply buried.

It was not safe to love and may never be in their current incarnation. Send them love anyway. Send them your love. Make it soft so it can squeeze in. This is living in love Dear Ones. This is the awareness that is required to be coming from love in all your experiences. It is easy when you are among like-minded people and you resonate with who they are. When you are with others who are out of resonance with you then it is more challenging. And yet, you must explore why they are coming into your experience. The attractive young nurse must ask why she is working in such a harsh environment. Is there an aspect of herself that is not loving the self that she is there to see? This we leave for you to explore.

We would like to clarify that we are not asking you to spend a lot of time with others who are out of resonance with you. That would not be healthy at this stage of your evolution. We are saying that, when you are in such situations, to look for love in everyone. See them as love. Know that you are all from the same source. Many of you now find yourselves working with people who are out of resonance with you and it makes the mornings challenging as you awaken and do not want to spend another day with them.

Know that judging them is judging yourself for being different from them. So, first have that awareness and let go of that judgment. Yes, you may be different, but find the oneness. Love them. As soon as you understand this and you 'get' it, then you will be free to choose another workplace. If you have been praying for another job, first receive the lesson that the situation is offering you and you will soon find that you are free then to change your circumstances.

Otherwise, you will repeat the same situation only with different people in your new post. This is loving yourself free. Love your differences right now. Know that those who are not in resonance with you are also souls on this earth doing all they can to survive this planet and all the lessons she provides. They are doing all they can to make their way in the world, just like you. If you cannot love them, where are you not loving yourself? This is the way of it Beloveds.

And now we would like to address another aspect of living in love. Many of you are living with someone who, at one time, you adored. And yet you see, in these ever-changing times, that your love is fading. You are beginning to find that you have more differences than similarities. It is becoming difficult to relate to each other. And we say to you Dear Ones, when you are in times of rapid change, everything changes. Love changes as well. And so we invite you to follow your hearts on this one.

This may seem to be in contradiction to what we have just written about loving everyone and yet we say, living with someone is different. When you live with someone that you no longer feel in resonance with, that disharmony is touching all aspects of your life. Staying with this person could actually keep you from moving forward the way your soul is choosing to. This would not be beneficial to your evolution. We wish you to know that the bottom line is loving yourself. You cannot love others more than you love yourself. If you are holding yourself restricted in a relationship which is then restricting other aspects of your life, you are not loving yourself. You are restricting yourself.

It may look like it is the other person doing the restricting of you, but it is you allowing that and therefore you are the one restricting. Sometimes leaving a relationship is freeing you both to the higher choices that your souls are desiring. We are discussing this so that you will know that living in love does not always mean staying in situations where the love is restricting. Just like understanding the lesson on the job with others that you are not in harmony with, the same is true in some relationships. You are there for a learning and then it is time to progress and move on.

If you develop and grow but do not allow your circumstances to change, then you are trying to move ahead while being pulled back. It becomes a tug of war. It makes the soul weary and it does not allow you to fly. And believe us Dear Ones, your souls are wanting to fly right now. That is what these times are all about. Expand, grow and spread your wings. This is the time to be your magnificent self. It is difficult to do that when you are holding yourself back. It cannot be done that way. You must be courageous and brave and take the measures in your life that will allow your freedom.

We are, again, not recommending any rash decisions. You must take responsibility for your choices and not say, well, The Council of Nine said I should quit my job and leave my relationship. You are responsible for your decisions. Do not leave a job without another if you have no back-up monetary support. Make wise decisions. What we are encouraging is growth. Do not hold yourselves back. The more steps you make to grow, the more that you will find new and exciting opportunities are coming to you. Stay focused on your dreams and believe that you can create them, because you can.

You have the ability Dear Ones. You are powerful creators. Just like you can create love all around you by loving everyone so too can you create all aspects of your life. Play with it with small things. Remember the bouquet of flowers? Play. Tell the universe you would like to receive a bouquet of flowers within the next seven days and see what happens. We love you so. We are here to support you in your growth into the Light. We see that you are learning and willing to be all that you came to be. This is your guidance. Use it wisely Dear Ones, for now is the time to fly. And so it is.

# Essay Sixty-three - COMING INTO WHOLENESS

And so it is Beloveds that we come before you once again. And again we offer our love to you and the joy of being called before the beautiful Beings of the Light that you are. And we say to you Beloveds, that this is the time for you to be asking yourselves, what is your purpose here on this planet in this time of great transition? What is your role in this transition? How can you best be serving the planet and all who walk upon her? How do you spread your Light in this world? It is time to find the answers to these questions, for they will lead you to the next step.

You are in times of discovery. People are discovering who they truly are. Parents are discovering the wisdom of their children. The world is discovering that change is upon us. In that discovery is the calling to your path, your role in this transition back to the Light. In order for Gaia to be all that she came to be, it is important for you all to be fully who you have come to be. Your part of the Divine plan cannot be fulfilled by someone else. You cannot hand it over, like asking a casual worker to take your shift for a day. It does not work this way with this plan.

You being you is required for all the parts to fit. So, stop hiding from your full self. What are your gifts, your interests? How do they serve the world? Let that be your guidance as to where you begin or expand your position in these times. By doing what you love to do or are inspired to do, you will be fulfilling your piece of the puzzle. For some of you this will mean having a profound role in the world. For others it may look like you are doing nothing at all. And yet we tell you, you are doing your part, many of you, just by being here.

Have you ever had someone tell you they feel better just by being with you? That is your clue that you are one who is accomplishing her/his role just by being. There may be more to it or there may not. Some of you are such healers that others benefit just by being in your presence. Others of you are narrators or orators. Some express your fullness through artful pursuits, be it music, painting, pottery. You are all unique and you all have something to offer.

We also encourage you to support your children in their journey by recognizing what their natural talents are. Please do not put your agenda upon them but allow them to show you what they are interested in. Take notice and then nurture what comes forward. Do they like to draw all the time? Are they good at organizing things? Notice who they are, not who you want them to be. By nurturing all the natural interests they have you will be doing them a great favor. You will be leading them, through your loving support, to that which they came to do.

Let go of your desire for their education or extra-curricular activities. Let them lead the way, for it is then that you will find out who they are and the skills they have brought into this world. The children of today are coming in fully aware of who they are and they do not have the same level of forgetting that their parents did when incarnating this time, so allow yourselves to learn from them. They have much to show you. It is by allowing these changes to be and to flourish on the earth at this time that you will find your way back to the Light.

There are those among you who are deeply psychic, so much so that they have a hard time functioning in the third dimensional world. Do not quickly assume that you know who they are and label them with some dysfunction. Look beyond what shows itself by trying to fit it into your current social norms. Many of the children of today are here to show you a new way. If you try to fit them into the old system you will cause great harm. Open your minds to receive these new children being born today and allow them to show you who they are.

Do not create a box for them but see them. Truly see them as individuals. They do not fit the old paradigm and they need supportive souls – people on their team – so that they can find their way in this world. It can be so difficult for sensitive souls to navigate this world, especially in these times when you are shifting into the new way of being. In a hundred years they will fit just fine, but for now they are breaking new ground and it is a difficult task. Those of you who are aware can be very helpful by creating understanding of the new children and helping others appreciate who they are. By doing so you are leading the future.

These children are your future more than ever before, for they come with a different genetic makeup. To say the children are the future has never been more true. Love them and support them so that they may step fully into that which they came to accomplish. Those of you with children who are very sensitive, do your best to understand them. Read about the crystal children that are coming in. Educate yourselves on how to parent these children. Be gentle, kind and yet firm so that they have loving boundaries on how to blossom into this world. And so it is.

# Essay Sixty-four - THE BLANK CARD

Just as you can draw the blank in the tarot, we have no title for today. Consider it to be like the blank card in the tarot. And what does that card represent to you? Is it nothingness? Is it the potential of pure Light? Is it new beginnings, a clean slate? We say to you Dear Ones, there are always personal interpretations beyond the traditional significance of any card when it relates to an individual. And so it is with this transmission having no title so we can go anywhere with it. We can go to the moon and back. It is free rein, run where you will, so to speak.

And so we say to you Beloveds, where we would like to run with you this day is not to the moon but to the stars. For you see, far above you, deep into the heavens, lie the stars that you see at night. For some they bring great comfort, for some magic and for others deep yearning. They have different significance to different people. And, deep into outer space, are planets where many life forms live and flourish. There are planets with people much like yourselves. They live differently. Their technology is more advanced than yours. They do not live with governments that keep secrets of technology.

And yet, they also do not have the heart that humans have. There are other beings that resonate in pure love and those are the beings that are here right now, watching over your planet and your evolution, assuring your success in moving into the Light of ascension. These Light beings have been here for eons of time, doing what they can to assure that you make it back to the Light. It is of these nations that we speak of now.

The love that is being transmitted onto your planet is what is allowing you to move up the ladder of ascension at this time. It is this love that has planetary alignments and powerful eclipses that awaken the human soul to much more than you have been living. These Beings that are of the Light may soon reveal themselves to you. For some this will be very shocking, so it will happen slowly. It will start with small appearances to groups that gather in the name of calling in Beings such as ourselves. There will be contact with such groups in the beginning.

And even then, there will be fear, for the human thinks it is ready when in truth it is not. It is only because your governments have created so much fear around ETs and what they truly are. And indeed, most people think of groups of ETs that are not so benevolent for the earth. And yet we say to you Dear Ones, most of the Beings that desire contact with you are Beings of the Light. To discern you only have to ask. Are you a Being of the Light? They cannot lie to you. Do you have the best interest of humanity in your intentions? By asking you will get your first inclination of who the Beings are.

Then, we say to you to trust your intuition. This is why we send our love to you through these transmissions. We want you to know what it feels like to be in the energy of loving Beings so that you can discern the difference if need be. Do you feel love? We say to you that when contact begins it will be the Beings of the Light that come before you. We are ready to offer you much wisdom and to support humanity on this journey back to the Light.

By revealing ourselves to you, we are able to reach larger groups and to share our wisdom of ascension. Once contact is made your media will not be able to cover it up and so everyone will have to awaken to the possibility of life outside your planet. It may be shocking to many, but they will soon learn that there is nothing to fear. That is why contact will initially come to those who understand this and request contact. They will be able to allay the fears of the masses and to discredit government statements that would create fear.

Trust your own hearts Dear Ones. This is the best way always for you to navigate these ever changing times. If there is any doubt then do not give of yourself to a Being that does not feel fully and wholly loving to you. If there is any doubt, then trust your feelings and walk away. Do not be in fear as you walk away. No harm will come to you now. The battle is won. You are moving to the Light and nothing will stop that now. Earth is climbing the rungs of evolution into the higher realms of the fourth and fifth dimension. It is going to happen. The only ones who will not make this leap are those who choose not to. This is the choice of the individual.

However, for those who stay behind, there may be great regret once they realize what they have given up. It is hard to desire ascension when you do not know what it means. So let us tell you. It means living in love all the time. It means living in peace and harmony. It means being the creator of your life. There will be no bounds to what you can create. Your life will be as joyful and happy and exciting as you will allow it to be.

You will be surrounded by others who love you and you live in harmony with them. You will be appreciated for all that you are and you will not go to work every day doing something that you are not inspired to do. No, you will do only what you enjoy doing – what comes naturally to you and brings you great joy. There will be no more slavery of any kind. You will be the master of your own life and only that which you invite in will exist for you. There will be only love and joy. All that is challenging for you in your life will disappear at will.

However, to stay in the 3D earth will be pretty much exactly as you are living now. There will be wars and famine and greed and killing. There will be earth challenges and climactic upheavals. There will be economic burdens. And so, knowing this, what will you choose? It is for this reason that we drew the blank this day. It is like a clean slate that you can create whichever life you choose. It is by knowing more of what the two choices offer that we believe that you will see the reason to want to ascend.

And so, Beloveds, stay out of fear when you see things changing on your world. The changes are required to create a new system – a new Light way of being. And, when Beings from other planets begin to show themselves on the earth, be not afraid. For indeed, they have been walking among you for eons of time, they just disguised themselves as humans. The dark side has always being hanging out in the ethers so seeing Beings in front of you does not mean that they are harmful. They are the ones that are not afraid to be seen and want to serve you and support your transition to the Light.

We will not say when this will begin to happen. That is up to you and your willingness to receive our support. There are many creations that would support free energy and so much more on this planet. It has all been hidden and lives have been lost for trying to bring it forward to the masses. It is time for that to stop. It is time to stop the destruction of the planet for the sake of less than one percent of the population. It is time for the earth to claim her rights to be well and whole before she is destroyed.

When you look for evil, know that it has existed on this planet for far too long. You need not look for ETs to find something evil. How many people on this earth are tortured each day? How many young girls live in a hole, useful only for their orifices? Oh, there is evil on this planet so do not fear the unknown. It has as much a possibility of salvation as it does anything else. Be wise about the world so that you can see what needs to change. When you consider this, why would you resist moving into a world full of love?

These are your options Dear Ones. Choose love. Choose ascension. Heal yourselves so that you may know what you deserve out of life. As long as you carry the beliefs of not deserving you will not see the difference. This is why we ask over and over for you to do your healing work. When you see fear in yourself, look within to what needs to be healed. We want so much for you to find the wholeness within yourselves Beloveds, you are so deserving. You have given so much to be here on this earth – to serve the Light.

Claim what is rightfully yours. Know that you deserve all the happiness that you can hold. That is the truth of being human. You can have all that you ever yearned for and rightfully so. Know it and believe it and then create it. Clean out the old beliefs and bring in the new. Heal thyself great masters that you are and step into your Light. You are magnificent beyond your greatest imagining. That is why we love you so. And so it is.

# Essay Sixty-five - BEING HOME

Greetings Beloveds. Greetings from the Love and Light of the Creator. Greetings from the Great Central Sun as we come before you in joy and delight. For you see Dear Ones, we are honored to stand in your presence. We are the ones who are privileged to be standing before you with this opportunity to share our energies with you – to bask in the Love Light that is humans on this earth.

You are Creator Light. You are the spark that we are. We are of one source so how could we not love you? Even those on your earth who have strayed far from their original essence, we love them too. We love all of creation for we are linked to the oneness that is all things. We can see with eyes that are not human eyes but the eye of All That Is. We are connected to the All Seeing Eye that knows all and is all and so we resonate with you and with all of creation.

And so today we speak of your piece of creation – the piece of creation that is human and we say to you Dear Ones, that you are perfection. That is not what you think you see when you look in the mirror but we say that it is what you are. We do not think that you should look at yourselves and see anything less than perfection. Every wrinkle, every roll of skin, every ache or pain is perfection. It is all for your human experience. It is not that you desire to be walking around with aches and pains on a conscious level, but on the unconscious level you have made this choice.

Your soul is seeking experiences and they come in many forms. Each is a teaching. It is all part of what you have chosen to have as a life experience so that you may grow and expand and come to a place of fully loving yourself. As soon as you love your aches and pains they can leave.  Love them free.  Love yourselves free.  Love all that is.  Love the one who hurt you as a child.  Love the one who hurts you now.  Love them and walk away.  Thank them for the gift that you have been shown by loving them.  As soon as you do then you no longer need the experience that they are offering.

Oh, we do simplify this process.  For you cannot simply say, OK I love this pain and it will leave.  That is truly an over simplification.  The truth of it is that you must love yourself enough to love your experience.  You must heal the experience to the point where you can fully love it.  Once you see the beauty of the experience then you know that you have healed it to the point where you can love it for what it taught you and then you are done with it.  You need not have that kind of experience again because you have learned from it.  You 'got' it and so it can leave.  This is the truth of loving it free.

And in so doing you are loving yourselves free.  Do you realize how free you are after you do the healing work that allows all your painful memories to leave?  You are like butterflies coming out of the cocoon.  You have finally released yourself from the burden of the memories that have held you back, clipped your wings.  Once they are healed and released then you are free to fly.  And soar you will.  Without all the burdens you will fly to heights that you have never imagined.  And this is the reason to love your pain and your experiences.  They are showing you the way to your freedom.

Do you have a sore knee?  What is it trying to tell you?  What do your knees represent in life?  Are you holding yourself back from walking forward in your life?  Well, let the body show you – with love!! – what you are doing.  Let the body show you where you need to let go or release so that you can move forward the way your soul wants to journey.  What a beautiful gift that sore knee is.  What a delightful experience the soul has chosen to show you the way. Are you listening? Are you paying attention? Nothing is by chance – n.o.t.h.i.n.g. So, pay attention Beloveds so that you can find your way back to the bliss that is the healed human.

What do you think replaces the pain after it is healed? Love! Pure love residing in a human body. Oh, that is when life is fun. When you are able to reside in a place of pure love, oh what joy. This is what we desire for you beloveds. Nothing less. We wish the greatest joy for you. Bliss is your calling. It is not just some idealistic thought - it is a full possibility for you, especially in these times. Never before has it been so easy to find a place of bliss upon this earth. But you must be willing to make the changes that are required for you to be a clear and open vessel for the bliss. It will not find its way to a cluttered or dirty vessel. The vessel must be prepared for it to enter. And you prepare by doing your healing work that then makes space for love and bliss to enter.

Waste no time Dear Ones. The earth cannot wait forever. She is waiting for you very patiently. However, there is a time line – a final date when she must make her shift to the Light. You want to be ready when that time comes. Be ready to go along with her. It will be so easy when you have done your healing work. You will be ready without even knowing it when you have done your healing work. Otherwise it may be a more difficult journey to keep up with her. Otherwise you may find that you are scrambling at the last moment and it can be confusing and shocking to the soul. That confusion may keep you from taking the journey with her back to the Light. Make the choice and then act.

And so, what does it look like to make that choice? Are you choosing ascension? If so, then the choice is to prepare. It is to do the healing work like we have said without delay. It is not time to say, oh, I'll just live my life the way I have been doing with some thought about what needs to change and it will be done. Oh no. It will not be this way unless you have done enough work already for it to be this easy.

Once the greatest mass of healing has been accomplished, then it does get easier and easier. It does take time to get to this point for most of you. That said, you could do it all in an instant with an understanding that it is possible - if you would allow a full and complete understanding of the possibility of that it could happen in that way. The point is to do the work and then reap the rewards.

For those who have done this already, we know you are feeling the bliss. We know you are seeing life become more and more exciting as it unfolds in ways that bring more joy. How exciting it is for one who has struggled for years to see life begin to unfold in grace and abundance. This is what lies ahead of those who have done the work and who live within a peaceful heart. Once you do this work, there is no fear, no false beliefs of hardship, no comparing your life to others. You walk your own path with confidence. You are confident in yourself and in the knowing that you are cared for in every moment.

Imagine living with no concern about anything – ever. This is possible when you believe. And it is what you believe that you create. So why not go for it? Change those beliefs that would have you living anything less. Seems impossible? It's time to explore why. Take a look inside. Ask yourself why you are living a life that is anything less than what you would desire your life to be. It's yours to change Dear Ones.

Jump on board and join the ride. Life will carry you easily once you are ready to allow it. That is the way of it. When you expect love and joy in every moment then you will begin to create it. Why expect anything less? It is folly to expect anything less than love and joy in every moment. Make the change. Speak to your DNA so that it may change. Tell your DNA that it will accept nothing less than love and joy in every moment and see what happens.

Oh, it will not happen if the underlying belief is that it is stupid or impossible. There is more work to do then before it will happen for you. For those of you who think that maybe you can believe it is possible, give it a try. Tell your DNA that you now magnetize nothing less than love, joy and abundance. Lock it in. See your cells dancing with the truth of it. Celebrate what life feels like now that you have anchored this in. Love it. Live it. Be it. And so it is.

# Essay Sixty-six - LIVING IN LOVE III

And so it is Beloveds that we are called before you once again. And once again we celebrate our coming together in this space of words on page. And we say to you, even though you are only reading words, you are, in truth, reading our energy. The essence of who we are resonates off the page as a vibration of love. We could write garbled words and still give the same vibration. It is the vibration of love and it is meant to lift you into deeper understanding of who you are. Some of our transmissions are encoded with deeper understanding. Some are not, so that you may have a rest in between – a time of incorporating the transmissions which are deeper.

And so it is that, today, we wish to tell you of another level of love. For you see, we talk about love a lot, and you interpret it in terms of human love. However, that is not the love that we speak of. The love we speak of is a love that is of a higher resonance than human love. It is creation itself. It is the love of All That Is and it is the essence of life – the prana. And, in this time upon the earth, after your grand shift into the higher levels of awareness, this love is more predominant on your earth than it has been for eons of time.

And so the love on the earth has changed. With your shift of late 2012, the energy on the earth changed and so your perspective of love is changing as well. Many of you will find that you are loving deeper. This may mean being in tears much of the time as you feel the joy of being alive in these times. This may mean that your heart is so open to everyone you meet that you feel like you are bubbling over at times. This may mean that you are loving yourself so much that you are strong in your convictions and know what you deserve and have no doubts whatsoever about who you are and what your expectations are from life.

This is the way of living in the full resonance of unconditional love. Loving the self unconditionally is what it is all about. When you step fully into that you see nothing in anyone else that you could possibly criticize. In order to do that you would have to see less than love within yourself. If you are nothing but love, that is all that you see. Oh, it is such a wonderful way of being. Never again will there be any need to think ill of anyone, for you see them as perfect as they are. You see only things that you like about them. You look at their qualities as an individual and you sit in deep reverence for who they are. You look at their actions and they all look beautiful because that is what you expect to see. This level of love is going to be expanding and growing on the earth now that you have shifted. It is the way of the new earth and it is what you are growing into.

For those who are not resonating at this level, we wish you to simply show them your loving grace. See their pain through the eyes of love and compassion. Know that something within them is choosing to stay in fear for just a while longer and that is OK. It is their path – their journey. Send them your pink heart love and wish them a soft journey. Open your heart and send them a ray of compassion. They will feel it. They have so much judgment for themselves that they cannot find their way by themselves.

By sending your unconditional love and compassion, you will touch them with the energy of acceptance and perhaps open a crack where the love can find its way in. The choice is theirs. There is no need to try and convince them or to rise above them. Just send kind, gentle thoughts of acceptance for who they are. That is the softness that they are seeking. When it comes from outside, it is shown to them as a possibility – one that they can then step into if they choose.

The world is changing quickly now toward the Light and it is a journey that holds extremes at this time. That will also soften over time as more and more find their way to the Light. You who are reading this are the ones who are leading the way and you are the ones whom we invite to gather into circles of love. Celebrate love and the new earth and envision the world full of loving beings who support each other and who admire each other.

This is the way of the new earth. And you are now on the new earth. It may not look so different yet but it will. It will be changing, day by day, so that, 100 years from now you will not be able to remember these challenging and difficult times. The minds of humanity will not allow you to go back there and connect with this energy and why would you want to. It may be recorded in history somewhere for posterity sake, and that is fine. But, in your day to day interactions your only desire will to be to continue to grow the love. There will be no reason to go back.

And so we say to you Beloveds, in the near future we will give you some understanding of what this new world will look like beyond your feelings and the essence of life. We will begin to share what some of the possible changes are in your financial institutions and your economy and your energy sources and natural resources. Much will change. Not only will the very essence of the human being change, but that will also demand a different lifestyle than you are currently living. You are currently living a very third dimensional existence.

When you are vibrating in the higher dimensions of Light, you will no longer tolerate the lifestyles that you are living now. It must change with the times and change it will. It will be delightful to see your beautiful planet return to her pristine beauty. And, as well, it will be wonderful to see the human body become more radiant, reflecting the fullness of being and the love energy that is expanding within the hearts of man. Much is changing. Celebrate every day Beloveds, for you are creating this new earth. The more you celebrate the easier it is to shift into these magnificent times of being Living Light. And so it is.

# Essay Sixty-seven - LOVING WHAT IS II

And so it is Beloveds that we come before you this day in joy and delight. We see before us the Kings and Queens of the Light and we rejoice. We see you singing like that royalty that you are and we celebrate. And, as you navigate these times there is much reason for celebration. For you see Beloveds, you have made it. You have climbed the ladder of ascension and you have found your way to that place where love reigns. You do not see it in every experience, but it is waiting.

You are residing in a plane of existence that allows great growth, but in a more gentle and loving way than what has been on the earth for eons of time. That is why we celebrate. That is why we are so delighted. It is a time of renewal for humans. It is a time of resting after all your morphing and changing in the years leading up to December 21, 2012. It was a time of great transformation in the human biology and psyche and it was draining.

You are still going through changes but not to the same degree. This is what allows a bit of rest from all the changing. And yet, there is still a lot happening. A lot is shifting and you are still morphing as you reside in the higher planes of Light and you feel the love Light that surrounds you now. This is the joy of these times. You are able to reside in a much better place of grace than before. For those of you who prepared yourselves by doing your personal clearing work, you are now reaping the rewards of your efforts.

You are the ones who are being gifted with a world full of love and grace. This is the way of it. You are being rewarded. Those who are still seeing fear in their experience will continue to create scenarios that offer their fears up to them. It is like creating a banquet. Whatever you order you receive. Sometimes you don't know what to expect at a banquet. You don't understand that you created the experience with your thoughts. Some – many – are still living this way. They do not understand yet that they are creating their lives with their thoughts.

The greatest challenge now is to make this a conscious awareness. The more you work with this, the easier life will be. When you slip away from this you will fall harder into self-judgment because you have seen farther above it now. The differences become more extreme because you are able to reach up higher now. When you slip back down it feels as if you have fallen farther. And indeed you have, for you have touched the higher planes of existence and it does not feel good at all to fall back into the lower third dimension.

The fourth dimension is much more beautiful and graceful and joyful and so falling back is most uncomfortable. Good. That means that you won't stay there for long. It means that you will do what you can to make yourself feel better again and get out of that hole. We do not want you to be comfortable there. It might be too easy to stay. We doubt that many of you would truly want to stay there once you have reached the higher dimension and know what it feels like to be there. It would be a very few who would not choose to stay there.

And so be gentle with yourselves in the times when you fall back. It is still a human experience and it brings all types of feelings. Some days you are on top of the world and others you fall off. We haven't forgotten you or betrayed you. We are still here ready to hold you up and to guide you to the Light. Just reach out to us and ask for help. We will be at your side. And so it is.

# Essay Sixty-eight - WHAT IT IS TO BE IN LOVE

And so it is that we come before you once again Beloveds, in the name of love and grace. For we see before us the queens and kings of Light in this world and we rejoice. And again we say to you that you are the saviors of this earth. There is no waiting for some outside savior of the Light to come and rescue you Dear Ones. It is already done and you did it. There was no king of heaven coming other than yourselves. The second coming is the time that you are in. It is the time when your DNA shifted so that you could hold more Light and be your own masters and you are here. You have done it.

Oh, you may look at your lives and think nothing has changed, and we would ask, has it not changed? Think of what your life was like ten years ago. Have you changed? Are you different? Do you think differently now than you did back then? We are sure the answer will be yes. For you see, the awareness around you – the prana, the breath of the earth has changed and so you must be changed as well. The energy of your surroundings has changed and so you must change as well in order to be in resonance with your environment.

For those of you who feel out of resonance with your environment, we say to you, look at your surroundings and ask where you are out of sync? Where are you out of sync with your soul choices? If your soul is choosing a change in your way of living, your way of existing upon this earth, and you are not flowing with that desire for change, then you will be out of harmony with your soul's desired destiny and you will then feel that disharmony in your life.

So, if your life feels out of harmony, look within and ask your soul what changes it is choosing. You will know the truth of it in your heart. It is your unwillingness to look at it truthfully that keeps you eluded. It tricks you into thinking you do not know the answer. You definitely know the answer. The question is, are you willing to know the answer? And then are you willing to make adjustments that resonate with the answer – to begin living the life that is in harmony with what you have come to do? And so, if you are feeling discontent or out of harmony with life, it is time to explore inside.

The answers are not outside of you. That is running away from the truth of the answer. You will not find any solution there. You must look within to find the grace of your existence. You must look within to find the truth of your heart's desire. Then you will feel fulfilled, because you are filling up from the inside out instead of the opposite.

Trying to fill up from the outside in is trying to find joy out of clothes, and things, and people and addictions. It never brings fulfillment. It usually brings self-hatred as a matter of fact. You shop and then regret it. You have sex and then feel empty. You drink and then realize your problems haven't gone away. The only place to find fulfillment is within. And the only requirement to find success is willingness. As soon as you are willing to truthfully look at that which is keeping you from moving forward, it will be revealed to you.

The moment you are ready to grow as a person, your helpers will arrive. The way will be shown to you. All you have to do is recognize the signs and the people when they arrive. Know that it may not look like what you think it will. Know that your helpers can come dressed in different packaging than you would have chosen. Trust Beloveds. Trust that Spirit knows what it is doing. The way to the Light is not the way you have been living so allow new situations to come into your life. Allow new people to come.

Follow the understanding in our heart. Does your heart say yes? Sometimes the truth is so profound that it takes days to absorb the experience. Sometimes it feels like fear because the soul recognizes deep change. Do not be fooled into thinking it is wrong. If you feel fear, ask is this fear or excitement? Ask, is this leading me to my highest good? If, when you ask that question, you feel a sigh or feel lighter, then the answer is a yes. If you still feel fear or feel heavier then it is not the best choice for you. Believe in these tools and learn to discern these feelings.

There will be times when the truth can lead to tears that almost feel like fear, but it is the fear of stepping into the highest possible aspect of who you are. It is a fear that knows that your life will never be the same, but in a good way. It takes courage to step totally out of the old you and into the new, more magnificent you. One would not think that it would be a fearful thing, but it is because you know that you will not walk this earth in the way that you have. Things will change. Even though they will be changes that you have yearned for or they would not be coming, still change means something new.

Change means something unknown and the physical body likes the familiar. The spiritual body is ready for the change, for it has a knowing of what lies ahead but the physical body does not believe it. It thinks the only safe place is where it has been, so it does not see the potential. And so you need to learn to listen to the spiritual knowing and not the physical body. Do not be limited in your life dear ones. Everything that you have ever desired is possible and waiting for you to step into the fullness of you so that it may come to you.

Your deepest desires will not come to the small you. They are out of range for that part of you. It is by stepping into your fullness that you then are big enough to hold those grand experiences. The small you can only hold the past experiences. In order to grow you must make room. When you grow, you do make room. So think of it that way. You are growing as a person to make room for the larger experiences of life.

Imagine someone who has a dream of going hot air ballooning but never believing it is possible. Then imagine someone who desires that and believes that it is possible and will happen. They know that in order for that to happen they must be someone who lives like someone who goes hot air ballooning. They must behave like someone who lives an exciting life and has the funds to do so and knows people who would like to do such things.

They must expand who they are to embrace hot air ballooning in their experience. It is like they must expand their field so that hot air ballooning can fit in. This is the way of it. Expand and be the full potential of all your desires. If you are choosing a romantic relationship, then expand your life to include that. Expand the energy of your home to make space for someone. Expand the energy of who you are so they can feel you. In this way they can find you. Expand out and out, shining your Light, magnetizing them to you. This is what we mean by living fully. This is what we mean by being all that you are. See yourselves as huge balls of energy and all those things that you desire are living within those balls of energy.

This is beautiful Dear Ones. See it now as you read these words and then read them again and again so that it becomes a part of who you are. Expand and expand and inside that ball of you energy is everything that you ever dreamed of. Sit and meditate on this now

Beloveds and know that you are magnificent and we are here at your side, witness to the brilliance of you. It is our delight to come before you and to see your radiance and to be your brethren in this grand evolution back to the Light. And so it is.

# Essay Sixty-nine - ALL THE WORLD IS LOVE

Love, love, love. The Beatles sang about it years ago and here we are to say keep on singing that song. And so we greet you this day Beloveds and say we are here once again to talk about love. And yet, we say to you, everything is love so how could we talk about anything else? We could connect all our transmissions to love as we do. There is a reason that we are stuck on the love button. You need to hear it. You need to know how important it is.

It is a word that carries much baggage in your society so we are doing what we can to turn the vision of the word love into a new meaning. Love is equal to pain for many people. Many do not know what true love feels like and are afraid to find out. They do not believe it is possible to experience true love on this earth and we can understand why. Many generations have you been on this earth without really feeling the love of home – the love of All That Is that pours down upon you from heaven you could say. So few of you have truly felt what that is like. It is no wonder love is a dirty word for many. So we are here to change that. We are here to help you understand what love really feels like.

Love is such a beautiful energy that those who do touch it in this lifetime are moved to tears. Those who touch love in meditation are often moved to tears. Those who feel our love as we connect with you and offer our grace to you are often moved to tears. And why the tears? Because it is a love that is like nothing that you feel from the mental perspective. It is a love that touches the heart. And it is so pure and so full of the truth that it touches your soul and that is where the tears come from. The tears are recognition of the truth of what you are feeling. Now, some experience this in relationship and that is truly beautiful.

Some of you experience this during your sexual interactions, when you are connected to spirit and with your beloved, and that is beautiful. That is what was kept hidden from you for so long, for the sexual communion of two souls who are truly loving each other is a powerful connection to the divine if you wish it to be. It is so powerful that it can awaken much within you that is divine.

It can awaken kundalini energy and send you into bliss. This, however, does not come from casual sex so do not use that for your excuse to have many partners, claiming you are connecting to your bliss. Sex from a mental perspective instead of from the heart is the opposite of bliss. It can be painful and harmful to the emotional body.

So we talk of love again. And again we say that the kind of love that we would lead you to is the love from the Creator. You find it within your heart. How often do you sit and connect with the heart? Just sit in meditation with the intention of connecting to the heart. You can do it, just have the intention of feeling deep love. Think of something that makes you very happy. Maybe it is a child, or a loved one, or your favorite place in nature. Just feel it in your heart. You will know when you have made the connection because it sends a rush of energy through your body that is a warm fuzzy.

It is soft and you feel like you have connected with the Divine. The Divine is within you. It is within your hearts. Use this as the launch of everything you do in your daily activity. If you could start your day with a heart connection and then have the intention of living from that place, your life would change dramatically. Even if it is not until you get to work, connect with the heart and then start your day. When you are meeting friends for dinner, sit in your car and connect before walking into the restaurant or into their home.

It is easier the more you do it and it can bring all your desires to you because when you think from the heart you are not in duality. You are then in unity consciousness. In that state you are connected with all that is. In that state you are the trees, and the plants in your house and the ant crawling over a log in the jungle. The more you drop into the heart the more you come to fully understand this. And you are now residing in the energies of love that will support you making these changes.

Never before has it been so easy for you to do this work. You are not as deep into the darkness now as you were in your past incarnations. Use the benefit of this energy to launch you into ascension by connecting with the heart. From that place, all life unfolds in divine grace and there are no worries. You will come to trust that what comes to you is perfect for you and that which is not in your best interest fades away. When you connect with the love space of the heart you also believe in yourself more and you live accordingly.

You do not allow others to walk all over you because you love yourself too much for that. You do not stay in unhealthy relationships because you love yourself too much for that. When you are walking in the love space of the heart, your life changes. You are looking through rosy glasses and all is wonderful. It always has been but it did not look like it. From the heart, you understand that all the challenges that present themselves to you are opportunities for growth.

You see the perfection as things play out in your lives and you celebrate every challenge, every argument and all self-judgment because you know it is an opportunity to see an aspect of your life that is ready to be released. And how do you release it? Surely we have talked enough about that. The first half of this book was about just that. We knew we would move through that to the good stuff – love. Love is the good stuff. Love is the stuff of which you are made and it is the stuff of which you will expand into as you approach this time of ascension.

Prepare yourselves Beloveds for the ascension. Be ready by loving yourselves and going into the heart and seeing not only yourselves from that vantage point but everyone else as well. And not only people but the animals and the earth. Everything is made of love. It is your creation so why not love it? And if you cannot love it then change it into something that you can love. You don't have to keep creating what you do not love. Change your thoughts about it and change it in your life. You may say it is not that simple, but it truly is.

You just have to do the healing work that continues to draw the experience to you. If you are not willing to do the healing work – to honestly look at the truth of what is leading you to the choices you are making - then you will continue down the same road. But do not say it is not possible to change. Say you are not willing to change, for that is the truth of it. It is important to be honest with yourselves. Do not kid yourselves, for you cannot change your experience when you do that. You just continue to kid yourselves into repeating your days over and over. That is only a good choice when you love your days. Until then we suggest you might want to shake things up a little.

And so we believe we have said enough this day. The time is coming near Dear Ones when you will be asked to make a decision. Ascend into the fourth dimension or stay where you are. And if you do not understand this talk of ascension, please learn about it so you can understand what we are sharing with you. The time is coming when you will have to make a choice. We have discussed the benefits and outcomes of that choice. We hope you have made a clear decision. We love you dearly Beloveds and we are always at your side supporting you in this journey called life. May it be joyous and grand. And so it is.

# Essay Seventy - BEING IN THE ENERGY OF LOVE

Greetings Beloveds. Greetings from the Love and Light of the Great Central Sun. Greetings from Home. For indeed, Beloveds, you are in the arms of Creator Light right now on planet earth. You have shifted and many of you have felt it. Many have not, and it is to both we speak. The energies of the earth are now residing more in the energy of love than fear. You really have no idea what a delight it is for us to say that to you.

For thousands of years you have been holding your Light in a very dark world called earth. And now, because of your willingness to walk the talk and stay strong in your belief in the Light, you are now walking in Love. Oh what a delight it is to see this earth unfolding now. You will find more and more that whatever you wish for is coming to you easier, sooner and with more grace. Notice every little thing that comes to you through your thoughts Dear Ones. The more you notice what you are creating, the more you will create consciously.

That is the reason for gratitude. It is to notice what IS working so that you can create more of it. Having your focus on gratitude takes you away from fear. And yet we say to you, you cannot have two grateful thoughts a day and 100 fear-based thoughts and see more of what you are grateful for. You must make the switch from focusing on what is not working to what you are choosing to have in your life. It all boils down to the majority of your thoughts creating your life experience. And yet, in these times of more love than fear on your planet, it is becoming easier and easier to stand in the place of receiving through love and requesting through love.

And so, this day, we would like to speak of creating through love. What does this truly mean? We have touched on this before. We have spoken of connecting in the heart and then working from there. This is how you create from love. It is a unity method of creation, one in which you create from a place of oneness so the polar opposite of what you create need not happen. When you create from the heart, you are creating only a loving experience with no need for the opposite which is what happens when creating from the mind.

So, how do you get into this heart space to create this way? You take time to quiet the mind. Sit somewhere where you will not be disturbed and take a few deep breaths. Better yet, take 7 breaths, breathing deep into the body and releasing all the air as you breathe out. Then tell yourself that you are moving into the heart space now. Feel your consciousness drop into the heart. You will know when you have done it because you feel the difference. There is an energy shift. Once in that space then you can imagine that which you choose for yourself. Envision it as if it already is.

Do you wish for a new relationship, smile in the warmth of the feeling of that relationship. See yourselves together. Pay attention to what you are doing. Feel the love that you share. Just enjoy the experience. Then, simply release the experience and trust that it is on its way. Afterward, all you need do is be the person that your beloved would be attracted to. Just exude the energy of that person.

Our dear Rashana has just set a statement for herself that is: I walk in the fullness of my soul expression. Every day she reminds herself of this many times and what it does is allow her to step into the highest aspect of who she is. We wish the same for you. Every step can be in that place of being your full soul expression. From that way of being, wonderful experiences will also walk into your life. They simply must show up because you are calling them in with the very essence of who you are.

Do not be in a hurry for the things that you desire to show up. From this place it is more of a dance of seeing what the universe has to provide. It is your higher soul that is bringing the experiences to you and they will be more wonderful and beautiful than you could have dreamed up. However, your dreams and daydreams are helping to magnetize the energies to you that will attract what you wish in your life.

So it is a balance of both - knowing the qualities of what you desire and knowing that or something better is on its way into your experience. This is the way of it Dear Ones. This is walking in the Light of Love. For this way of living is loving the self. There is no emptiness when one walks this journey, so if you are feeling lonely or empty, that is a signal to you that there is more healing work to do.

Walking in the fullness of one's soul expression is indeed full. There are no empty spaces. Oh, there are invitations for new experiences and for loved ones to enter. It is not that there is no room for such, it is that there is no deep yearning. It is more from of a place of wholeness. This is your signal to guide you in the journey forward. Every time you feel incomplete, know that there is some exploratory work to do to find the source of that feeling.

Go back into your childhood once again, or later experiences, to see where you first felt that way. How far back does it go? Was it one instance, one event, or was it a family pattern? All this exploring, over and over and over, will lead you to the place of fullness. It can be a long journey and requires commitment on your part to become all that you came to be, to persist with every emotion that is anything less than love, to find your way out of the old patterns and into the new you. This is the whole intent of this book Dear Ones. It is to help you find your way back into the fullness of you.

For only then are you truly living your soul expression. All the dirt has been washed off the window so that we can look through and see the true you, not all the emotional protection and pain that you had to put up so that we could not see you. You did not want to see yourself or for anyone else to truly see you because there was pain in there and you knew you were not the wholeness of you. By releasing, you are washing away the debris so that you shine out into the world more fully. This is the beauty of souls healing and this is what will be more and more on this new earth.

You are being guided back into the whole, brilliant, glorious self and from there you have nothing to offer but love. And where does that love come from? It comes from loving the self. When you are totally loving the self, there is no need to defend oneself. There is no need to prove you are better or to demand to be seen in any way. You are at such peace within yourself that you are at peace in all your interactions with others. This is the way of it when the wounds are cleansed and released. We wish this for all of you for it is such a peaceful existence. So heed our words Dear Ones. Love yourselves free and illuminate the world. And so it is.

# Essay Seventy-one - THE UNIVERSE SUPPORTS YOU

And so it is we come to you again Beloveds. We come in love and Light and in the glory of heaven. We come to watch over you and protect you and lead you back to the fullness of you. Oh, it is such a delight to stand before the dear humans who are working so hard to be all that they can in this world. It is such a delight to stand before those who choose love and nurture each other in this journey called life. There are so many of you now, standing in Love and Light.

The world is becoming brighter and brighter with your love Lights. You are sparkling gems on this beautiful planet that you have the great privilege of living upon. For indeed, Mother Earth could have shrugged you off long ago. She could have said enough of this disrespect - enough of this selfishness and greed, but she did not. She loves you like any mother loves her child, regardless of their behavior. And she is gleaning the reward of her patience, for the entire human species is morphing into love.

The entire human race is changing, ever so slowly, to resonate with pure love. And the most wonderful thing is that this growth will happen exponentially so that within a matter of a few short years you will see that you are living on a very different planet than you are even now. More and more families will offer loving kindness to their children. More and more people will love themselves and so there will be no need to be hurtful to others as a way of punishing the self.

This is all changing and as the world begins to resonate more in love, Mother Earth can take a big sigh of relief. For, along with that loving of the self, is the love of the earth. You will become caretakers of the earth once again instead of raping of the earth. The methods that you currently use of supplying energy for yourselves simply will not be tolerated in only a few short years. Everything will begin to change as humanity becomes more loving. As you love yourselves and each other this also resonates out to all the creatures of the earth.

Great reverence is about to awaken for all life and it is so beautiful we cannot begin to tell you how it warms our souls. From our perspective, the earth becomes a sparkling jewel once again. All that the darkness tried to strip away has been lost and that is why Mother Earth was so patient with you. She wanted to prove that Light prevails just as much as you did. That is why she held on almost to the point of destruction. She could feel it. She knew it was on its way and so she held on and held on and here you are.

Celebrate Beloveds. Celebrate your return to the Light. All of humanity is now on its way back to the Light and the Light is love. It is inevitable that some will leave. Those who are not ready to walk in love will leave to have a different experience on another level of existence. That is perfect for their soul plans so do not despair. For you, love is on its way. How delightful it is.

Every day we talk about love because love is all there is. Love is it. That is the foundation of everything so why would one not want to talk about it every day? Just try to imagine how your lives would change if you talked about love every day instead of all the bad things that happen to you or all the things that are not working in your life. If you talked more about love every day your lives would morph in an instant. It would be incredible, the speed in which your lives would change. So, why not look for the love in every experience? What would love do in each situation? What would each experience look like from the viewpoint of love?  Explore your life this way.

Let us say that someone runs into your car on the way to work - just a little fender bender.  Now you have to go through insurance and get your car repaired and miss the morning meeting.  All of this is running through your mind.  How could you look at this from the perspective of love?  Well, first you would trust and know that each person involved had chosen this soul experience for some reason.  That could put your mind at ease just a little, knowing there is some lesson in it for you.

Then you would realize that someone else would have to speak on your behalf at the morning meeting.  Perhaps it would be someone who normally likes to hide behind you but now will have to be seen and it will lead that person out of their shell, so to speak, and lead them to a deeper awareness of their abilities.  Wonderful.  And perhaps, when your car is being repaired, there was a recall that you weren't aware of and so that is fixed as well, saving you from a potentially harmful accident.  All these things are underlying every experience.

So when you view it through the perspective of love, you trust the universe knows what it is doing and is offering you valuable lessons or experiences that support your personal growth and development.  And to add to this, the more you are seeing your life from the perspective of love, the less challenging these experiences become because there are fewer lessons needed to guide you to the place where your higher soul wishes to be.

So we invite you to begin to look at your lives in this manner.  The more you do the easier life will become and the happier you will be.  The universe is not out to get you.  The universe is simply here to support you.  It has no bias so it supports whatever your beliefs are. Why not believe that every experience is a loving experience and live that instead of believing in fear and creating scenarios that support your fearful thoughts.

It is really that simple and the ways of getting there are clearly outlined in this book. All it requires is action on your part. It is truly more difficult to hold onto the fear based thoughts than it is turn to love and watch your life unfold into that. It is just because it is less familiar that you do not make the changes. So practice. Every day take one aspect of the teachings in this book and practice. It becomes much easier than what you have been doing, assuming you have been holding onto fearful thoughts.

It is with the deepest love and appreciation that we come before you with these messages. It is our mission to support you in your growth into the new human living on the new earth. Now is the time. How delightful that is. And how we rejoice as we watch you embracing this new way of being and stepping into the fullness of a life lived with ease, grace and joy. What more is there than that? We leave that for you to explore. And so it is.

# Essay Seventy-two - LOVING IN THE LIGHT OF CREATOR/ALL THAT IS

And so it is Beloveds that we have the great privilege of coming before you this day. By the time you read these words you will have passed through the shift of December 21, 2012. And so we write for you, the reader, with the knowing of what is on the other side of that timeline. That is to say, we write in the moment that you are reading this work. And we rejoice at the coming together of souls who read these pages and who step into the desire to be all that they came to be and to serve their Divine purpose on this earth.

Yes, we rejoice at the calling to spirit, for it is by living in the connection to spirit that you find the fullness of life. The human mind does not lead to fulfillment Beloveds we can assure you of that. It is your connection to source that is where the love comes from and each heart yearns for love. When you do not have it within yourself you look outside to find it there. What comes to you from outside is simply a reflection of what is within, so therefore you do not find it there either.

It is from within yourself that you find true love. It is by learning to love the self that you find fulfillment. It is by healing the wounds of the past that you get to the place of loving the self. Do not carry resentments about your past. It was all your chosen experience. It all took you to a place of perfect experiences for your personal growth. So do not begrudge, but find the reason – the lesson in it all. That is where you will find the release. Take a good long look at it and discover what it was teaching you. What was the gift Dear Ones? It is there somewhere.

As we may have told you, our channel Rashana had a traumatic event in her childhood that forced her to be disassociated from her body for most of her life. She could not fully relate to people. She was quiet and shy – unsure of herself. But she did the healing and found the gift. After 50 years of being disconnected she found the gift as she was coming back. And that gift was to be so connected to spirit. That gift was to live a life knowing only love. For you see, from her perspective connected to spirit and not the physical world, everything was love.

So now, as she learns what it is like to be fully embodied, she also knows the gift of her ability to channel so clearly came from being disassociated. This is what we mean by the gift Dear Ones. Her pain led her to disassociate which led to her connection with spirit which led to her channeling abilities. The gift is there somewhere. Do not hold onto the pain as if it is some victory rite.

You are not hurting anyone but yourself by doing so. Let go. Seek out the source of the pain and forgive yourself for choosing that experience. Beloveds, we say to you that you are in magnificent times. This new era on earth is one in which many changes are going to begin to occur. Be ready to hop on board. Be ready to step into your role in this divine plan. You each have something special to offer. Do not hide behind your pain.

And so we would like to speak to you more about the experiences that are being human on the new earth. We say to you that it is time to have more appreciation for water. It is being discovered that water is much more than was thought. There are people like Dr. Emoto who are showing the incredible properties of water to hold intention. What do you think this means in your life? Knowing that your bodies are mostly water, what could this mean to you? Could you program water to bring what it is you desire into your life? We say to you this is possible, and we will tell you why.

It has been discovered that the properties of water are more like crystal. As many of you know, you can program crystals to hold your intentions. Think of where crystals are now used – in computers and a diversity of technology. So, if water is of a crystalline property imagine how you could use it to change your life considering all the water in your body. Not only that, but your very genetic structure is becoming crystalline in nature. So, you can literally program your bodies to hold what it is you choose to have in your life. It is human thought that changes the water structure in Dr. Emoto's work. Prayer has been shown to heal polluted water and beautiful music has been shown to create harmony in the water crystals.

This is the way of the future Dear Ones. We offer you a hint of it here. Use your imagination to consider the depth of this knowledge. You can change your world through the water. You can start with your own body. Program the water to bring about health in the body. Program the water to magnetize to you that which you desire. There is so much to discover that has been hidden. Much that has been buried, both literally and figuratively, is being revealed in these times. That is part of what is so magical about this new earth and the evolution that mankind and all of creation is currently experiencing.

You are rising up in awareness and the vibration is causing the rising up of that which has been hidden. You see the play on words. Words are creation. Use them carefully! There is a reason that Rashana does not use the word 'want'. Instead she types desire or choice. It is because the dictionary meaning of 'want' is 'to desire without having'. We tell you this so that you may speak consciously. It is important. Ignorance leads to more ignorance.  Inform yourselves to heal yourselves.

There are many of you who are leaders on this planet. As leaders you have the responsibility to be aware of your teachings and what you are showing the world through your life and your choices.  Also, you have taken the time to know thyself and do the healing work that places you in a position where you can offer guidance to others.  This is an important characteristic of one who shows the way for others.  We invite you to use water in your own life and see the results and then spread the word.

It is time for the world to awaken to all that is possible. Do not let your logic mind limit you.  There is so much that the logic mind cannot reach out and find.  It is the subconscious that knows all.  The conscious mind goes there to retrieve its information.  And where do you think the subconscious is?  Ah, that is a conversation for another day.

It is our deep honor to come before you Beloveds and share our wisdom with you.  We are your guides back to the Light.  Let our words speak to your heart and if they do not then trust what is truth for you.  It is yours to discern what resonates with you and what does not. Always make the choice that is best for you.  We love you so.  And so it is.

# Essay Seventy-three - STANDING IN THE LIGHT OF GRACE

And so it is Beloveds that we have the honor of being present with the beautiful beings who are the ones who are changing the world. We say to you Beloveds, you are Light and love in this world. We see you shining and we say to you that the heavens sparkle brighter because of your reflection in the stars. For you see, you are the stars themselves. Oh, you may think that we are just being kind and poetic but we say to you that what we speak is the truth. The Light of heaven is within you. The love and Light of creation lies within your cells.

You are made of the same stuff as the stars in the heavens and the soil beneath your feet. You do not think of yourselves as being the same as the stars but you are. When you look at the base of your atoms, there is very little difference between you and the stars. All of heaven is within you. You can find it by going into the heart. When you close your eyes you can find your way back. We tell you this so you will understand that all of creation is from one source. And if all is from one source then all is connected. Your mind creates a grand illusion that makes you feel separate.

If you feel alone you have lost the understanding of this connection. Be at peace Beloveds. We love you so. We see into your soul and we know that you are Light. We look into your hearts and we know that you are love. And we wonder why you cannot see this for yourselves. This world of illusion has certainly played a trick on you. Many of you are stepping out of that illusion now. Many of you are understanding that you are so much more than flesh and bone. For those of you who are connected to the divine aspect of who you are we know how difficult it can be to pretend to fit into a world that does not understand you.

The chasm is growing between those who reside in the Light and those who simply do not understand the way of the Light. You cannot explain to them who you are and you cannot live in their world. Do not despair. Simply find your family – the family who understands you. Find your soul family so that you will feel more at home here on earth. As the divide grows it is vital for those who are resonating closer to the fourth dimension to be with those who understand who you are. It is discouraging to the soul to be elsewhere.

It can be challenging when families do not resonate at the same level and friends begin to drift apart. Understand and let go. It is time to be with those who understand you. It is challenging for people who do not understand each other to try to remain friends. You can no longer support each other because you simply do not fit together. So agree to let it go and be at peace with it. This is more challenging when it is family but you must honor yourself and who you are. It is of no value to anyone to force yourself into situations that make you recoil.

If you find that it is that challenging to be with people then give yourself permission not to be there. Create situations where you must be somewhere else. It is OK to honor yourselves this way Dear Ones. It is more harmful to force yourself into social activities that do not resonate with who you are, especially when there are close ties in those situations. Without close ties it can be more playful and manageable but for many these are family ties that are shifting and changing. Accept what you feel and allow forgiveness.

You are morphing. Not everyone does this at the same rate. There is some cross over between those who are ascending. Some are ready and some are not nearly even considering it. For those who do not even know what it is, some are still ready because they have loving hearts. For some they are lost to the ways of the fourth dimension and not prepared to ascend. So your world is becoming torn between two kinds of people. The hope is that all will come to understand what these times are about and all souls will agree to rise into the fourth dimension.

For this reason, there will be a period of years when this divide is felt. It is ironic that as you find your way back into unity thinking you feel the division between people as stronger. It is because, as you come to live in the fourth dimension and experience its magic, you cannot be the same person in the 3D world. You simply cannot make yourself go back and connect with that. It is happening to more and more people.

So, the bottom line here is to be patient with yourselves and forgiving. If you find that you cannot tolerate being in a certain social circle, do not be a part of it. It is vital to protect your sensitivities at this time. Many will not understand you and that is OK. They cannot because they are not relating to who you are. And as much as they cannot understand you, it is hard for you to relate to them, so it is a two way street.

Do not take all the responsibility for being different or weird. Let others know that as much as you are different from them, they are different from you. This is a natural part of the ascension and it is helpful to understand it. As always, do what is best for your soul, your heart. Be the love that you choose to be and everything else will fall into place. We love you all. We are your support in changing times, with guidance on becoming the new human. And so it is.

# Essay Seventy-four - BEING IN LOVE WITH LIFE

Greetings Beloveds. Greetings from the Great Central Sun as we come before you this day that is time out of time. For we say to you, whenever you read this message, the message is in time with what we say. Let us explain. We may say that you are on the brink of a great discovery of how life flows. That is appropriate for each of you who read the words, regardless of what year you read them in. These words may be written some time in 2012 and you may read them in 2013 or 2014. It matters not. That which you read is appropriate for you at the time. That is the magic of how life works. The soul makes choices.

You choose to read this book when the messages are appropriate for you. There is no competition of who read it first or how long ago it was written. That is just an illusion of truth. The truth is that the time is perfect for you right now as you read these words. And so we commend you for being here and we say we are delighted to stand before the essence of you. We feel you. We hear your song. We are illumined by your grace and we delight in the presence of you. And so Beloveds, stand strong in the power of life unfolding in grace. Stand strong in the knowing that every little desire that you have deserves to be fulfilled and every step forward is leading you to the higher aspect of who you are.

These times of evolution upon this planet earth are all about discovering who you truly are. It is not who you thought you were or who you used to be. The truth of you is so magnificent that you could not accept it before. And certainly your world would not have supported it, for most of humanity was not ready for the fullness of you. But, these are changing times. These are the times that allow and support you in moving into the fullness of the truth of you.

So, you must look within and find who that is. Do you know the truly divine, magnificent and incredible you? Who might that be? If you were to allow yourself to think so well of yourself, who would that be? Many of you are learning how to clear the unsupportive patterns of the past and as you do then the real you is unfolding right before your very eyes. And we say to you, you will know this is happening when you see relationships change, when you can barely tolerate places that used to be OK for you. It is because you are changing but not everyone around you is doing the same.

As you change in these energies of now, it is by leaps and bounds. It creates a great divide that makes it somewhat unbearable to do what no longer feels right for you. Good. Do not do what does not feel right. Do not buy into the thing about being selfish or inconsiderate. Should you really be more considerate of someone else over your soul desires? The only time you should do for others is when you choose to do so. If you do so from the heart desire to give then it is beautiful. If you give out of obligation you are only giving resentment. We pity the receiver. They will feel the energy of your giving as insincere and wonder why they don't feel good about receiving.

It is time to be sincere to yourselves in every situation of life. We know those to whom we speak. We know you are not the ones who will only think of yourselves and never give again. That is not the nature of who you are. Those reading these words are the caregivers of the world. You are those who have come to be of service, and so we can say these words to you without being concerned that they will be misinterpreted. We know who you are Beloveds and we adore you. You are the ones who have come to lift the world into the dimensions of love and you are doing a fabulous job.

The world has ascended and you are on your way. Oh it is delightful to see you glowing and growing. It is delightful to see you stepping into the fullness of your soul expression and being brave enough to offer it out to the world. Oh how we rejoice. It is with these words that we congratulate you for having come this far. We congratulate you and yet we say to you, the work is not done. Do not sit back on your laurels just yet. Oh, it is getting to be fun and things are flowing so why stop now? It is just getting to the good part.

It is just getting to the part that we can start giving you everything you have ever dreamed of. Actually, it is not us giving to you but you giving to yourselves. You are doing so by believing in yourselves. That is our whole intention of these transmissions is to support you in believing in yourselves. That is all that is required. Once you are there anything is possible. And we mean that. Anything IS possible. If you can think it and then believe in yourself, that is all that is required. Then it will happen. There is no other way of it. And so the key here is to believe in yourself. The more you heal and clear out the old stagnant beliefs, then the more you can believe in yourself and create every dream you ever had.

And how do you create that? Simply by being. Once you are believing in yourself, you will find that opportunities just walk into your life. Life becomes synchronistic. You have a thought of something you would like to accomplish and two minutes later the key shows up that leads you to that creation. Oh how glorious it is. And we say to you, it is practice for being in the fourth dimension. It is the playground where you learn to navigate the finer energies that reside in the higher dimensions.

We are delighted to see you playing with it and expanding your abilities. As you expand your beliefs, then you step into the endless possibilities that are the life of creation. You are genius, you just don't accept it about yourself but it is true. Each human is pure genius. Why not accept it? Why not believe it? If you cannot believe it, what is keeping you back? What limitations are you placing on yourself? Where are your doubts? Look at them and clear them up. Is it from not understanding the way of the universe? We think not.

Once you believe in yourself the way of the universe shows itself to you. You do not need to have cerebral comprehension of how all this works. Actually, that could be a detriment. You just have to believe in yourself and then watch life unfold in wondrous ways. It is in the experiencing that you will come to understand, not the other way around. You do not need to understand so you can experience. Just believe, clear and experience and then you will come to understand more fully as your experiences increase. As life becomes more synchronistic, then you will gain more understanding of how things work when you are in the flow.

And so we are delighted that we were able to offer this message this day. We are delighted that we are able to connect with you day after day. We are delighted to see you unfolding those wings and exposing them to the sun. It is time to fly. Soar to the heights that you deserve to be in. Life is grand here. Come join us. We are waiting. And so it is.

# Essay Seventy-five - BEING IN LOVE WITH YOURSELF

And so it is Beloveds that we have the deep honor of coming before you once again. And we say to you, it is a great delight to be in your presence this day. It is a great joy to stand before the Beings of Light who call themselves human. We say to you Beloveds, you are such magnificent Beings. You have no idea what you have accomplished as a race of man. You fell into the deepest levels of darkness and, unassisted to the greatest degree, you found your way back to the Light.

Oh, you have no idea what that truly means. You are the only species who has done this. If you consider what that means you would be astounded with yourselves. You would see why there is such celebration and why Beings from universes everywhere have come to witness what is happening on Earth at this time. For you see Dear Ones, you are the first to do so. You were a grand experiment as many of you have heard, where it was decided that you would be allowed to have no interference from the Light to see if you could find your way back.

There was to be no interference from the dark either, but they do not always play by the rules. And so, there was some interference that meant that the Light had to step in at some point to assist you. But, overall, this was the doing of man. You found your way back to the purity and grace of Love. This is an accomplishment beyond your current level of understanding. It is going to affect all of creation from this day forward. And so it is that we say it is our great honor to connect with you – to stand before you and witness all that you are on this earth.

And this also leads us to our topic for today, Loving the Self. It is where all love is created. For you see, within your heart is all of the universe. And also the deep love that is creation itself. You cannot feel the love from someone else that you do not have within your own heart. It is your heart emitting the love out into the world that you feel coming back to you. It is your love reflecting back. So how could you ever love someone else more than you love yourself? You cannot. We would like you to understand the opposite as well. When you look at someone and you dislike that person, you have that same dislike for yourself.

Somewhere, deep within your psyche, you have those same traits within yourself that is your shadow side that you are not willing to look at. So instead you pretend it is someone else and you put your hatred or dislike upon them. The mirror is always reflecting back to you Beloveds. So be willing to look and be honest about what is reflecting back. And when it is love, admit that you love yourself that much. It is a good thing to love yourself. Loving the self is not selfish. Selfishness actually comes from not loving the self. When you feel lack, you are selfish.

When you love the self, there is no sense of lack. You feel connected to the Divine which is Love and there is no feeling of needing anything. Instead you desire to serve all of humanity as much as you can. When done from the fullness of self, your very essence impacts the planet with Love and you are doing your service just by being here. And so this is why we would like to see everyone walking in the love of self. We would like to see everyone walking in the knowing that they are complete and pure love.

Then you are all willingly giving to each other, knowing that you will also receive in return. It is a cycle. Always giving but not receiving is not a loving act. Those who always give but have no need to receive are not loving themselves. They are trying to prove that they are worthy of love by giving, in the hopes that they will look like loving people. The giving and receiving is balance and all life must exist in balance to be considered harmonious. This is what we wish for you Beloveds and this is the reason for our transmissions.

And so here we are. We have been writing for many days now. Rashana has noted that, after today, there are twenty-one more transmissions. So, we are currently writing Essay Seventy-five and almost all of our transmissions have been about love.

How could we write about love day after day after day? As we have told you, the reason is that you do not fully understand love. You do not have a deep concept, many of you, of what love truly is so we are trying to decode your social patterns that have falsely determined what love is. There have been many rules around love that are not only unhealthy but have led to the demise of your society. It is time to turn them around, and the biggest one is the guilt that is dished out around loving the self.

Hogwash. Loving the self is all there is. If you were to look truthfully at yourselves you would soon understand that EVERYTHING you do is out of selfishness you could say. The person who is the busiest volunteer in the community is doing it for themselves. It is the fulfillment that they feel for doing service or for the vision that they have in the community. It does not matter the motivation, it is assured it is self-centered. That is simply the truth and there is nothing wrong with it. So, coming to learn that everything you do is for the self, as it is for everyone else, why would selfishness be such a nasty concept?

The thing that we would like you to understand is that when you consciously love yourself, and fill your heart to overflowing with love and live without any self-punishment, then everything changes. Suddenly life is easy and graceful and full of love because that is what you are sending out and so it is reflected back. Can you see this? When love comes back to you it is because you are loving yourself that way. It makes your life easier and more joyful and then you have more love to give and then more love comes reflecting back.

Can you see how this is so much better than thinking that being selfish is a bad thing and that you are somehow taking from others by being selfish? The opposite is true. When you do not feel full and complete within yourself then you are giving to others out of guilt or commitment. Then that guilt and false commitment to others reflects back to you. Guilt reflecting back is not a pretty picture. When you look into the guilt mirror you do not like what you see. That leads to more guilt and a nasty pattern of self-hatred. Do you really think you have more to give the world when you do not even like yourself?

Impossible. It is the one who is full of love for the self that truly emits love out of every pore of their body and sends that love around the world. They not need do anything else but emanate love and they are having a positive impact on the entire planet. This is the grace of loving the self. We hope it brings you more clarity of what it is to be in love. All love begins with the self. Then it is reflected out into your hologram that you call your life. It is all your creation.

Why not love yourself and make it more joyful and playful? We are supporting you. If those around you do not understand it is OK. Eventually they will see the change in you and they will have to wonder how you came to be so much Lighter. Then they will pay attention for a different reason. Be the beacon that you are by loving yourself. Let the love Light shine from within your heart and you will change the world. And so it is.

# Essay Seventy-six - LOVING FROM THE HEART

And so it is Beloveds that we are here talking about love once again.  What a delight it is for us to stand before you once again in the realms of Light and Love. For Beloveds, we wish you to know that the place where you currently reside is of a higher dimension than it was when you first started reading this book. With each transmission your resonance is amped up. For you see, each transmission comes with a vibrational trigger that lifts your level of resonance up a notch so that, by the time that you finish this book you will be ready for our next.

In the second book you will find that the messages go much deeper.  In preparation for that, each of these messages also comes with an incremental frequency of Light.  You may not be aware of it but it is so.  By reading these words you are increasing your frequency and thus preparing yourself more fully for ascension. You are lifting yourselves up to the Light and Love of Creator.  In this process you are also lifting the planet and all life everywhere up into a higher frequency.  This is the way of it.  As you lift yourself, you also lift all of creation.  For indeed you know and your physics is proving that all life is connected.  Each person who falls affects the whole and each person that finds their way back to Love and the frequency of Light lifts all of creation up with them.

So pat yourselves on the back Dear Ones, for your willingness and determination to be all that you came to be and for being the essences of love that you are.  For without those of you who are walking consciously on this earth right now there would not be the invitation to ascension.  It is those of you who walk in the Love Light that are lifting all of creation into the higher frequencies that bring you closer to Creator – to love. And so it is our delight to be here offering this understanding, offering our vibrations to you so that you may ascend even higher into the realms of love. And so, Beloveds, we say to you to be love in every instance. That is to be in love with the self.

To do what is right for you and to see in all that is around you, the creation that you call life. Look at it with eyes wide open and a heart that is willing to see the truth. Who are you really? Are you angry? Are you love? Are you indifferent? All that you are is pure love. It has different appearances and it has a different resonance but it is all love. All experiences are leading you to where you have chosen to be. Love all of it. Whether it looks good or bad is only a judgment of the ego mind. In truth it is all pure love and it is a grand opportunity to be whole.

You are fixing the lost pieces that were left behind from past lives and past experiences in the current incarnation. As you heal all those pieces you walk more fully in the Light. As you walk more fully in the Light you become more reflective of who you truly are on the other side of the veil. When you are walking as true spirit you are pure, radiant love - each with your own personality still but in the vibration of love. You know what it is and you know who you are in that vibration because you have been there many times. You reside there between incarnations, awaiting the next lesson for the soul.

You walk there reconnecting with lost loved ones and remembering who you truly are. Then you agree to forget and become human again. This is all changing now. In this new era of Love that the earth is now moving into, you will not have so much forgetting. You will not need to forget as much as you have in the past. Therefore you will bring more of the love that is you into the human incarnation and this is what will make the earth such a beautiful place to be. This is what brings the thousands of years of peace. For as you find your way back to your true nature, which is love, then your earthly experience will be lighter.

It will be more joyful and playful. This is part of the essence of who you are in truth and with the healing that has been done on earth and with the ascension, you will have a different experience on this planet from this time forward. It will still be a school but the lessons will not be so dense and painful. There will be less recovery time required after the lifetime has ended because the journey will not be so difficult. What a delight that is and it makes us happy to bring this news.

No longer will there be suffering on earth in the way there has been in the past. Even for those who do not choose to ascend at this time, the density on earth will never fall as far as it did for those of you who have incarnated here many, many times. And so it is time to celebrate. It is time to commend yourselves for your commitment to the Light and the rewards that it brings. Life will keep getting better and better. Love will grow deeper and deeper and bliss will be yours.

You have endured much Dear Ones. It has been a long and arduous journey out of the darkness. The rewards are deserved and the love that you will feel for each other and all life will grow to the point that you may feel at times that you cannot contain it all. But we say to you, your hearts are able to hold so much love. It is just that you have not been in the vibration of love like you are now. It is all new. The physical body must learn to resonate at the level of love that is now available on your planet.

Your bodies are learning to walk in love instead of fear. They are a bit timid but the heart is leading now. The heart is assuring the physical body that it is OK. The heart is all knowing and the body will catch up. The more you open to the Light of Love the more the body will be willing to come along. It will feel good and the body will soon recognize that this is even better than what is was used to. It will learn to hold as much Light as it possibly can so that it can experience more and more of this great feeling that is the Love of Creator. Oh, it is delightful to behold and it is all your creation Dear Ones. You have delivered this to yourselves.

The second coming has arrived and it is you awakening to you. It is was within you all the time – so close you could not see it. We say to you now to look in the mirror and say hello to love. You have saved yourselves. You have brought yourselves out of the depths of darkness into the Light. What awaits is magical beyond anything you have ever imagined. Be in love so that you will be prepared. Only those who can hold the Light of Creator within their hearts may step into the Light. That is not out of punishment or any hierarchy. It is your choice. Only those who resonate in harmony with the Light can stand before the Light of Love.

It is a vibration so pure and strong that you must be prepared. Those who are walking this earthly journey in intent and in love are the ones who will be prepared to hold that Light within their hearts. Be the beacon that you are and your heart Light will illumine all those around you. We love you beyond measure for we see before us the Kings and Queens of the Light. We see before us Creator's great reflection. You are the Divine. You are Love. You are our brethren. Feel us dance upon your soul and remember. We are One. And so it is.

# Essay Seventy-seven - LIFE IN THE HIGHER REALMS

Greetings Beloveds. Greetings from the Love and Light of the Creator. Greetings from the Great Central Sun as we come before you this day honored to stand before those who read these words. And we say to you Dear Ones, you are the sacred souls who have chosen ascension at this time. You are the brave ones who are willing to step out of the old paradigm and walk into the new world of Light. And it is to you we speak this day. We have asked our dear Rashana to bring forward the topic for this day by stating the title of this essay.

And we would say she has chosen well. For indeed, what is it to live in the higher realms so to speak? She knows, for, in many ways, she is doing it. It is to live in a place of faith and trust that all that is required in your life will find its way to you. It is to live in the faith that, whatever happens in your life, it is leading to something that serves your highest good. It is to live day to day, moment to moment in the trust that all is unfolding according to Divine Plan. It is to live knowing that all you need do is be willing to walk a life of service and great joy and delight will be yours. It is the knowing that one must heal in order to find their way back to the fullness of who they are.

It is the willingness to take responsibility for everything in one's life. Life in the higher realms is a life where each person is honored for who they are. It is a world where no person is discriminated against for how they look, how they dress, what they do, where they come from or who their parents are. It is a world where each person is worthy of care. It is a world where each person is raised to believe in themselves and step into the power of who they are as human. It is a world where invention is freely offered to expand the world and to ensure longevity and survival without destruction.

It is a world where all of nature is respected and honored. It is a world where you will not have forgotten your origins. It is a place where you know of which you came and where it is easy to love. It is a world where the only pain that must be endured is pain by choice of learning. It is a world where earth is pristine and everything is created from beauty. It is a world where every soul is worthy because of their presence in the world, understanding the value of all. It is a world of unity, where creation comes from the heart and the mind is allowed to expand. It is a world where nature leads the way to health and prosperity. It is your world Dear Ones. It is a world that you create.

Life in the higher dimensions is a life where you know that you are creating your world and so you make it beautiful and full of love and joy. It is a world where you honor yourself and that honor then befalls every person you encounter. It is a world where the language is formal, for you understand the power of words. It is a world where all one's needs are provided for, for lack is a false concept of the mind. The higher dimensional living is a life where love of mankind is for all and not only those who can serve you in some way.

It is a world of willingness to be of service to the all, with no hesitation, to what is best for the entire village and not for only yourself or your family. So much is different in the higher realms. Love is pure and unconditional. It is a world where sacrifice is unheard of because one gives freely from the heart. It is your world turned upside down.

Many think of the dimensions as layers. And so, if you were to look down that would be the third dimension and looking up would be the fourth. And so if you turned your world upside down you would be in heaven, so to speak. This is what the higher dimension is like. It is like living in heaven. Only it is you who are creating that heaven. That is why the scribes of the past have talked of creating heaven on earth. That is where you are now Beloveds in your journey of ascension. As you vibrate at the higher levels of resonance, you create a life that is in harmony with who you are.

When you resist your growth and the truth of what it is to be a creator, then you repeat the patterns of the past and create much hardship. It is difficult for our scribe Rashana to watch her loved ones suffering in this vortex of creation when what is being created is painful. And yet she knows that, beyond being an example of what can be, there is nothing she can do to change it. She speaks her knowing when she can but it cannot be forced.

Each soul must come to its own conclusions about what life is and the choices that they make. Each soul must come to its own understanding, through its own process of growth, as to the way of the world. It is a huge dichotomy now between those who are finding their way into the new way of being and those who are holding on to the past. All you can do is offer your love and be an example of love in this world. When you see others suffering, send them your love. Love them free of their pain if you can.

Beloveds, you are going to see more and more discrimination in the world as the earth shifts into two dimensions at one time. Those of you who are choosing to rise up into ascension will be living different lives than those who are staying in the third dimensional world. This will continue to expand, creating a great divide between the levels of living and the appearances of what life is. It is the only way that this can happen without a great loss of lives.

It is the way that ascension is offered this time as souls freely choose their destiny. We understand that the human condition is what is causing some to forget and stay behind, but we say to you, each soul has had the same support from the higher soul and the Guides who watch over them. Each soul has been given equal opportunity to step into the Light at this time. We cannot affect the outcome of their decisions. Nor can you.

You have only to care for yourselves at this point in time Dear ones. Make the choices that support your own personal growth. For life in the higher dimensions is upon you. Many of you are feeling it. Many of you are seeing your life as synchronistic and free flowing. The joy is your indicator. And so Beloveds, we commend you for your place on this journey back to the Light. Have compassion for all and choose wisely in your own life. Step out of fear and into your heart's desire.

That is what leads you to your own true destiny in these times of great transition. The journey has been long but the rewards are many. Stay in the love Light of your own true divine spark and all will unfold with grace and ease. Be a warrior of the Light. Stand strong in your own knowing of your journey. Do not falter in the belief that you are the creator of your own experience on this home planet of yours. Gaia wants to take you with her. Hold on and enjoy the ride. As you rise up into the heavens we await you with open arms. And so it is.

# Essay Seventy-eight - LOVING INTO THE LIGHT

Greetings from the great central sun as we come before you in love and joy. And we say to you Beloveds, this is the time of great change. This is the time that your earth is moving into a whole new dimension. As such, you are having to expand and grow along with her. To resist is to cause much hardship for yourself. We know that we repeat this over and over, have you grasped it yet?

Have you been doing your healing work and releasing the patterns that hold you back from your magnificence? Many of you have and many more have not. And so, when you find that your lives are seemingly falling apart and nothing is going the way you think it should be, then you know there is more to do. It is a choice Beloveds, and the choice is yours as always.

And so this day we would like to talk to you about what it is to be Loving into the Light. That is to say, what it is to be loving from the place of a whole and healed individual. For we say to you, that loving from that place is different from how humans have loved in the past. For in the past your love was needy. Loving from a place of wholeness has no neediness to it. It is strong and pure and it is love in its own right. That is, it is love for the sake of love, not love for the sake of protection or worthiness or need. Loving in the Light comes only after you are fully loving yourself.

Once you are in that place of being in love with yourself then you can accept others exactly as they are. You step into a place of awareness that each person is doing the best they can and if they are mirroring anything to you that does not look appealing, you understand that you have some work to do, not the other person. So, being in love in this way is much easier, for it does not expect others to behave in a certain way and be this or that or look like this or that.

You accept and allow people to be in your life who resonate with you. And when you are within such harmony within yourself there is no need to change anything. You accept what is and so you accept what the people in your life are reflecting to you. When you are full of love for the self what do you think they will be reflecting to you? Love of course. They are mirroring as always.

Beloveds, we wish you to know you are the miracles of the 21st century. You have changed the world – indeed the universe. You have walked into this time of the great shift with grace and determination. This is to be rewarded. You will find that, as you move more and more into the understanding of these times, that you are living a very different life than you did a few decades ago. This is relating not only to the advancements in technology, but to the human species as well. It is as if the technology is a reflection of who humanity is.

You are more connected to the ethers now than ever before. That is no coincidence. It is the way you are living. Those who spend a lot of time together and who are resonant with each other are finding that they can communicate intuitively without saying a world. Words are still used for the comfort of doing so, but the feelings are exchanged in mutual understanding. This is happening more and more for many people. You will see many such changes as the earth moves into the fourth dimensional reality. Trust your intuitive knowings, for they are correct. Learn to believe in yourself when you have a whim and find that you were correct. Pay attention to these unfoldings.

And so Beloveds, we delight in this coming together. We delight in the time that we have together to share our energies and intertwine in the ethers. This is indeed a great way of coming to learn and understand what life is moving into. By sharing with you this way you are coming to feel the energies behind the words and to feel the intentions of the messages. This is good. This is leading you to be more intuitive in your everyday activities and to have more faith in your way of being in this world. This is just the beginning Dear Ones. Step onto the train and enjoy the ride. You are on the expressway to the heavens. And so it is.

# Essay Seventy-nine - YOUR HEART'S DESIRE

Greetings Beloveds, it is our great privilege to be here with you – interacting with humans at this time in your evolution. You are souls of great Light who have come willingly to bless the earth with the grace of your presence. And it is our delight to tell you how magnificent you are. We are the ones who are honored to be here with you, sending our love tones down upon you and interacting with the dear souls who are Love on this earth. And we say to you Beloveds, it is your Light that shines so brightly that calls so many Beings from diverse universes to the earth at this time. It is your beautiful, soul resonance that calls us to be here with you this day.

For you see, the more you shine, the easier life becomes. And the more who see your Light and choose ascension for themselves, the more Light you shed into the world and the less darkness there is. This is the beautiful way between choosing the Light and staying in the dark. It is always the Light that illuminates the dark and not the other way around. So the more Light there is, the less darkness. The darkness cannot find its way through the Light without being illumined. That is why, when you bring your past wounds up to the surface, you bring healing to it.

You illuminate it and so it can no longer vibrate as darkness. And so it is that as each one of you finds your way into the fullness of your soul expression at this time, you become more Light. Being more Light in the world, you help all of humanity ascend into the fourth and fifth dimension with the love essence – the love rays that you are. Love and Light are synonymous Dear Ones. The Light reflects Love of All That Is and the Love shines forth as Light. So it is no wonder that so many of your way-showers are signing off with the little adage, in Love and Light. They know and have for some years now, the truth in those few words. In Love and Light is peace and joy and harmony and grace. In Love and Light is the new earth. And on this new earth your love Light shines brilliantly.

And so we wish to talk to you today about being all that you are. We would like to talk to you about being every little thing that you could ever want to be. What would your heart's desire be if you were living your life fully the way you would dream it to be? What would your life look like? It is important to think of every little thing in your life and how it would look. Where would you live? What part of the world would make you happy? Why would you be happy living there? What would you be doing with your days? Who would you be with? Where would you go? Who would you hang out with? What would you do to express your soul's mission every day? Consider all of this so that you can find your way.

You cannot find your way to your heart's desire without knowing what it is. You may be focusing on only pieces of the picture and so it cannot come together for you as one complete package. You must hold in your awareness the complete picture with all the pieces in place. Every little detail should be considered. Then you connect with the feeling of your life when you are living that way and wait for that experience to come.

The picture may not come just as you saw it but the feeling should be at least what you imagined. It will very likely be even more wonderful than you imagined it would be. How fabulous! We don't think any of you will be complaining about that. It is the focusing on what you do not want that brings about the complaints. So, discover what your heart's desire is and focus on that.

For many eons of time humans have lived lives full of despair to the point that many would not even dream of what they wanted. They felt it was too painful to have all these dreams knowing they would never come true. Well they were right. Your dreams will never come true if you do not believe that it is possible for them to come true. We give you a 100% guarantee on that one. Many are still afraid. They have not realized that you are in new times where you can create your dreams. Or they are not willing to take the action that would see their dreams come true.

This is a sad outcome Dear Ones, for this is a great opportunity to move forward in your soul evolution. Hold onto the past and your soul will become stagnant. Your energy will not flow and you will have to make a change because your body will stop functioning properly. When you slow down and halt the energy of your soul, which is the life force within your body, then the body begins to weaken. The outcome will show you in some way the connection. The body has expression which has been identified by many. We would say to you to look at the symbolic action or non-action that your body is telling you.

For example, this morning our channel Rashana worked with someone who can't drive right now because the body is not able. This person can walk with a cane but not drive. So, one of the questions was related to when this person would be able to drive again. The answer was as soon as she started walking in the fullness of her soul. She had stalled her soul, not expressing her truth in her life, and so the body became stalled as well, which then expressed itself in her immobility of not being able to walk without a cane or drive a car. She had stopped everything. The answer to when she could drive a car again was when she allowed herself to move forward in her life.

This is how it works Dear Ones.  If you do not go willingly into the soul expression that you came to be, then the body will respond in a way that will lead you back to that truth.  The choice is yours but we wish you to know that the reason that these things happen is because your soul wants to grow and expand at this time.  The earth has expanded already and to be able to walk upon her in harmony and peace you must be in resonance.  To resist this is what causes despair at this time.

So, your heart's desire is your soul's desire.  What is it?  Explore that for a few days.  What does your heart truly desire?  Does it want to burst free out of your life and be someone totally new?  Hooray.  Let it happen.  It may not shift overnight but little steps will at least let your soul know that you are listening and you are willing.  Does your soul want to leave the city and live in a small community with a garden in the back yard?  Make it happen.  Do not let false beliefs keep you cemented to the city if this is your desire.

The only thing that will hold you back will be false beliefs.  I cannot leave my job.  False.  Why not trust that something far better awaits you?  My children will miss their friends.  Perhaps so, but they will make new friends who may be even better than the ones they have now.  My wife will not want to go.  Share the dream.  Bring her into the dream.  Speak of all the possibility the move will bring.  Every excuse is just that.  There is a way if you desire it.  If it is your soul's desire, the way has already been laid out.  You just need to step into it.

The problem is that you cannot see the path before you and so you hesitate.  But, with each step you take, the path is created.  It is all your doing.  If you start down the path and all is going well and suddenly things take a turn for the worse, we would say that you lost your faith and so you created something from your past that felt more comfortable than the uncertain journey of creating as you go. However, if you take step after step, confident each time that it is leading you to your heart's desire, the road just becomes more and more luminous, as if paved with gold.

That is the way of the new world that you are living in. Try it with something little. Believe that some little thing that you desire is on its way to you and experience it for yourself. Perfect it with the small things before moving on to the big things. We wish joy and happiness for you. Hardship can come when people take the steps without the true faith, so test yourself to see where you are with your faith. But follow your heart's desires and know that it will lead you to your bliss.

We love you so. We are always at your side. And so it is.

# Essay Eighty - FREEDOM

And so it is Beloveds that we are going to speak today of freedom. We wish you to know that you are free to make choices in your lives and do things differently than you have in the past. You are free to step out of your own box that you created for yourself. You built it, so you have every right to tear it down. And do not start over! No more boxes. Crush them. Stomp on them and have fun doing it, for it is time to release all the boxes that would put you in categories of how you must live your lives.

You are free as well to make any choices that you would like. But, we see one major block that keeps you from stepping out of your boxes and doing whatever you wish. Can you guess what that would be? Can you see what keeps you confined to your self-created boxes? It is your concern about the opinions of others. How can you be free to be who you are when you are worried about what someone else might think about the new you? As long as you hang onto that concern, you are trapped. You are confined within the judgment of others (which, as you should know by now, is a judgment of yourself).

So, take a look at the beliefs that built the walls of your box. Let us say you are feeling particularly happy today. Would you express that happiness by dancing down the middle of the street? We think not, even though it might be something that you feel like doing because you are having such a great day. One brick in the wall. Let us say that you just got a raise. Would you walk out of the boss' office doing your happy dance?

No, because the norms say that you should keep it a secret and others shouldn't know because then they will be jealous. Another brick in the wall. All these things are how you keep yourselves confined to your socially inflicted prison. Step out Dear Ones. Dare to do something unconventional and see what happens. Pay attention to the bricks that have built your walls. You cannot break free of the box if you don't even know what the box is made of.

Some of your parameters of behavior are so deeply entrenched within your psyche that you don't even know that they are there. And yet, the more you begin to look and explore, the more you will see. The more you decide that you are choosing to be free in this life and live by your own set of standards and not the standards of others who do not even know you, the more you find freedom. Life will become more and more joyous. And we say as well, in these times of higher resonance that you are finding it more and more difficult to do what is not in harmony with who you are.

So find out what is keeping you in that box. Slowly start to remove the bricks and eventually you will find that there are no walls. For a while you may still stay within the imaginary walls, not fully trusting that you are free. You might step your foot outside of the box and then pull it back in very quickly in case someone sees it. Over time you will become more and more comfortable living within your own sovereign self, your own state of being in this world. You will come to trust in yourself enough to know that, by choosing to do only what is in harmony with who you are, that you are becoming stronger and attracting to you those who are ready to live the same way.

You will find yourself surrounded by new people – people who are also living outside the box. You will find your new family and together you will be collectively free. This is the way of the new earth Dear Ones. This is what you are moving into. Do not be afraid to be among the first to show how this is done. It is what you came for. It is because you hold such Light that you can be the beacon for all. Be not afraid of stepping into your own truth and out of the false paradigm that has kept you restricted for so long. We are here with you. We are watching over you and cheering you on. When others condemn your actions, know that your A team is here cheering you on and saying "Yes"!

We love you Dear Ones and we wish the very best for you in this human incarnation. It is by being brave enough to walk in your own truth and no one else's that you will find your way to peace. There is no peace in living your life according to someone else's standards. You know who you are. Live your life accordingly and watch the universe open up to you. For when you are walking in your truth – walking in the fullness of you – the very beautiful expression of life that you created in the higher realms can then become reality for you.

 It is as if you are finally stepping through the veil into the life that you envisioned for yourself long ago at the time of your conception. As soon as you step out of the 'have to' that others put upon you and into the 'I shall do what resonates with me', you walk into the fullness of what you have come here to be. It is beautiful to watch this happen Beloveds. It is beautiful for us to witness you as you walk this path back to your glory.

For we see the joy and happiness that comes from this full expression. We see the great burden that is released from your shoulders as you honor you and do what is in your truth, no longer carrying all the 'have to's and 'should be's that have been bestowed upon you by dysfunctional social norms. Such a deep and heavy weight that is. It is as if you can hardly stay on the ground once you release that and allow yourself to walk in the truth of who you are.

We wish you to know that, as you do this, you are showing others how it is done. You are giving permission for others to respond to life in the same way. You are freeing up society as you free up yourself. You are changing the world by changing yourself. It is the only way that it happens and it is beautiful. We love to see humans walking in the glory of who they are with no apology. You are magnificent. Recognize that within yourself and know, in that radiant truth that you are, you deserve to shine your Light your way. No one else can tell you how to be in this world. They do not know you. You know you.

Claim your right to be whole and walk in the strong knowing that it is OK just to be you. There is no need to be like anyone else, or like what someone else likes, or think like others think. What would be the good of that? The world is pretty boring when there is no truthful expression. Be who you are. The world needs you in the truth of who you are. We do not need clones. We do not need everyone accepting the same norms in life. Diversity is vitality. Embrace all ways of life, all beings, all choices and you will see the world change.

Oh we know you could say, how could I embrace a murderer? And we say to you, the sooner you embrace those who murder and offer them compassion, the sooner there will be no more murders upon this planet. That which you condemn seems to perpetuate does it not? You have been condemning murders forever. Is there still murder? Oh yes. So obviously that way is not working. Why not try loving every expression of life? When you do, then all expression becomes love. That is the way of it. It is so simple that most cannot see it. Many are not ready to be it. But some of you are. And to those of you we say, shine your love Light strong, for when you do, you are illuminating all those who struggle as well.

You cannot trick yourself into being so loving. It must be sincere and come from a full heart space of acceptance. So do not fool yourselves into thinking you are loving of all if you are not. You are just fooling yourself and then not stepping into the truth. Where you have judgment, look within. Where is that judgment within yourself? Oh you could say, but I am not a murderer. So, look within and ask what that murderer represents to you? Where do you end the life of yourself? Where do you cut yourself off from life? That is the mirror that you are seeing.

And so we leave you with this untitled message. Did we jump all over the place? Perhaps. Was it worthy? We believe so. It was worthy of some inquiry if nothing else. And so we leave you with our encouragement to tear down the walls of perception and step out of the box that tries to claim who you are. Each day is a new day and each day can be a new creation of you. You can be someone totally different each day if you choose. No boxes and no parameters. And so it is Beloveds. And so it is.

# Essay Eighty-one - LIGHTWORKER

And so it is Beloved Beings of the Light that we stand before you once again and we say to you, it is our great honor to be here witnessing who you are on this earth. We see you. We love you. We adore you for all that you are doing to be pure love on this earth. These are challenging times for many and yet you stand strong in your faith that all is well in the world. And you will be rewarded for that faith. Mother Earth feels you and she loves you. As such, she will protect you and make sure that you are cared for.

For those of you who offer her your loving support, she will return that support to you. When you see severe weather patterns, it is not that she is punishing anyone - not at all. It is that these patterns are called to energetic centers that, in a way, magnetize them with the overall consciousness of the area. That is the way of it with most of your storms and weather patterns on this planet. Some of the weather is manipulated but that is another matter altogether that we will not discuss here.

And so Beloveds, today we would like to talk to you about your roles as Lightworkers upon this earth. Those who are called to read these words are those who are awakening to the fact that they are Lightworkers on this earth. And what does that mean? It means that you are open to ideas that perhaps do not resonate with everyone around you. It means that you have an understanding of what is beyond the physical plane and an acceptance that life holds much more than is visible with the physical senses.

You no doubt are highly intuitive and opening up more and more to those abilities. That is what it is to be a Light worker. Also it is to be keenly aware that you have come to be of service to the Light. Yours is a life where you are supporting others and have a deep willingness to make the world a better place. And we say, to most of you, that is accomplished just by being here. For most of you, your hearts are resonating such deep love that you are changing the planet just by being you. How wonderful that is.

And yet, you desire to do more, to be of greater service. This is how you know that you are a Lightworker. There are more and more of you waking up to the truth at this time and we say, good. We need you. The earth needs you. Those who have been the first to walk in the knowing of what we speak need you. It is time. It is time to stop hiding from the inner truth that you are resisting because it does not fit with the social norms.

Those norms need to change and you have come to be a part of that change, so step into it Dear Ones. Stop hiding from yourselves and spread your Light into the world. The world cannot change if no one is willing to be different. Your lives will not change if you are not willing to live differently. Your relationships will not change if you are not willing to change your relationships. There is so much fear of what others will think that keeps you minimized and small. It is time to expand and grow.

Oh we wish you could see how beautiful you are. We wish you could see your radiant Light that shines up into the heavens. We sit here and we look down and wonder how you could ever doubt yourselves. We see the great, radiant kings and queens who held such regal positions in times past acting so small at this time. Do not allow others to diminish you. If you know that you have a great gift to offer the world, step into it and believe in it. Others will not see it until you see it within yourself. Remember, all the world is a mirror.

When you believe that others will accept what you do and see it as worthy, then that will be the truth of it. What are you afraid of? We see so many of you afraid to step into your power? Is it the responsibility? Is it living up to it all the time? We say to you, when you are doing what you love and what comes to you so naturally and what you have wanted for so long, it does not feel like a burden. So let go of the fear of the responsibility. And living up to it is easy. It is who you truly are so it is no challenge to stay in the truth of it. Consider this deeply. Let yourselves explore these issues so that you can walk through the hesitation and just be.

Think of people that you have seen or know who do accept all that they are and who stay true to themselves and who express who they are to the world. What do you admire about them? What are they showing you? Does it look difficult or desirable to be living the way they do? This too will lead you to the place of greater understanding around this. No one is going to walk up to you and say hey, you're fabulous unless you believe it about yourself. And when that does happen, you are showing that person how fabulous they are! If they did not recognize it within themselves they would not see it in you. It is a beautiful give and receive rhythm that is created.

Today we would like you to list ten fabulous things about you. Then we would like you to share that list with some of your friends. You are not asking for validation from them. Your worth does not come from outside of you. You are going to ask your friends to have a list as well. As each of you reads your list, you are to affirm for each other that you have those qualities. This activity is to get you over the idea that you cannot brag about all your great qualities.

This has been taught to most of you by your society. It keeps you diminished and we are ready to see you expand. So, share your best qualities and hear them affirmed by your friends so that you can accept them more within yourself as truth. That is the purpose of this activity. Have fun with it. Have a 'pumped up' party where you praise each other. Do not make mockery of it, for that will diminish the purpose of you truthfully believing these qualities about yourself. So make that clear, it is not a mockery. It is like a rite of passage, a passage into believing in yourself. Write your list today and accept the wonder of you. And so it is.

# Essay Eighty-two - CELEBRATE

And so it is Beloveds that we greet you from the Great Central Sun. We greet you from the Love and Light of the Creator and we say to you Dear Ones, all is well. The world is going to stay. Many are still waiting for doom and gloom and we say to you, those predictions are not going to happen. Your world is now growing into a planet of pure love. Oh this will not happen overnight, but it is happening none the less. And so it is our delight to tell you that, from our perspective, life just keeps getting better and better for you.

You have lived through a time on the earth that will never happen again. This is quite incredible since history has a habit of repeating itself. But, this marker that you have moved through is one that takes you out of the pattern of repeating the past. You have now stepped into a new reality that could not possibly manifest the same patterns of long ago. And so celebrate. Celebrate each day as you awaken. Say hallelujah, this is a new world I am living in today. Then ask what you would like this world to look like? What will I create this day knowing that anything I desire is mine to create.

Say yes to life as you see more and more wonderful things happening. Celebrate the little things that show you that your life is changing. Every little thing that is a positive step toward your dreams, celebrate it. That will bring more and more things for you to celebrate. The mere fact that you awaken is reason enough to celebrate but there is so much more. Do you see where your life is opening up to your desires? Do you see the rewards of your healing work? Each day that you get through in joy is reason to celebrate. Then there is more joy.

And so Beloveds, living on this new earth is a magnificent gift. You are living in the most incredible time for you are creating this new earth with every day. Because you are not repeating history then you are creating the future. That is the way of it now. So keep your thoughts pure and positive so that you can create a life of bliss and joy. Keep your mind in conscious creation during the day. If you find your thoughts wandering to creations that you do not choose to experience, change them quickly into something else. Very often old patterns come up to be released and they mull around in the mind for a while. By releasing them you then make room for the beautiful thoughts that will create the life you are about to live.

All your tomorrows are created today. It is each thought you have that is creating your tomorrow. That is why it is vital to stay in the moment. When you are living in the moment, most often it is an easy and joyful place to be. So the more you stay there the more ease you are creating. And as you do this habitually, you will come to find that life just flows and you begin to trust that more and more as it does. It becomes easier to trust in the rewards that come into your life and to know that ease and grace is your way of existing. The longer you stay in those thoughts the greater delight will be your experience.

We would invite you as well to consider who you surround yourself with. Do they resonate with the life that you are choosing for yourself, or do they drag you down into despair and lack of faith in your ability to create a joyful life? If so, then you must work harder to maintain your level of knowing that life is beautiful. So consider this in your choices through the day. If you believe that you can be surrounded by people who resonate with your beliefs and can step into the creations that you are choosing for yourself, then you will find those people being attracted to you.

We are not asking you to put people down or to reject them, but to use discernment in your decisions so that you stay in resonance with your highest choices. Those who use this discernment are those who love themselves so much that they will look after their creations this way and look after their energy field in this way. As long as you are coming from a place of love in your decisions, the outcome will be beneficial. You may find that some friends simply drift away and it is best to let that happen, for it usually means that your time to learn from each other has ended and something new is coming for each of you.

This again becomes a matter of trusting the universe or your oversoul to lead you to the highest and best choices for your life at that time. So these are the changes that will continue to happen quite a lot in these times. As the energy of the earth shifts as much as it has, humans are at different levels of understanding and working with this. Because of that, there are many changes that are happening in relationships and it is best to know that each change is for the best for all.

That is why we tell you all is well. Some of you mourn what has changed even though, at some deep level, you know it is for the best. The attachment to the past and the hesitation to move into the new you is what causes this mourning. For many it is the fear of moving forward. It does mean more responsibility because as you move forward, so to speak, you are stepping into the higher power of who you are. As you do this you become afraid of your brilliance. It is time to stop hiding beloveds. Now is the time to be radiant Light.

The world needs you and you need the radiant you. You have come here for this. You do not want to have to start over in another lifetime. Do it now. It will be joyful once you get the hang of it. It is time to stop wading at the edge of the beach and just jump right in. Once in, the water is always more welcoming than you thought. You will not get sucked in by the undercurrent, unless of course that is your expectation! You are the creators after all. Decide how brilliant you are and then step into it Dear Ones. We are here waiting and watching.

There are only fourteen more transmissions in this compilation of essays. Our scribe Rashana is asking us for a taste of what is to come after this. We will say to you that the messages will become deeper. They will carry a different resonance – one that will take you much deeper into the truth of who you are. We will consider offering a few of these in the days to come. In the meantime know that these transmissions, if used consciously, will change your lives and prepare you for living in these times. They are here as guidance for living on the new earth.

For this planet you call home is not the same planet she was last year. December 21, 2012 was a shift into the new earth and so here you are. Do you feel it? Do you recognize that things have changed? If not, please follow our guidance so that you will come to be in resonance with what is. This is the greatest opportunity that has ever been given humanity to shift into an ascended being while incarnate upon this earth. We do not want you to miss it and that is the reason for our repetitive messages and guidance on moving into the shifts and changes of the fourth dimension. We offer our love in that guidance. And so it is.

# Essay Eighty-three - TODAY WAS CREATED YESTERDAY

And so it is Beloveds that we come before you once again. And once again we say to you that this is the time of your life. Do you realize that the times you are in have never been experienced before on this planet? That is to say, the energy that you are currently residing is entirely new for your planet. Of course you could say that every day is new and it is. And yet, the energy has been the same energy going round and round for eons of time. Now you are in something different.

You are living in a higher state of resonance. Your earth is changing right under your feet and therefore you must change as well. For every piece of the microcosm impacts the macrocosm. When one person in a family changes the entire family must change. Such is the way with humans living on the earth at this time. The earth has shifted into a higher level of resonance and therefore you must shift as well. That is the way of it. And it is of great benefit to you because Mother Earth is doing all the work for you. Your earthly mother has done all the work by making the shift herself so that you can simply lift up with her.

By changing her resonance field, you, living in that field, are changing as well. What a great mother she is. And you can be good children by willingly walking into the loving grace that is available to you now. We say this with some jest. There is no such thing as good and bad. There just is. And yet we say to you, many of you still judge your lives as good or bad. And we would say to you, if you would consider your life as bad, it is because you are still believing old thoughts and still repeating the beliefs of the past which is then creating your todays. Today was created yesterday and the day before that and so on back in time. As we have said, the more good thoughts you have today, the better life will be tomorrow.

It has never been easier once you get the hang of it. And it has never been harder if you do not get the hang of it. The reason is, as we have said, you are manifesting much faster today than before. So, you are seeing the results of your thoughts within a matter of a few days most often. Some things of course have been years or months in the making, but, for many of you, you can have a thought today and see the manifestation of that thought tomorrow. If it is not happy thoughts you are having, well, life is probably not looking so joyous. So pay attention Dear Ones. We are wishing a life of bliss for all of you.

Find your joy for tomorrow by being in joy today. Find more of what you desire tomorrow by being grateful for what you have today. Find more love in your life tomorrow by loving yourself more today. This is the way of it and it is grand indeed. And your dear earthly mother has led you here. She had no choice but to step up the game so to speak. It was her destiny to ascend. It is yours as well if you will join her.

Many will choose to leave the planet instead. They are weary of the journey and ready for something new. That is perfect for their soul plan. And yet, for many of you who are choosing to stay, you are doing so for the lessons that you can garner by being here. You can get those lessons slowly and live a life that does not hold much joy, or you can embrace a life of change and healing and walk into your joy. It is your decision Dear Ones.

Decide which life is best for you at this time and then use the messages in this book to help you get there. We are waiting for you in the fifth dimension which is not that far from where you are now. Awaken to the possibilities of life. Imagine all the love and joy that you can stand and then call it your life. Think big Dear Ones and then step into that vision. It is you creating life. Surround yourself with your vision. Allow it to be your reality. And so it is.

# Essay Eighty-four - WHAT ARE YOUR DREAMS?

And so it is, Beloveds, our deep honor to come before you this day and we say to you that this session is being received at a monumental time upon the earth. For the date this day is December 10, 2012. And we say to you that we recognize that all of you who are reading this are reading after this time and yet we say to you, our messages are synched into the time when you will be reading. We also say to you that this day of December 10, 2012 is such a powerful time because it is leading into this time where all of humanity is shifting.

Certainly all those who are willing are shifting into the brilliant Light that is the earth after the shift – after the magical date of December 21, 2012. For many of you we recognize that you have not found one day to be any different from another. And yet, to those who would understand, we would say that who you are has shifted. Who you are has stepped into another deep level of resonance with All That Is. And so we are delighted to address you this day.

Our intention is to help you ascend, for once you do you will no longer need the support of anything outside of yourself. You will have full understanding – full awareness of what is. You will have your soul's mission – your soul's journey – but your understanding will be expanded to a point where you will be able to create for yourself and you will be able to touch into the All That Is – the wisdom that is available to all in 'the field'. It will all be yours to access. And so you will no longer need the outside support.

And so the support that we are offering at this time is to help you – to elevate you to the level of energetic vibration that you may resonate higher. And that has been our intention through all these essays. So here we are with only eleven days left to complete the essay quota for this book. Eighty-four transmissions from The Council of Nine to date. And with each transmission the energy has resonated at a higher level. As you read them your energy is being magnified. And so we are delighted to be here this day to bring this information forward to you and to say to you, Beloveds, hang onto your hats.

For what is unfolding on the earth at this time is so joyfully delightful. Be prepared for all your dreams to come true. What would your dreams be if that were possible? Many of you do not even know what your dreams would be. And so we say to you Beloveds, let your imaginations go. Allow yourself to fall into the space of your heart and see your dreams that are lying there. You cannot create them if you do not know what they are. And so discover your dreams when you allow your imagination to fall into the possibility of absolutely anything. What would your dreams be in that space? Do not allow any restrictions.

Do not allow the mental deceit of the mind to keep you from stepping into all of the possibilities that are available to you as a human. And now, more than ever before, everything is possible. And so take this day to dream. Take this day to expand. Take this day to imagine what you are going to create for yourself in this new dimension in which you are currently residing. Oh, it may or may not feel new to you but we say to you that it is. There is no doubt whatsoever that it is. It is only your own choosing that is making it feel new and magnificent or just another day.

And again we say to you, if it feels like just another day then be aware of your thoughts all day long. If your thoughts all day long are creating just another day, the same as yesterday, by going over all the old patterns, all the old beliefs, all the unbeneficial self-talk, all the worries, the concerns, the beliefs that things are not going well, that things are falling apart, then of course, that is what you are going to create. And so it is about learning – having the strength and the courage to unlearn that way of being – to be strong and determined enough to have something new in your life, something different.

This is where we say to you that it does not come with ease Dear One. It takes work, it takes dedication, it takes your determination. It takes your effort to turn it around. And so if you are one who is reading this who feels despair in your life then you must grab the bull by the horns, so to speak, and have the determination to change it. You must have the determination to be aware of your thoughts in every moment.

And when they are leading you into despair, turn them around and see the Light. Turn them around and know that there is love and joy available to you if you will believe it. Turn it around and know that is fear that is creating this. Then ask, what would love look like? Love would be a day that is supported. It would be a life where you know that everything you need is provided for you. It would be a life where everything simply falls into place. It would be a life where you would follow your heart yearning, not knowing how to get there, but trusting that the universe knows how to get you there.

So again, we take you back to discovering what you would dream – what your heart yearning truly is if you could dream - if you would allow yourself to go there. Find that dream and then believe it's possible. You don't have to create it, you just have to believe it's possible and the universe will bring it to you. This is the trick Dear One. This is what needs to be learned. Many of you think you need to know *how* it will happen and in your mind you cannot fathom that and so you don't believe it's possible.

And so we would like you to learn a new method. That is to believe and know that it is possible, because you couldn't imagine it if it wasn't part of your reality. If you can imagine it, it is part of your reality. And so if you can imagine it, then the universe has a way of providing it for you. All you have to do is believe it is possible. That's it Beloveds. Every day just believe it's possible. Every day catch all the negative thoughts and turn them around into what you truly desire and to believe that it is possible.

Let us imagine that your thoughts are, as you get up in the morning, that your boss is going to be cranky again and make your day miserable. The turn-around would be to catch this thought and consciously turn it into a positive thought. You would change that thought to the idea that your boss has suddenly changed into a new person and every day when you go to work, she smiles at you and is pleasant and compliments you on your work.

This is the way you recreate your lives Beloveds – day after day after day. It won't happen from just one day of following this practice. It would be easy to slip back into the old patterns. It will happen after many, many days of this practice so that it will come to the point that you truly do believe that it is possible. And that is why you must celebrate every little moment that tells you that you are on the right track. Every time somebody says something to you that feels positive or is in response to something that you have wished for – every little thing that tells you that you are on the right track must be celebrated so that you will get more of those.

And so it is a gradual process. But it is a gradual process into the joy of life instead of all the energy it is taking to hang onto what life has been in the past. And so this is what we offer you Beloveds, through these transmissions. We offer you the possibility of a new life and we can give you the information and we can energize the truth with our transmissions but we cannot do it for you. You must take the action yourself. And the only action that is required is to find your dreams and believe in them. If you would allow yourself the grace of believing this, it is really quite simple.

And so Beloveds, we say to you that we honor you. We understand the challenge that it is to be human. And we understand how difficult it can be to learn to live in a whole new way – to hold the responsibility of being such a magnificent Creator, starting with your very own life. We understand and yet we say to you, now is the time and the energies are supporting it. There could not be more support for you ideally – really, than the energies that are resonant upon the earth at this time. So take action. Love yourself and create your new life, knowing that everything you need is here for you and everything that you ever could dream of is possible. And as soon as you believe this, it will show up for you. That is the way of it Beloveds.

We are at your side, today and forever more, with great pride and respect for all that you are. For all of you are magnificent. Just surviving on this planet is a magnificent accomplishment, so do not ever diminish who you are on this earth. We have so much admiration and respect for you Beloveds. And we want so much for you to find your way in this new world. And so we offer you the grace of our loving hearts. And we offer you the mirror to see the beauty of who you are, reflecting back to you. The moment you love yourself the way we do your life will turn around and you will know that only loving deeds will come into your life. That too is the way of it. And so it is.

# Essay Eighty-five - BEING AUTHENTIC

And so it is Beloveds that we come before you once again in great joy and delight. For we are The Council of Nine and we come in love to share our messages of joy with those who inhabit planet earth. Again we say, this is a time of great magnitude on your planet earth and it is a time to step into the full evolution of humanity at this time. We see who you are and what you do and what you think and how your lives are going.

Many of you say that you understand the new ways and yet your lives are not changing so much. Why do you think that is Dear Ones? Could something be awry? Could there be a stick in the cog of the wheel so to speak? For if you understand the new ways of manifesting and you have great dreams, why are they not coming true? We invite you to ask yourselves this question and to be honest about the answer. It is only in being honest with yourself that you will find the answer. Many of you live double lives.

There is the true self and then the social self and you think that you are deceiving others with your social self when in truth, you are only deceiving yourself. What others think of you has no matter in your life. The opinions of others have no place in your life. Do you understand this? You can throw a fancy party and think you are impressing others but the only true way to impress anyone is with your authenticity. This is what people look for. This is why you are only deceiving yourself if you are anything but authentic. And so, let us look at the truth of what you believe, not only about yourself but of your ability to change your world or create that which you truly desire.

You may be saying oh yes, I know how to make this happen. But do you really? It all sounds so simple.

And for those who truly do understand how to manifest their greatest desires it is so simple. But for those who think it in their mind but do not yet manifest it in their lives, we are speaking to you. We are asking, what is it that you are not willing to believe in order to truly create the life of your desires? Is there doubt in your abilities? Is there doubt in the process at all? Or, is your limitation created by your thinking that still relates to the past?

Or are you connecting to what appears as real – your day to day life - as opposed to what you desire that appears to be not yet manifest in your life? These are questions to consider. It is not until you believe with every core of your being that you are the creator of your life that you will be able to turn it around. Once you fully grasp that, then you can slowly begin to create the life of your dreams and allow the fullness of possibility to come into your reality. It is with this understanding that you will allow yourselves to become the grand beings that you truly are.

If you could see yourself from above you would not doubt who you are. Let us offer you an activity in this moment. In your imagination, rise up above your body, up above the roof of where you are now sitting and rise up into the heavens far enough that you can look down onto your house and see you sitting inside. Now see all the possibilities that are available for you. Ask to see what possibilities are available to you in this moment.

Maybe it will appear like a bubble over your head. Maybe it will just be a knowing if you are not a visual person, or it will be a feeling. Each of you has your own unique way of receiving this information but you all have the ability. So take time right now to do this. What seems like your imagination is as real to your mind as the reality that you see with your eyes. How does it feel Dear Ones? What is waiting for you in the ethers, just hanging about waiting to become your experience? This is a wonderful activity for you to undertake.

We offer you this so that you can expand your thinking out of what seems to be your present reality and allow it to grow into something more. If you try this activity and receive nothing, that is OK. Keep trying and it will help you expand your mind. For you see, all that you create in your lives first becomes manifest in the ethers so to speak. First it is a vision for the quantum field to hold and then, as you add to the vision with your continued belief in the possibility of it, it becomes more and more solid in a sense. The more belief you add to it, the more it becomes manifest and eventually shows up in the physical field that is your human experience. So, the more you are used to going into the ethers and using your imagination the more you will be connecting with this energy of manifesting.

And so beloveds, we leave you this day with this activity. Play with it. Grow with it. Use it to create that one thing that you would like to manifest this week. Go into the ethers above your home and look down and see yourself receiving that one thing that you are going to playfully manifest this week. What will it be? Just have fun and allow yourself to be light in this activity. You know how to do this. You absolutely do. Have fun and know that we are always at your side cheering you on. And so it is.

# Essay Eighty-six - BE JOYFUL

And so it is Beloveds that we are present before you once again, and we say to you that we are delighted to be in the presence of beautiful human beings. Human being. What does this mean? What does it mean 'to be'? What do you do when you are be-ing? Do you dance and play? Do you work? Do you do nothing? Just what does it mean? We would say to you that it means whatever it is that brings you joy. That is your number one task in life is to be joyful and playful.

What is it that keeps you from living this way? Is it all the responsibility you have? Can you not be playful and responsible at the same time? Is it that you do not enjoy your career or perhaps you have fallen out of love with your partner? We would then ask you to explore why you stay in the job or the relationship if it does not bring you joy? Can there be anything more valuable than that? We think not and yet we see humans sacrifice their joy for many material things that do not go with you when you die.

Your joy does. When you find your bliss and you live in joy, you take those qualities with you when you pass over the veil. You do not take your possessions or your jobs. None of that goes with you. So where is the true value? This is something we would like you to consider. You could live a life of poverty but be happy with the way you are living and be much farther ahead, from our perspective, than the millionaire who lives a lonely, empty life in his mansion. The qualities of life are what you take with you, not the things in your life.

So here you are. You have your big house, the all-important job, the two and a half children and the good looking spouse and you are miserable. What do you do? How do you change all that exterior perfection for internal peace?  This is the dilemma for many of you. And many of you just give up trying to make it happen. You give up on being happy and put on your social face that tells the world all is well when really all is falling apart.  It is you to whom we are speaking now.  You will, in these energies that you are currently living in, begin to find that your life will become a reflection of the truth and not the image that you try to present to the world.

You can no longer keep it together to create the façade. The truth of you will come shining forth and in that, if you are miserable, it will become very apparent.  This is because the earth is now residing in a higher level of vibration.  And, in the level of vibration that you are currently residing in, only the truth is supported.  If the truth is that you are happy, it will be written all over your face and your life will just bring more and more reasons to be joyful.

But, if the truth is that you are miserable you will create more and more scenarios that make you miserable. This is what we have been saying all along.  We are relating it to a different aspect of life now in that even when you have been able to put up a good appearance for others, you may find things crumbling.  This is because you are placing your values on things that cannot support you.  New clothes will not lead you to the truth. Another drink will not lead you to the truth.  It is by doing the internal work that you find your joy and you step into truth.

So Beloveds, look within the heart for the answers that you seek.  You can find guidance through others but the wisdom of you lies within.  Be not afraid to seek. You have never been so supported in this journey.  And so it is.

# Essay Eighty-seven - LOVE GAIA, LOVE THE SELF

Greetings Beloveds. Greetings from the Love and Light of the Creator. Greetings from the Light of heaven that is you. For indeed we say to you that the stars you see shining in the sky are also in your heart. The great sun shines as well in your heart. And the beautiful earth – Gaia - is your very nature. Your physical biology is part of the earth. And so when you disrespect the earth you are disrespecting yourself. This is a significant aspect of your self-reflection.

When you see how polluted your world is and how much plastic is floating around in your oceans, it is a reflection of humanity. It is a reflection of how you have lost the love of self. You can only love others as much as you love yourself. The way you treat planet is a reflection of your self-love. And so you can see why we spend so much time asking you to find the love for self. For indeed, you need only look at the state of this planet to see where you are, as a species. And yet we say to you, there is hope. You are changing.

You are realizing what is truly important and you are realizing that your true nature is connected to the Divine and to your lovely planet. The more of you who step into protecting your planet, even in the smallest ways, the more you are loving yourselves. You will begin to see this more and more. Material possessions are going to start losing their worth and you will find that humanity is moving back to the core values of living. You will see that, as you lose the blinded love of possessions and walk into the love of yourself and all the life upon this planet, she will begin to look more pristine.

As you elevate your own aspect of Being you will see a new sky and a more beautiful earth. It is all based on the vision that is held within. You could use this analogy. You look at the world from inside your head you could say. The physical eyes are in the head and the images are interpreted by the brain. If the beliefs that are translated through the brain are that the world is full of love then you must see love. That is your interpretation and the images come from your interpretation. The eyes alone do not interpret what you to see. The energetic signal must run through the brain.

Therefore, the vision is also related to that energetic signal that comes back from the brain to be interpreted by the eyes. Have you ever pointed to something that another person could not see? Maybe it was a bird in the sky. You pointed it out but the other person had trouble finding it and then the bird was gone. That bird was not fully in that person's brain interpretation of that moment so that person did not see it. This is the way that your vision works. This is related to everything we have been telling you in that you create your world. And so, knowing this, we would say to you that the way in which you conduct your life, in every way, is a reflection of your love of self.

We are delighted to have this opportunity to share our messages with you and to be with you day after day. It is our intention that these essays will lead you to a place of allowing yourselves to love you. It is a rethinking, for many of you, of what you have been shown by the outside world as you were growing up. Many children were taught, either by actions or words, not to be so bold as to love the self. Anyone who is not in love with their self cannot see someone else in love with the self. Their pain will not allow it.

And so you become a mature adult and you must re-learn who you are. This is not a simple task but one that most adults come face to face with at some point in their lives. We would say to you, the sooner the better. Get rid of those false beliefs that were planted into your psyche that you are not worthy. You are worthy because you are Creator itself. You are created through love so how could you not feel worthy of love? Your electrons resonate from pure love. It is your interpretation of what should be that turns them into something else.

In the beginning, they are love energy. So we invite you to decide to love yourself. Be gentle with this. You cannot demand love. You declare love. There is a difference. To demand is to believe you do not have. It has a fighting essence to it – a neediness. To declare comes out of knowing.

I declare that I am worthy of love and therefore, from this moment forward, I love myself. Then ask what self love would look like. What does it feel like to be loved? What does it feel like to love myself? How do people respond to me or treat me when I am living in the love of self? What do my daily experiences feel like now that I am in the love of self? How do I respond to others now that I am in love of self? What do I expect my day to be like now that I am walking in the path of self love? You must know what it looks like in order to create it. So, take the time to answer these questions so that you recognize it when it appears in your life.

By answering these questions you are creating boundaries for your experience in life. Anything that falls outside of the boundaries of acceptable experience can then be altered to fit your love experience. If someone says something to you that falls outside your experience of feeling love, then ask where are you not loving yourself? You need not address the other person, although, at some point, you may choose to change that relationship. All your experiences come from within. Remember that your eyes are interpreting your experiences from the filter of your brain. So look within and ask where you could be loving yourself more to change that experience.

When things happen that feel out of the love boundary, they are a great opportunity to change the pattern within and thus they are a blessing. In this way, all of life becomes a blessing. This is done without self punishment. You cannot say damn, I have failed again! That is not love. A more loving response would be to say, wow, I see this is an ongoing journey back to loving myself. That's OK. I'm growing and learning as I go. That is being gentle with yourself, like you would have chosen to be treated as a child. Be the kind and loving parent to yourself. The more you do this, the more you will see your world change.

We say to you Beloveds, that we see within your hearts. We see the beauty that resides within. We offer you only love for we see that worthiness of you. Find it within yourself. Do what must be done to see that love within. Perhaps it is from walking in nature that you realize that you are that beauty also. Perhaps it is in the eyes of a loved one that you see your beauty. Know that it is there. Believe that it is worthy of a gracious life. Begin the change back to love. That is what it's all about. And so it is.

# Essay Eighty-eight - CHANGING REALITY

And so it is Beloveds that we are coming to the close of our transmissions in this collection of essays. It has been our great delight to come before you in this way. Never again will we pass messages such as has been collected here. For humanity is quickly moving through this time of change – of expansion - and you will soon be ready for the next level of messaging. For, after this collection we are going to step it up a level and we are going to offer you more teachings about who you are now that you have walked into the fullness of the new energies that are available.

We are going to teach more about the world that is awaiting and the person that you are in this new expression of being. For you see, life will never be the same again. This planet upon which you live has shifted and so she is supporting a new level of life. All life upon your planet has changed with her. It must. And, along with that, humans are changing as well. For many of you it is not obvious because you are changing right before your very eyes. Day after day, you have been gradually changing. Actually rapidly would be a more appropriate expression of that change, but it has happened in a way that some have not realized. You do not realize how different you are today than you were yesterday and especially a year ago.

You simply adjust to what is and do not have a level of comparison. The time will come soon when you will realize. That is because very soon you will be doing things that you never imagined possible. You will be communicating with people intuitively. Someone might tell you something but you will know that it is not the truth. There will be no more secrets in this way. You will be open to believing in things that you never thought possible. That is because the vibration of the earth has changed and so, being in resonance with the earth, it is possible for you to connect to the vibration of things that at one point would have been out of your field of comprehension. This is delightful Dear Ones and we anticipate this time with great joy.

And so let us begin our transmission for today. For you see, today we wish to tell you about the truth of creation. You have your different stories and ideas of creation. Each religion tells it in a different way. Your scientists have a different way of explaining it and today we offer our way of understanding this as well. And we say to you Beloveds, creation comes from your own mind. EVERY aspect of creation comes from your mind. For many of you this will be hard to fathom. We invite you to allow yourself to find space for this in your belief system.

There will soon be people on this earth who can choose to live in two different realities almost at the same time. They will be able to experience a situation from two different perspectives almost while being in each experience at the same time. You will be able to be sitting within an experience and decide that you would like a different outcome of that experience and it will immediately shift into the more desirable outcome. This is possible and within your abilities at this time. This is how much your world has changed and how much you are changing.

And so, in our next compilation of messages – the next book – we will address more of this type of understanding. We will be talking about the new you and the possibilities that are available to you. By bringing the possibility of what you can do into your awareness then you will be able to see it when it shows up for you. It is like creating a language. Once two people have spoken the same word then it becomes part of your reality. And so it shall be with the abilities of the new human that you are. As more and more people play with the possibilities of what you can do in these new energies, it will become more a part of the awareness of the whole of humanity. Those who read these words will be the way-showers. You will be the ones who will be showing the masses how this is done.

These are such exciting times Beloveds. You are here at one of the most magnificent times of creation. For us, watching over you, there is great joy in guiding you back to the full expression of human. Much was lost with your willingness to walk into the grand experiment of free will. And here we are guiding you back to what you were before the fall from grace. That fall from grace was simply the forgetting of who you truly are and all your abilities. Now that you are becoming more aware we say to you that there will be no more manipulation upon your planet.

You will no longer tolerate the few who sit at the top dominating the life expression of the whole. Their lies will be revealed through your own deep awareness of the truth. They are trembling as we write this, for they know what is ahead. And so it is that we say to you to trust your own inner knowing at all times. Ask your heart what is truth and do not accept that which feels like a lie or deceit. The time for those games is over.

Love reigns on the earth at this time and never again will you fall to the level of darkness that existed on your planet. Mother Earth has reclaimed her rightful place in the hierarchy of heaven. She sacrificed much for the sake of humanity. Love her back now with your concern for her wellbeing. Do what you can, with your inventions and your intentions, to support her in the journey back to her pristine self. She is your mother. She deserves your love and support.

And so Beloveds, we leave you this day. We leave you with the words that will wash over your minds like oil across canvas. They will leave images as they pass. Those images will be malleable and change as more ideas and thoughts pass over them. In the end you will have a beautiful painting of life created anew. There is nothing you could think of that is not possible. And there is much that is possible that you have not thought of. Be open and follow your heart. That is the way of it Dear Ones. We love you so. And so it is.

# Essay Eighty-nine - A NEW LEVEL OF EXISTENCE

And so it is Beloveds that we are delighted to gather once again. And once again we say to you how joyous we are that we have the privilege of standing before the beautiful humans who are recreating the planet. For you see, it is your willingness to change and become something so grand that all of the heavens are watching, that has led to the new earth. Yes, you are residing on a new earth. You are living on a new planet. She has morphed and moved into a higher resonance and so have you. Now, she could have done it without you, but not with you unless you were willing to grow and expand along with her. And we are so grateful that you were willing. It was a bit of a ride. The year 2012 was full of downloads as you like to say. It was full of energy transmissions that knocked the physical body a bit hard at times. But now here you are. You have made it into the higher dimensions of Light. Your world has changed and so have you.

There are many who do not recognize the change. Actually, for many, things do not look very different. That is not because they are living somewhere else in the physical sense but in the energetic sense of what they are creating in their lives, they are. They are repeating the past over and over and over. They do not realize that they can create something new now. They do not know how because they do not even have the awareness that change is possible. Those are the people who are struggling in these times and finding life difficult. If they are open to hearing of a new way, we would recommend sharing your experiences of life. Share how, when you expect something new in your life it arrives and how, when you let go of your old beliefs, something new can become your reality.

For those who are lost in the way of fear and despair, send them love so that they may feel it and it can offer them hope. And for those of you who know that the world has changed and can feel the new energies of earth, congratulations. You have brought yourself to a new level of existence. From here it is a joyous ride of discovery into a new way of living. It is like being a child again, learning how to be in the world. For those of you who very consciously grow and expand, you will have the most fun. For you will see yourself changing almost daily. One day you may feel a deep connection to Spirit and another day you may feel like there is no connection at all. As you become more powerful within yourself, you come to understand that all is within. There is no need to look outside of yourself for anything. Not for love, not for information, not for comfort. It is all within.

In that level of existence there is great peace and contentment. Life is just an experience without attachment to anything. Every day offers new opportunities of discovery. There is no expectation of what it will be and a great acceptance of what it is. This is the way of living in the higher octaves of existence. This will continue to grow and expand within you as you integrate these energies and bring them into the fullness of your knowing. This is the possibility you are currently in. You have passed the marker and now are growing into the new way of being. You are growing into the thousands of years of peace and harmony. How delightful it is for us to witness these changes and see all the humans around the globe, stepping into this new opportunity.

As this continues to grow and change, you will see many world governments begin to change as well. There are many governments and bureaucracies that cannot survive in this new energy. They have no choice but to change. Do not be fearful about what you see but stay in a place of peace and harmony within your heart. It is the old crumbling to be replaced with a system that is more in resonance with the new earth upon which you are currently living. It is a new system arising that will be in support of all of humanity and will have concern for all life. The system that is crumbling almost destroyed this planet.

It may be a rough ride for a bit through the transition but, considering the near destruction of the earth, is it not worth a few challenging years as it changes? Indeed we believe you will agree. For you see, as all these changes are taking place, the human heart is opening. It is feeling safer to be true to itself and it is feeling safer to be in love – the love of self that allows you to then open yourself up to the world. As it becomes safer to be fully loving in this world, then, of course, there is more love in the world.

For you see Dear Ones, everything is energy. You are energy and your thoughts and feelings are energy. As you offer love out to the world know that it then becomes part of the experience of the all. It doesn't just tap on the door of your neighbors, it travels the world. For those of you who yearn to travel, just send out your love Light and know that it is travelling the world. Send it to those places that you so yearn to be and your own energies will magnetize you to that place. This is the way of the world in which you are now living.

It is important to understand that there are no barriers, no limits to what you can do with your energy. You can impact the entire universe if you choose to do so. In some way, you already are. And so be playful. Use your love energy to bless all of humanity. Send your love energy to the earth every day. Ask that each step you take is a blessing for Mother Earth and then know that to be true. When you state such an intention, you are indeed marking every footstep with love. You leave a trail of Light, like fairy dust, as you travel and go about your day. It is so easy to offer your love to the world. It just takes intention.

Intention is a powerful tool for your growth. Intention is creation. The particles that make up your reality respond to intention, even when you are not aware of it. The particles that make up matter are only responding to your intentions in every moment. So, this is another reason to be very aware of every thought. What are your intentions toward other people? It is all your experience so if your intentions are not always pure and loving, you will feel them. It means that you are not purely loving yourself. So be aware in every moment of what your intentions are with your thoughts as well as your deeds.

This is our transmission for this day Dear Ones. As always, it is our joy and delight to come before you and to share this understanding with you. Stand strong in your convictions to be whole. Raise the sword of your majesty in this world and claim your position among the place of kings. End the pandemic of being a small, disempowered human. You are creators. You are magnificent Beings of the Light. Feel your majesty and use it to be a loving beacon to the world. It is your experience that awaits you. It is your divine path that lies before you. Claim it Dear Ones. We love you so. And so it is.

# Essay Ninety - BE THE BEACON

And so it is Beloveds that we come before you once again. And once again we come in love and grace. We come before the beautiful Beings of Light that call themselves human and we say to you Dear Ones, the time is here. You have moved fully into the Light of heaven and now you are becoming a new human. This will not happen overnight but it is happening. And it has been happening for some time. Soon you will notice. Soon everyone will notice that most people in the world are happy to learn about that which was hush, hush only a few short years ago.

No longer are people afraid to express who they truly are. Those of you who are leading the way are standing in front of the crowd without hesitation now because you know the energies of the day will support you. You know that you will not be ridiculed out of existence or shamed into retreat. Oh no, you are now living on an earthly plane that supports your wisdom and your knowing. People are ready to awaken to your understanding of the world. So share who you truly are Dear Ones. You then give others permission to do the same. As long as you keep yourselves in the shadows you are not allowing others to see the truth of who they can be.

You are all mirrors of each other. If you show others your Light then you give them permission to find that truth within themselves. And by seeing their Light, you are making them that Light. By seeing them for the very best they can be, you are turning them into that because they must fit your experience of them. This is how Jesus healed. He saw everyone as complete and whole with such conviction that they then had to become that vision of what he saw. This is what you are moving in to. This is what the new earth is

358

becoming. What you see in others they shall become. And even more important is that whatever you see in yourself you will become.

So make sure you pay attention to all your redeeming qualities. Give careful attention to all your so called good attributes. Play them up. Why not? If you are creating why not be the best of you? So, what do you most admire about yourself? What are your greatest values that you know you hold within yourself? Perhaps it is artistic abilities. Perhaps it is your kindness and the goodness you see in all. Perhaps you are good at gardening. Play it up and claim your place as a great gardener. The more you believe it about yourself the more you will become it.

So why not take it further and state that you are in a way, even better than what you believe you are. Say you do not think you are very good at managing books and keeping track of your personal accounting. State that you are a good bookkeeper and manage to balance your accounts every month. Just step into it more fully than you really believe so that you can broaden into that. Or, perhaps you do not think of yourself as a very good swimmer. Next time you go to the beach say that you are a pretty good swimmer. You have a strong breast stroke and enjoy being in the water. And watch your swimming improve. You can use this method with what you see within yourself and what you see in others.

We hope you see these times that you are in as fun and playful. There is so much that you can do that is yet to be discovered. By being playful you will allow this to unfold more and more. It is the lightness of being that allows you to expand. Do not get stuck in the seriousness of this work. Life is meant to be fun and playful. Your human experience, when you take it lightly, is a much more pure experience. The mind is what creates the heaviness and the seriousness. The heart is playful and light when it is not crushed with hardship and pain.

That is why we have asked you to do your healing work, so that you can find your way back to that joyful and light heart. That is where you will be able to spread your wings and fly so to speak. You have not seen an eagle soaring with rocks anchored to its feet. That is not possible. You cannot carry the burdens of the world and still take flight. Your duty is not to cure the world. Your duty is to work on yourself and then, as proxy, the world is served in the process. Do not think that your duty is to anyone but yourself.

And so we anticipate the day when we give our last transmission for this collection of essays. Our hearts sadden in a sense, for we enjoy these transmissions immensely and we know that they are beneficial to all who read them. It is only a short break for our scribe Rashana and we will put her to work again, with her willingness of course. And so Beloveds. Stand strong in who you are and who you desire to be. Know thyself and grow thyself. Be the fullness of you. And look into the eyes of another and know that they too are the fullness of you. With each person who stands before you, see the perfection that you know is you. That is what you are - one being from one source having multiple experiences. We love you so. And so it is.

# Essay Ninety-one - BECOMING REAL

Greetings Beloved Beings of the Light. Greetings to the great ones who call themselves human. Greetings to all who reside in the Light and read these words and know that you are the new wave of the planet earth. You are the generations who will turn the earth into the pristine gem that she is. You are the generations that have already morphed the human vessel into a more crystalline nature. And you are the generations who are remembering the truth of what it is to be human. For you see Dear Ones, as many of you know, your biology was robbed of its true essence eons ago.

You have been living on this earth for hundreds and hundreds of years only partially whole. The strands of your DNA that were disconnected are available to you once again. And as you reconnect all the strands of your DNA you become the true human once again. There is so much potential in the human that you have lost. There is so much that is you that is hidden. Do you know that the human biology was created to live for hundreds of years? Oh you see your diseases and your bodies failing and you wonder how that could ever be so.

We say to you that, once again, it is your belief systems that are creating this scenario for you. You believe that you must get old and die and so you do. If you believed that your body lived in vitality for 200 years, then you would not be over the hill so to speak, until you reached 100. If this was your belief system, then 99.9% of all humans would still feel pretty young. If all you felt very young then it would become the reality of earth that seventy year olds are still young. You can see this already beginning to happen on your planet. Sixty is now considered to be the young-old and not until the eighties are you old-old.

It is starting to change.  And it will continue to change.
So how delightful for you that you are not really aging at
all, unless you believe you are.  If you choose to decide
that your body is failing because you are a certain age,
well then you will create whatever it is you believe.  On
the other hand, there are those, such as Rashana, who
never attribute any ache or pain or fatigue to age.  She
knows that, if she decides not to use her body very
much then it will not be as strong.  It has nothing to do
with age but what actions you take.  This is what we
mean.  It is not that the biology does not have the
capacity.  It is that the mind has adopted a false belief.
Change that belief now and become younger every
day.  It is much more than possible.  It is the truth.

And there is much more truth that we would like to
share with you.  Let us look at relationships.  You
believe that you must be with one person all your life
and feel guilty when relationships break down.  And yet
we say to you, in the natural rhythm of life, when two
people grow differently, it only makes sense that they
would grow apart.  When two people come together into
Divine union to serve as one, then they are growing
together and it may be a relationship that lasts for
hundreds of years.  The truth of relationships is that
they serve as growth meters.  You magnetize people
into your personal experience who can serve you at the
time.

There are times when it is only a short time when you
have received all that you need from that relationship
and so it begins to dissolve.  On the other hand, when
two hearts join from a place of true love, in service to
Creator, then that love can last forever.  The way
humans have been doing relationship is very self
serving.  When the relationship is based on a bigger
picture of two very independent souls coming together

to be even more united as one, they walk with one vision of what their life together means.

When two souls come together in self-serving ways, they begin to repel each other because the vision is not of one service. The vision is not of one purpose. It is two very individual visions and in such cases they can quickly deter away from the other. This is fine. There is no criticism of this. It is better to leave a relationship that no longer resonates with who you are than to stay and live out of harmony. You are not supporting the world when you are living out of harmony with who you are. So, relationships can be lasting when the greater vision is for humanity and in being of service to all.

The reason is the individuals in those relationships do not look to their beloved to fill them up and make them whole. They are already whole. They look to their beloved to harmonize what they already are and to amplify their love to even greater levels of resonance. In this case, the couple amps up the love energy of the earth and all benefit. There is no clinging in such relationships because there is no emptiness. Two complete beings serving love together. This will begin to happen more and more as humanity heals and you find the love you seek within yourself. Once you are whole and complete within the self, then you are ready to share in wholeness as opposed to in lack. It is a beautiful sway into fullness that is slowly unfolding on the planet at this time.

And so Beloveds, there is one more thing we would like to share with you this day. Walk in the truth of who you are. Do not pretend by doing what you think needs to be done to fit in to what is in style or acceptable by the cool ones. You are all cool. You are all unique. You all walk to your own song and you all have your own song to sing. Be free. Let go of the shackles that are worrying about what others think. There is no greater prison than a life lived for what others think. Free yourself out of that way of thinking and just be you. There are thousands of people who will be attracted to the energy of the true you.

So many of you feel like you will lose all of your friends if you are who you truly are. We say to you, the opposite is true. When you walk in the truth of who you really are, more and more people will be attracted to you because you will be authentic. All the people who are searching for someone quirky and fun just like you will be so happy they found you. Everyone who is searching for someone who is truthful and stands up for what they believe will rejoice in finding you doing that. It is only by you being you that you will find authenticity in your life. Once you start living the authentic you, everything starts to fall into place in your life.

You find out what it is like to float down the river with the current. It is so easy. Life just flows gracefully. This comes from your authenticity. So many of you will not make the changes that will lead you there because you are afraid. You are fearful that if you leave your job to do what you really love that it may not pay as much or it will be hard to find something or you will be leaving your pension behind. Let go of the fears and everything will fall into place. It cannot happen though if you do not believe in it. Once you step into the fullness of you, life becomes a joyous game of 'I wonder what today will bring?' The beauty of that is the joy of accepting what comes and not having attachment to thinking that you must create it.

You are co-creators with the higher aspect of your soul and together you create joyous wonderful amazing lives! You just have to believe it. There is so much you can do. We would say there is nothing you cannot do. You just don't believe it. It will be shown to you Dear Ones. More and more it will open up to the truth of being. So be ready. Say yes to the truth of you. Be willing to be the honest expression of who you are. Step into fully loving yourself and watch your world change. You are love Dear Ones. And we are honored to walk by your side, witness to this grand evolution of earth and mankind. It is very sweet Beloveds. Very sweet. And so it is.

# Essay Ninety-two - YOUR EXPERIENCES ARE YOUR CREATION

And so it is Beloveds that we have the great grace of coming before you once again, dancing in the Light of who you are as humans. We see you and we delight in the presence of you. For you see Beloveds, you are the ones who are allowing yourselves to be recreated as you live day by day. And you are the ones with the great courage to step out of all that you have known and welcome a totally new reality into your world. We are delighted with who you are and we are delighted to be guiding you in this next part of the journey. For you see, you have passed through the marker and into love.

You have moved out of the density of the third dimension and now are holding the attributes of the fourth dimension. Have you noticed more serendipity in your life? Are you noticing more harmony? These are fourth dimensional attributes. You think something and a couple of days later things fall into place related to that thought. Or you have an idea and a couple of days later the opportunity to live it reveals itself to you. This will flow very beautifully if you are willing to live in the trust of your creations that are currently available to you. If you continue to doubt yourself as a creator then you will most likely cling to past thoughts and belief patterns and so your life will be one continuous cycle that never changes.

Look at the main complaints that you would have about your life right now. Are they the same as they were five years ago? Are your finances the same, your relationships the same, your job the same, even though you are not happy with any of them? If the answer is yes to any of these then you can be sure that you are living out the old beliefs. It is time to release them Dear Ones and to look at the truth of creation. Your experiences are your creation. That may be hard to hear for some of you. You do not want to take responsibility for the aspects of your life that you do not like.

And yet we say to you, it is only by looking at it truthfully that you will ever change it. You are in charge of your lives now Dear Ones. The miracle of the lottery will not happen if you believe you are poor and in debt. You must make the change. It will not be done without you doing the work. And so it is out of love that we offer these messages. We wish you to understand that, until you take charge of your mental being you will continue to repeat the same life over and over.

There are many of you who are seeing harmony in your lives. You are in the joy of non-attachment. You are in the place of having released the issues of the past and ready to step consciously into creating your life. When you walk this path, you will see more and more that things fall into place and each day offers a new experience. You are no longer repeating all the old patterns of the past but, from a clear and open heart, you are allowing life to bring experiences to you that will reflect your current beliefs. If you believe that life supports you and is good to you then you will begin to experience more and more goodness in your life. If you believe that you are lovable and deserve love then it will be magnetized to you.

And so it is that we say to you, from the depths of our hearts, so to speak, that you are loved beyond measure in our realms of existence. For you see, you are the most incredible species. What you have accomplished in your free will is miraculous compared to how it could have gone. We held the vision for you for a long time and you saw it and grabbed onto and made it reality. This is why we love you so. You are wonderful beings who do not see your value and your magnificence at all.

If we could offer you one thing it would be for you to see the true brilliance that you are. You are amazing beings of Light and we are honoured to stand before you. We are honoured to guide you and to share our wisdom with you. Believe in yourselves Beloveds. Know that anything is possible because you are human. You are so much more than you realize. Think of the most grandiose thing that you could ever do and then believe that you can indeed do it. Then just wait for it to come about in your life.

As we come to the time of closing for this book we wish you to know that there is nothing to be afraid of. Do not let doubt and worry keep you from your magnificence. Do not let anything keep you from your dreams. Dream big Dear Ones. All that you could desire is already yours. If you can dream it, then it already exists on some level. It must, or you wouldn't have the vision. So, knowing that, what will you do with your dreams? Knowing that the dream already exists somewhere, then believe in it. Wait to see it in your personal experience, for surely it is on its way. And it is, if you will believe it. Do not put your own parameters on it such as the length of time it will take or how it will happen. That is not for you to worry about. Just dream it and wait, knowing that it is coming. That is the way of it. Play with this Beloveds. We love you so. And so it is.

# Essay Ninety-three - BE CREATIVE IN YOUR CREATIONS

And so it is beloveds that we are delighted to be standing before the dear human that you are. It is our great delight and joy to be addressing you this day. And we say to you, the reader of these words, that you are the joy and delight of Mother Earth. You are called to these words because you are among the few who are consciously raising the vibration of the earth with your open heart. You are the ones who are intentionally creating this beautiful and wonderful new earth. Watch as your world unfolds into glory and grace. Watch as your worries fall away.

In their place comes ease and grace and a life that flows with joy and delight. This is the way of residing in the new levels of awareness with consciousness. This is the way of being a new human on this earth. Nothing is the same. Everything has changed. Can you feel it? Are you aware? Do you see how much has changed? Turn off your news. Shut off your TVs and just be in the world. Just listen to your own heart. Just take in the experiences around you. Just be more present in your own piece of the world. That is where your soul resides. That is where you have impact. You can watch the news and get lost in the misery or you can be in your own small community and make a difference.

You can give your power to the media or you can give your love to your community. We think that you can see the difference between the two. Basically, one is giving your power away and the other is giving your love away. It is not your power that you are giving to your community by being a loving citizen. You are gaining your power in that situation, and you are changing the world. You do not change the world by watching all the horror that is happening around the world, except to make it more fearful. The last thing humanity needs is more fear. You've done quite well at creating that one.

Step out of the fear beloveds and walk into the grace of being an empowered human. You are creators. You know this, for we have told you many times. So be creative in your creations. Do not create more harm and hatred. Step out of that. Walk away from it. Walk away from the TV for it serves you not. It reprograms you into slavery. Walk away from it and become whole once again. Find your way back to you and you will begin to become who you are meant to be. Your media pulls you away from you. It pulls you away from your joy. It gives your power to your celebrities, as if they were anything to aspire to.

Use your great wisdom and aspire to your own dreams. What are they? Do you even know? Are you creating your own dreams or someone else's? Are your dreams your own creation or the creation of the society which dictates how you must look and what you must wear and who is important? You are all important. There is not one person on this earth who is not important. How can you think anyone is less worthy than another? We say to you they are not, regardless of who they are and what they do. The man who crawls on the street, eating off the ground is as worthy as you. He is as worthy as the banker who kicks dust in his face as he walks by. Love everyone. Love yourself and there will be love for all.

And so beloveds, we have gone on a rant again. For you see, we are so delighted to have Rashana who allows us to share in this way. You are ready to hear our words or you would not be here. Listen carefully to what we say. Use our words as a guide in your life so that you can find your way back to you. You know within the depths of your heart what is true. Find yourself there. Go back inside and find you. You will know you have found you when you see the beautiful, radiant, loving Being that sends only love. That is you. It is within each one of you. By finding your love for you then you will be finding your way back home. That is heaven on earth. Fully loving thy self and knowing thy self is heaven. After that, it is all just a grand game played for the fun of it – played for the experience.

After you are residing in love you will accept everything in your life as it is. You will know that each experience is coming from your own creation so why would you not like it? You will know that everything that becomes your day is just what your heart desired. It is such a grand game when you accept it for what it is. This is what all of humanity is moving into. It is such a wonderful thing to see what is becoming for Mother Earth and all her children. You are growing up. You are learning to care again for your mother as she cares for you. It is not all about you any more – although it is. But, it is about you in a loving way that also cares for others. It is you loving you that makes you love everything else – including your Earthly Mother.

You have made it dear ones. So many possibilities await you. Be in love with you. Allow others to love you. The world is your oyster as they say. Make pearls. And so it is.

# Essay Ninety-four - THE GREATEST MIRACLE

And so it is Beloveds that we are delighted to be with you this day. We see before us the beautiful beacons of Light that call themselves humans walking this earth. It is a glorious day Dear Ones. For you see, this is the 100th transmission that is the completion of this book (author's note: some were omitted which is why this one is numbered ninety-four). It is also the day of the Winter Solstice, December 21, 2012. It is a grand ending, making room for an even grander beginning. Today is the day that you, as humans, walked through the greatest evolution on this planet. You walked through it, many, without even knowing it.

Oh yes there was all the hype about the Mayan calendar but many ignored it and saw it as just another day. Well, it was not a day of tragedy and apocalypse but it was a grand day. For you see, this day marked the ending of a cycle. It is the end of a 26,000 year cycle that sees your solar system moving through the Milky Way Galaxy. It is the day that you moved from darkness into Light. Even more significant is that you rose up closer to the realms of creation. You moved into a higher dimension. So many Lightworkers were gathered on that day, offering their pure love to the ascension of planet earth.

Your hearts were felt dear ones. Your love tones were felt as you sounded for the earth and all of creation. Every heart beat that was rejoicing the new beginning was felt. Oh, we are so grateful for the brave way-showers who stand strong in the knowing of what is truly transpiring on your earth. We commend you for stepping out of the norm and into the truth of your own hearts. What were you doing on that grand day that was December 21, 2012? Do you remember? Yes, for our scribe Rashana, she is typing this on that date but we are transmitting for you the reader and that date has passed for you.

Our beautiful scribe celebrated on the eve of this day by being in a circle of sound. It was beautiful and Mother Earth felt their love tones. She celebrated on the day with a friend and joining online with Lightworkers around the world as they joined their hearts to ensure the great success of your transition closer to the Light. For you see, the more of you who gather, the greater the impact of your thoughts and intentions.

We have spoken to you of your thoughts and intentions through this entire series of essays. And, when you gather in large numbers, you are magnifying your intentions by the square of the number of people present. This is how you can change the world. This is how you can have such an impact when you gather. Not only are you supporting each other but you are supporting all of creation. Oh beloveds, we are so delighted to see what lies before humanity. From this day forward it is all downhill so to speak. The hardest part is over.

For those who are paying attention to our words, you will see your lives begin to flow with grace and synchronicity that will delight you. This is the way of the new world. Everything that comes into your experience is planned by the great hierarchy of your oversoul. It is busy all the time planning and placing things in alignment for the highest choices for you in this incarnation. You will see this expand more and more. As we have said before, if you see more and more hardship in your life then you must understand that there is healing to do. There is a need to change your beliefs and expectations of life. We have discussed this enough not to reiterate it here today.

Today is a celebration. Today is our opportunity to commend you for all your hard work. You have lifted yourselves into this grand opportunity of ascension dear ones. Pat yourselves on the back. Love yourselves for the great job well done. Please do a happy dance right now for all that you accomplished. It was not always a sure thing but you made it happen. This is why you are so marvelous. This is why so many nations, tribes and civilizations from other solar systems are here watching in awe. Truly, they are in awe because it was not believed that such an experiment would succeed.

And so it is a celebration indeed. We are dancing with you. We are embracing you with our love. We are at your side leading you from here. It is not over. It is just beginning. But it is a beginning like no other. It is a beginning into a new level of being that has not been experienced before on this earth. Grand indeed are those who are reading these words. Love yourselves for this great accomplishment. See the beauty of you. Look in the mirror and thank yourself for being here. YOU have made a difference in all life everywhere. Know it to be true. You are a master.

Beloved Beings of the Light, we stand before you in deep honour and respect for who you are. We stand before the greatest tribe in creation. Oh, we know that you have trouble believing this. But one day you will know. One day, when you pass from this current incarnation into the higher realms of existence, and you are witness to all that you have accomplished, you will know. And you will laugh. You will put your head back and laugh and laugh. For you see, once you pass over, you will understand what a grand game it was indeed.

You will laugh that you took it so seriously. You will laugh that you believed it all to be real. You will laugh mostly because it is the most natural way to respond to the deep knowing of the incredible feat that you, as part of the humans living in the time of the great shift, have accomplished. It is marked in the ethers of time – recorded in the records of eternity that you, the one reading these words, created the greatest miracle that humanity has ever been privilege to experience. And so it is.

# ABOUT THE AUTHOR

 Rashana lives in the beautiful province of Nova Scotia, Canada. She is an Intuitive Counselor, Channeler, Reiki Master, Certified Hypnotherapist, Sound Healer and the Creator of Rashana Sound Essences. She is a beautiful soul who presents her messages with love and compassion.

She channels the higher Beings of Light, including Ascended Masters, The Council of Nine and her over-soul. Rashana has appeared on national television, several radio shows and in front of large audiences. She has recorded 2 CDs and just completed her third book.

Her passion at this time is to empower others on their journey using channeling, sound healing and her most recent offering, The Freedom Release Technique, which she created to help her clients clear limiting beliefs that hold them back from the life of their dreams.

Please feel free to go to her website **www.rashana.ca** to get the book "Healing with Love – Messages for the New Earth" for free and find out more about the other books, CD's and other products on offer.